Touring Scotland
WESTER ROSS

By the same author

Touring Scotland · The Lowlands

Touring Scotland · The Unknown Highlands

Touring Scotland
WESTER ROSS

(Kintail to Torridon)

ROSS FINLAY

G. T. FOULIS & CO. LTD
HENLEY-ON-THAMES · OXFORDSHIRE

First published 1971

© Ross Finlay 1971

ISBN 0 85429 113 X

The text is set in 11 on 12-point Garamond

MADE AND PRINTED IN GREAT BRITAIN BY
MORRISON AND GIBB LIMITED, LONDON AND EDINBURGH

THE CONTENTS

LIST OF ILLUSTRATIONS

Maps

Acknowledgements for Photographs

The Author wishes to thank the following:

Scottish Tourist Board   4, 14, 15, 16, 17, 19, 22, 23, 24, 26
John Lang & Co. Ltd.   7, 9, 11, 12
Tom Weir   1, 2, 3, 5, 6, 8, 10, 13, 18, 20, 21, 22, 25

CHAPTER I

GLEN SHIEL

FOR MOST PURPOSES, Wester Ross begins away up in the high lonely mountain country between the Great Glen and the Atlantic coast. The road access from the Great Glen is good, either by the modern route from Invergarry by Loch Loyne, or along the older road through Glen Moriston. These two roads come together a little way east of Loch Cluanie, a recently extended hydro electric reservoir that straddles the boundary between the counties of Inverness and Ross.

There are high mountain peaks and ridges to north and south, imposing both in their barren times and when there's a light dusting of green to mark the new season's growth. Loch Cluanie itself, however, is a rather nondescript affair, thanks to the water-line that still hasn't had time to look anything but embarrassingly artificial. Even into the later weeks of June, pockets of snow can usually be seen in the corries hidden from the sun; Loch Cluanie in winter is a forbidding prospect, with deep snow often lying down to the roadside, and the remote-seeming peaks hidden in banks of mist or cloud.

Most of this is deer forest country; Cluanie forest, lying to the south of the loch, is part of the vast estates of Lord Burton, which are controlled from Dochfour on Loch Ness-side. Since much of the country described in this book is given over to deer, it may not be out of place as early as this to explain a little about the Highland deer forests.

Deer forests are not in any way like wooded forests; usually quite the opposite, covering great stretches of inaccessible mountain country where the only trees may have been planted by landowners of the past to ornament their wildly expensive shooting lodges, or to give sheltered winter grazing for the deer. There are something like two million acres of the Highlands given over mainly or partly to deer; it has been pointed out that

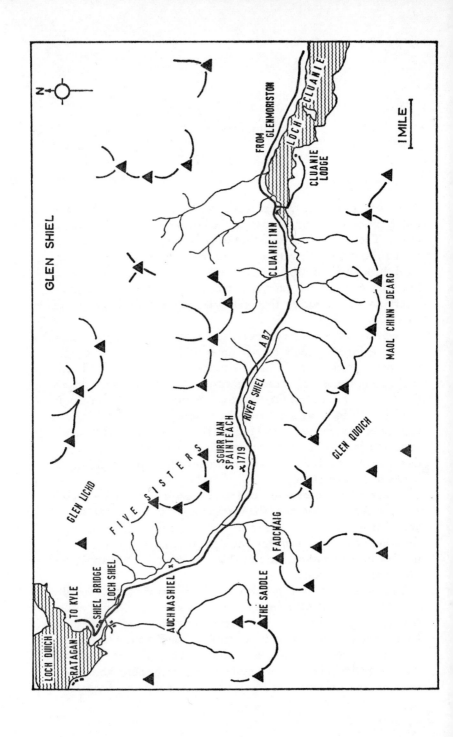

ninety per cent of this ground is virtually useless for any other purpose, being too high, too much covered in bare rock, bog or rubble, offering miserable grazing for other stock, and suited only to the red deer that are best adapted for it. In the Highlands there are also roe and fallow deer, but only in very small numbers.

Until fairly recently, deer stalking was done mainly for sport, although the carcases might be handed out to the tenants on the estates. Nowadays, with venison fetching higher prices than ever before, it has been said that a well-run forest may be able to meet most of its overheads from the sale of venison, and make a profit from renting out the shooting rights at a substantial fee to stalkers who are interested only in a good 'head' for their trophy rooms. Several of the deer forests in Wester Ross, as elsewhere in the Highlands, have come, with the changing times, to be given over partly to sheep or cattle, or even to plantations of conifers, either on the estates' or on the Forestry Commission's behalf. A once famous deer forest mentioned in this book has so far changed its tune as to allow keepers to go out with machine guns and slaughter deer by the dozen for their venison, a way of working normally associated only with the well organized gangs of poachers who operate in some parts.

In most of the forests, though, stalking is still carried on in a much more regular manner, with long hard climbs through rugged mountain country and the quick killing of a carefully selected beast. It's unavoidable that there are often clashes of interest between deer stalkers and visitors who want to wander over the superb mountains of Wester Ross. The trouble is that the hill stags are at their best only for a fairly short period in the year, beginning about the middle of August when they move up to the higher ground in the mountains, and lasting to the middle of October, by which time the rutting season is at its peak and the stags are losing their earlier prime condition. Whether they are being shot for sport, or for venison, or as part of the annual cull which has to be made to keep the numbers small enough for the available grazing, stags have to be killed during that period.

Anybody who wants to walk or climb through a deer forest in the stalking season should try to find out locally if he is likely to interrupt a stalk in the same area at the same time. Red deer are cautious creatures, and a blundering visitor can ruin hours of hard work for a stalking party. Most estates will be able to provide this information, and on most of them there is no restriction of access to the hills during the rest of the year; but it would be naive to suggest that there are no estate proprietors or their employees ready to make themselves thoroughly obnoxious to casual visitors to their sporting preserves. Guns have been waved ominously at targets other than deer. Nevertheless, as the Red Deer Commission have pointed out, since many hill walkers or climbers use paths through the mountains that were originally built by the deer forest owners, it is not unreasonable to expect visitors to make enquiries before using them during the stalking season.

The road from Loch Cluanie into Wester Ross has been greatly modernized in the last few years, and is now a fast, double-width affair that cuts out all the weary queues and delays that used to afflict motorists here until well into the 1960s. Almost at the west end of the loch is a side road over a bridge to the left, which used to be part of the main road from Invergarry until the reservoir of Loch Loyne was created in a great valley to the south, inundating the middle section of the old road. The new route from Glen Garry over the deserted hills to Glen Moriston is therefore a bonus from the network of hydro electric schemes.

Now the road over the bridge, although it has a perfect tarmac surface, is a dead-end. The county council no longer maintain the bridges, and it has reverted to private ownership, mainly to serve the shooting lodge of Cluanie, in a patch of woodland at the south side of the loch. Just beyond this road-end is the only occupied house along miles of the main road, the old-established Cluanie Inn that first opened for business in the middle of the eighteenth century and, in more modern terms, includes the only petrol station along any of these roads for a greater distance than many visitors are inclined to believe.

Some way beyond Cluanie Inn, where the much improved modern road takes a line lower down the hillside than the original military route, there's a forestry plantation hanging onto the steep mountain slopes to the right. Above and beyond this early part of the state forest of Glenshiel is a green hillside scarred with long gullies. At the far end of the plantation the road crosses one of the great West Highland watersheds, beyond which all rivers flow directly into the Atlantic, and begins its dramatic plunge down through the wild mountain valley of Glen Shiel, until it finally reaches Loch Duich, an inlet of the sea. The landscape is on a very grand scale here, the steeply contoured walls of the glen sweeping up on both sides towards almost parallel lines of summits that dominate the restricted view for miles ahead. For much of the way, the road is almost three thousand feet lower than the line of shapely summits that are little more than a mile away; so the sense of being overlooked is inescapable, even if there's no real impression of being hemmed in. Apart from the road and the series of forestry plantations lining the north side of the glen, and occasional patches of old arable land beside the river, there are no signs in these upper reaches of human occupation or activity.

As it picks its way down the course of the River Shiel, the road seems in places to be unguarded and vulnerable to attack from above. It has indeed been savaged from time to time by landslides and rockfalls; in December 1949, after a sudden thaw, a long stretch of road hereabouts was smothered under twelve feet of rubble and scree. Accidents like this are less likely now, because of the new line of the main road, the cutting walls specially built to prevent landslips, and the binding action of the Forestry Commission's trees.

This high part of the glen used to be regularly blocked by heavy winter snowfalls. The first Statistical Account of the parish of Glenshiel, written towards the end of the eighteenth century, recalled 'an extraordinary example of abstinence' that had recently occurred: 'A female of this parish, of the name of Isabella Macrae, of weak intellect, and a beggar, had left Glenmoristone, where she had been soliciting alms, at the beginning of a fall of snow, which lay upon the ground for the unusually long period of six weeks. During the greater part of this time, the poor woman was not missed, her friends in this parish believing that she was waiting in Glenmoristone for the disappearance of the snow. It was at last ascertained that she had left that country, on her way home; but it was only at the end of the period above-mentioned, that she was discovered under a wreath of snow alive, after eating all the heather within her reach. She was known to have had a small quantity of oatmeal in her possession, which, with the heather, composed the whole of her sustenance, during the time that she remained under the snow. Though she lived some years afterwards, she never recovered an erect posture, and it is also recorded, that when found, her chest bore the impression of her knees, in consequence of having been so long in a sitting and stooping posture.'

South of the road at the head of Glen Shiel, a succession of green, steep-sided corries, with elegant triangular summits linked by delicately curving saddles, marks the boundary between Inverness-shire and Wester Ross. This is all part of the Cluanie deer forest, which stretches over the ridge towards the lonelier country of Glen Quoich, itself so surrounded by great mountain peaks that it has the highest rainfall in the whole of Scotland. Directly south of the plantation that marks the watershed, the eastern end of the ridge is known as Maol Chinn-Dearg, and the hillsides that swoop downwards from it to the head of Glen Shiel formed one of the hunting preserves of the Scottish kings.

There were deer drives here, according to some sources, as early as the thirteenth century. Certainly, James VI had an interest in the place, because in 1573 he issued a proclamation forbidding entry to 'graziers, cutters of timber and peelers of trees'. Over the years, what timber there was has been completely cleared from that side of the glen, and in the second half of the last century, it became a strictly preserved deer stalking ground once again.

Beyond the watershed, the glen narrows substantially, and the roadmakers had a difficult task finding a reasonable route. Until the many improvements of the 1960s, this part of the road used to follow almost exactly the line settled a hundred and fifty years ago by Thomas Telford, which was itself based for much of the way on an earlier military road. Many of the old loops and cuttings and unguarded corners can still be seen. Telford noted that the road was three years in the building, at a saving of seventy-odd pounds on the original estimate of nearly fifteen thousand, which was by no means the rule hereabouts.

There comes a point where the latest version of the road takes the south side of the river, in a more open situation than its immediate predecessor on the north bank. Where the older, cut-off road crossed to the south bank over a narrow stone bridge, there's a National Trust for Scotland sign marking the site of the Battle of Glenshiel. This was the only real engagement of the miserable shambles in 1719 that is the least publicized of the Jacobite rebellions, an affair that resolved a tangled story of

European intrigue, plots and counterplots, midnight dashes and secret couriers, in one night of gunfire in this lonely Highland glen.

After the collapse of the much more famous rebellion of 1715, James Francis Edward Stuart, *Chevalier de Saint Georges* and Pretender to the British throne, went back to his threadbare 'court' at Bar-le-Duc in Lorraine. There were still powerful forces willing to sustain him in his claim, even if many of them were interested less in getting him personally onto the throne than in forcing the detested George I off it. James had support not only from the Tory party in Britain, but from France, Spain, Italy and Sweden as well.

After the failure of the Fifteen, however, French support faded out when the Regent Orléans, ruling the country after the death of James Stuart's supporter Louis XIV, made friendly noises towards the British government, whose assistance he realized he might need in a quarrel that was brewing with Spain. In this situation, the Jacobite headquarters at Bar-le-Duc was something of an embarrassment, and James was forced to move to Rome where, as a Catholic prepared to win back the British throne from the Protestant House of Hanover, he was made most welcome. Sadly, the French pension he had been granted by Louis XIV was stopped as soon as he crossed the border.

It was Sweden that provided the next offer of sponsorship for a Jacobite rebellion, now that the French finance that had paid for the Fifteen was no longer on tap. Charles XII of Sweden, who had a recent territorial grudge to settle with George I, was interested in any plot that might depose him. Charles's chief minister, Baron Gortz, busied himself in the winter of 1716/17 with plans for a Jacobite rebellion in England and an invasion, with Charles at the head of twelve thousand Swedish troops, of the Scottish Highlands. Catholic Europe rallied round: Philip of Spain's chief minister, the all-powerful Cardinal Alberoni, gave substantial support in gold.

British government agents were on the trail of this plot, of course, and on 29 January 1717 they intercepted and decoded some secret messages to Count Gyllenborg, the Swedish representative in London. That same evening, Gyllenborg's house was unobtrusively surrounded by a party of soldiers, and he was arrested. In command of the party was General Wade, later to become known in the Highlands as the builder of a great network of military roads, although not, despite the evidence of the Ordnance Survey one-inch map, of the one through Glen Shiel itself.

The cat was well and truly out of the bag, and the idea of a rising in the summer of 1717 fizzled out; but Jacobite agents were still sounding out the courts of Europe for support. The Duke of Ormonde, Prime Minister of the Old Chevalier's phantom court, went without success to Stockholm and St Petersburg, and by the following year the exiled Jacobites were running low in both money and morale. Suddenly, in the summer of 1718, European politics took another convulsion when British warships under Admiral Byng were sent to the Mediterranean to smash a Spanish fleet off Sicily, where Alberoni had perennial ambitions. The Cardinal, desperate for revenge, settled on another Jacobite attempt as the most economical way of getting his own back.

Ormonde was summoned to Madrid, where he and the Cardinal got down to the details of the rebellion which Alberoni had nominated him to lead. The much respected and popular Ormonde, an exiled leader of the Tory party, seemed to Alberoni to be the ideal man for the job; but Ormonde's character had flaws that were ill-suited to the leader of a great national revolt. As one of his associates wrote: 'He was so diffident of himself that he often followed the advice of those who had a smaller share of sense than himself; he was as irresolute and timorous in affairs as he was brave in his person, and was apt to lose good opportunities by waiting to remove difficulties which naturally attend great designs, and of which a part must always be left to fortune in the execution.'

Charles XII of Sweden agreed to support the plan. It involved an invasion of the west of England, which Ormonde was to lead and James Stuart himself, almost as an afterthought, was invited to join or follow. Ormonde suggested a secondary expedition to the West Highlands and that young George Keith, Earl Marischal of Scotland and something of a military prodigy, should be in command of it.

Alberoni had thousands of troops in Sicily, and always needed large home garrisons in case of trouble with France, but he finally offered substantial help for the invasion. He would provide five thousand men and two months' pay for them, three hundred horses, field guns, muskets and gunpowder, as well as the transport ships. With this force, Ormonde was to land in the West Country, gather the support that would almost certainly be available, and march on London. Keith was to be supplied with two frigates, a few companies of Spanish troops, muskets, ammunition and money for his landing in the West Highlands.

On 8 February 1719 the news spread through Rome that James Stuart and the leaders of the Jacobite court had been seen riding furiously northwards, and nicely confusing rumours went the rounds about the reason for his hurried departure. Before the party got to Genoa, just as they passed out of friendly territory, they were all arrested, when it was found that the 'Pretender' was himself a pretender: a mildly disguised member of James's staff. James himself, in one of the occasional romantic adventures that punctuated a rather dull life, had sneaked quietly out of Rome, a few hours earlier and in another direction. By the time the hoax was discovered, he was sailing out across the Mediterranean to Spain.

In a life that was not blessed with much good fortune, James must have rated this as one of his most disagreeable experiences. Admiral Byng's fleet was still snooping about the Mediterranean, and the Jacobite ship had many narrow escapes from the ranging British warships. Slipping in and out of lonely island harbours, almost engulfed by a series of storms that left James wracked with sea-sickness and fever, it took almost a month to reach the Spanish coast. On the way, it had been forced to put in at one of the islands off Hyères on the south coast of France, where the disreputable inn and its tough, unwashed customers were in the middle of celebrating a carnival. Poor old James, still fragile from his desperate bouts of *mal-de-mer*, had to put a brave if greenish face on things and dance energetically round the kitchen with his boisterous hostess. Although he was never a man of overpowering optimism, this four-week spell of unrelieved misery must have made him wonder if the game were worth the candle.

He would have been even less confident if he'd known that Charles XII had departed this life, shot through the head during one of the battles with which he perpetually occupied himself. Alberoni, on hearing this news, wondered seriously about calling off the whole affair; but his detestation of the House of Hanover decided him to continue with the fitting-out of the invasion fleet at Cadiz, which a series of hopeful 'leaks' tried to suggest was just another phase of his operations against Sicily.

James Stuart, as so often in his life, missed the boat; but this time, he did it literally. On 9 March he staggered ashore at Rosas on the north-east coast of Spain, to be given a royal welcome, but too late to join the invasion fleet that had just sailed from Cadiz. He was probably not too unhappy about having to spend more time than he'd anticipated on dry land; and, just for once, he was very lucky. On 4 March, King George's spies had reported full details of the entire invasion plan, and a British fleet was already patrolling the south-western approaches. The Spanish fleet never reached there. They ran into a terrible storm in the Bay of Biscay. It raged for two days and two nights, dismasted many of the ships, washed stores, horses and soldiers overboard, and finally forced the crippled and useless survivors of this miniature Spanish Armada back to their home ports.

Before news of this disaster reached Cadiz, Keith's expedition to the West Highlands had already sailed. It reached the Island of Lewis towards the end of the month, and at the Earl of Seaforth's island castle more detailed plans were laid. By 4 April it had been joined by another group of exiled Scottish Jacobite leaders who had travelled secretly from France, as well as by others who still lived at home. Already, trouble was brewing. There was a great deal of argument about who was actually in command, but by 13 April they had established their mainland base at the Earl of Seaforth's castle of Eilean Donan, on the shore of Loch Duich half a dozen miles from the foot of Glen Shiel.

At a council of war four days later, the leaders were still arguing among themselves about who should have been bossing whom, and about what their next move should be. Since there was no news of Ormonde's expedition to the west of England, some of them, including Don Nicolas Bolano who was in command of the Spanish troops, wanted to hurry back to Spain and safety; but Keith would have none of it, and settled the argument on 30 April by sending the two Spanish frigates back home.

Next week, a British naval squadron commanded by Captain Boyle arrived on the scene. Two of its five ships anchored in a sea loch some way to the north, and the others, the *Worcester*, *Enterprise* and *Flamborough*, mounting one hundred and fourteen guns all told, sailed into the mouth of Loch Duich. A longboat was sent to demand the surrender of Eilean Donan Castle, by that time garrisoned by men of Don Pedro de Castro's regiment. The Spaniards fired on the boat and wouldn't let it land. On 9 May a day-long bombardment reduced the castle to a pile of rubble, the Spaniards surrendered, and the gunpowder and ammunition supplies fell into government hands.

Meanwhile, the main body of Jacobites had moved up Glen Shiel, and were busy protecting their strong natural position near the present-day bridge with a series of barricades and trenches. With their escape route to the coast cut off, they were in a pretty hopeless position. News had finally come about the fate of Ormonde's invasion fleet, and the Jacobite Highlanders whose support had been canvassed were none too keen to throw in their lot with such an obviously doomed expedition. The fact that the Old Chevalier had shown up none too well during the Fifteen was no incentive to join him this time. The Jacobites had no more than a thousand men, gathered from Perthshire, Stirlingshire, Argyll and Lord Seaforth's territory round about. Among them were a group of followers of Rob Roy Macgregor, most famous of the Scottish outlaws, who had come to lend his support.

The Jacobites had a long and nerve-wracking wait, because it wasn't until 5 June that General Wightman marched from Inverness with a government force of about the same number of men: some English, some German and some from loyalist Highland clans that had no sympathy for the Stuart cause. Four days later the Jacobites, having been warned of the advance, took up their positions in Glen Shiel, on the hillside north of the bridge; by this time they had been joined by two hundred more volunteers.

That evening, one of their outposts reported that Wightman's troops were camped almost at the watershed, about a mile west of Cluanie Inn. At two o'clock in the afternoon of 10 May—White Rose Day, the Chevalier's birthday—the two forces were in sight of each other, half a mile apart in one of the narrowest and steepest sections of the glen.

Wightman was dismayed to see how well protected the Jacobite position was: 'Their Dispositions for Defence were extraordinary, with the Advantages of Rocks, Mountains, and Intrenchments.' George Keith recalled in his memoirs: 'Our right was cover'd by a rivulet which was difficult to pass, and our left by a ravine, and in the front the ground was so rugged and steep that it was almost impossible to come to us.'

After some 'softening up' by his four Cohorn mortars, whose shells set fire to the heathery hillside, Wightman sent his left wing up the steep slopes to the first barricade, where it was driven back. Another assault had as much success; but a third one on the same point, which the Jacobites had not thought to reinforce, broke through, and the government troops began a difficult advance up the 3,370-ft mountain of Sgurr nan Spainteach, the Spaniards' Peak, which reaches north and west from the bridge. In the face of this determined attack by practised and professional soldiers, the Jacobites were quick to retreat, although their marksmen had given a good account of themselves.

Once they saw that the game was up, the Highlanders faded quietly from the scene. The Spaniards, who had been standing their ground well, were forced to move higher and higher up, until by sunset they were almost three and a half thousand feet up the bare mountainside. Bolano offered at a midnight council of war to continue the fight, but the Jacobites were at the same time gradually disappearing homewards through the hills; one of the Scottish leaders of the expedition reported later: 'The Spaniards themselves declared they could neither live without bread nor make any hard marches thro' the Country, therefore I was oblig'd to give them leave to Capitulate the best way they could.' Unsupported, and with only the vaguest idea of the language, the Spaniards surrendered the next morning, and the last force of foreign troops ever to invade British soil were taken as captives to the south. Keith recalled that of his local supporters, 'every one took the road he liked best.' As for himself: 'Being sick of a feavour, I was forced to lurck some months in the mountains.'

From time to time, Jacobite weapons have been fished out of the deep pool above the bridge, where they were perhaps thrown by escaping Highlanders leaving the scene to take on the guise of innocent travellers. This is recalled by the name Eas nan Arm given to the latest bridge—the Water of Arms. Wightman spent the next week or two rampaging through the rebel countryside, reporting to the government that he had 'taken a Tour through all the difficult parts of Seaforth's Country to terrify the Rebels by burning the Houses of the Guilty and preserving those of the

Honest. There are no Bodies of the Rebels together, unless stealing Parties in Scores up and down the Mountains.'

One prominent Jacobite who didn't seem too put out about the utter failure of the attempt was James Stuart himself. Three months later, back in Rome, he married Princess Clementina Sobieski, and never gave anybody another chance to collect the price of £100,000 that King George had put on his head if he were ever seen in Britain again. The following summer Princess Clementina gave birth to Prince Charles Edward, who was to restart the whole business rather more romantically a generation later. Oddly enough, Bonnie Prince Charlie spent a short time in the glen where his father's earlier ambitions were finally shattered. In July 1746, having broken through the cordon of sentries trying to hem him in along the western coastal districts during his flight after Culloden, he spent a night in a cave on a hillside above the glen, while Redcoats patrolled the valley below.

Nothing of great note happened in Glen Shiel for many years after that, until the first day of September 1773 when a small party of travellers could have been seen making their way slowly down the glen. Samuel Johnson, James Boswell, Johnson's servant Joseph and a local man called Ewan Campbell, acting as their guide, came this way to the Skye ferry during what has remained to this day one of the classic Highland journeys, as recounted in Boswell's *Journal of a Tour to the Hebrides*.

Dr Johnson, a bulky man and no longer in the first flush of youth, was rather irritable during this long and difficult stage, and was to get more so as the weary day wore on. Boswell's diary noted several minor disagreements: 'Mr. Johnson owned he was now in a scene of as wild nature as he could see. But he corrected me sometimes in my observations. "There," said I, "is a mountain like a cone." "No, Sir," said he. "It would be called so in a book; and when a man comes to look at it, he sees 'tis not so. It is indeed pointed at the top. But one side of it is much larger than the other." Another mountain I called immense. "No," said he, "but 'tis a considerable protuberance." '

The splendid Yale edition of Boswell's *Journal* published in the 1960s notes that Johnson's harrumphing about the conical mountain was 'captious', as can still be seen today. The summit in question is Faochag, which got its name of the Whelk from its pointed top. It's in full view from the bridge near the old battlefield, an independent pyramid of a mountain two miles to the west-south-west. The good doctor's crack about the 'considerable protuberance' is one of the remarks that failed to endear him to generations of Scottish readers, suffering from the touchy native habit of taking other people's opinions much too seriously.

This was perhaps the toughest day's stage in their entire journey. They had spent the night in Glenmoriston, away beyond Loch Cluanie, and were on their way to the foot of Glen Shiel, where they had still to tackle the stiff climb over the pass of Mam Ratagan, towards the Skye ferry at Glenelg. Continuing down the glen, past the rocky and heathery scree-sloped sides of the Spaniards' Peak, they passed along the foot of Boswell's 'immense mountain', the spectacular ridge of the Five Sisters of Kintail which makes up the eastern wall of the lower reaches of Glen Shiel. The modern road takes much the same line, past the old stalker's house at Achnagart on the far side of the river, about a mile after which the party 'came to a rich green valley, comparatively speaking, and stopped at Auchnashiel, a kind of rural village, a number of cottages being built together, as we saw all along in the Highlands. We passed many miles today without seeing a house, but only little summer-huts or *shielings*. . . . At this Auchnashiel, we sat down on a green turf seat at the end of a house, and they brought us out two wooden dishes of milk. . . . Mr. Johnson imagined my dish was better than his, and desired to taste it. He did so, and was convinced that I had no advantage over him. We had there in a circle all about us, men, women and children, all Macraes, Lord Seaforth's people. Not one of them could speak English. I said to Mr. Johnson 'twas the same as being with a tribe of Indians. "Yes," said he, "but not so terrifying." '

They passed a pleasantly patronizing hour or so there, Boswell handing out snuff and tobacco, slices of wheat bread and then a penny to each of the children. 'I told Mr. Johnson of this, upon which he called for change for a shilling, and declared that he would distribute among the children. Upon this there was a great stir. . . . Mr. Johnson then ordered the children to be drawn up in a row, and he distributed his copper and made them and their parents all happy. . . .The people were much pleased, gave us many blessings, and said they had not had such a day since the old Laird of Macleod's time.'

And so the party went on their way, Johnson and Boswell telling each other what devilish fine fellows they were to have distributed their largesse so benevolently. Later, they were a little deflated to be told that the woman who had sold them milk, and to whom they gave an extra tip because she withstood her neighbours' whispered suggestions to charge them too high a price, was comfortably off, with what was in local terms a fairly substantial number of cattle. It can be said, without pointing the finger too directly, that this two hundred year-old story is not entirely without relevance today.

Auchnashiel has disappeared entirely, although the once fertile sweep of ground created by a swing of the river is still plainly to be seen, with lines of trees following the river's course. Just before the time of Johnson and Boswell's visit there had been more people in Glenshiel parish than they knew of; but in 1769 and again in 1772 a number of cattle-farming tenants had emigrated to North Carolina. There are vague traces of one or two cottages at the site of Auchnashiel, and it isn't long since a certain stone was pointed out as the exact spot where Dr Johnson sat supping his milk and wondering if Boswell had had a better deal.

It's rather unfortunate that the structure of Glen Shiel, since the narrow valley floor levels out a long way from the foot of the glen, makes it impossible to see Loch Duich from anywhere inside it; but this serves only to concentrate the traveller's gaze on the soaring hillsides that sweep up to the peaks of the Five Sisters of Kintail, the great mountain mass that forms the north-eastern wall of the lower reaches of the glen. From the depths of the valley, however, the lack of foreground makes them seem like just another lump of mountain, and not the magnificent group silhouetted against the sky they are seen to be from farther west.

The Five Sisters are the heart of the Kintail estate, once part of the great north-western properties of the Mackenzie Earls of Seaforth. Even after the noble line had died out, this was Mackenzie property for several generations, a strictly guarded deer forest that was usually rented to outsiders. Just before the first world war, there was what seemed at the time a very minor incident on the high tops of the Five Sisters, although it was to play a major part in the modern history of the estate. A young English climber called Percy Unna was ordered off the hill by Sydney Loder, who rented the shooting rights over Kintail for several years; Loder may have forgotten what was a fairly commonplace incident, but Unna did not.

A few years later the 21,000 acre Kintail estate was sold to a Lowland whisky magnate, Alexander Edward. Later still, he gifted it to the Northern Infirmary in Inverness. In 1944 Kintail was put up for sale again, and who should buy it but the same Percy Unna, by that time a wealthy civil engineer, but still an enthusiastic mountaineer who had been elected for a term as president of the Scottish Mountaineering Club, no mean honour for an Englishman; he had never forgotten his run-in with Sydney Loder in the feudal days at the turn of the century. Unna immediately presented the estate to the National Trust for Scotland, and ever since then the public have had free access to it. This was only one of Percy Unna's many gifts to the National Trust, since the Unna Trust set up after his death also bought or endowed the mountain estates of Torridon, farther north on the Ross-shire coast, and Ben Lawers in Perthshire. It is one of the unalterable conditions of the Unna Trust's gifts that these areas are to remain basically undeveloped mountain country, with no proliferation of hotels and similar facilities for 'armchair' travellers.

The National Trust for Scotland do not rent out the Kintail stalking, but call in the Red Deer Commission when a cull of the herds is necessary. Local opinion is that they make more money from the venison taken and sold in this way than would be possible from renting the estate out to sportsmen. There's an unusual clash of interests, as far as deer stalking is concerned, on the two sides of the lower glen. As owners of the east side, the National Trust for Scotland allow free access to climbers and hill walkers, and have no interest in the sporting possibilities; on the west side, the Glenshiel shootings are part of Lord Burton's deer forest of Cluanie, and are so affected by the movements of climbers and hikers that the deer shy away from them until round about October, almost at the very end of the season. Previously, stags were available from August onwards, but now they are so scarce that Dochfour estate have recently found it almost impossible to interest a shooting tenant in the place at all.

Down at the foot of the glen is Loch Shiel, which is not to be confused with the much grander loch of the same name in Ardnamurchan away to the south. The Ross-shire Loch Shiel is a pleasant and unobtrusive stretch of water at the foot of the immensely steep slopes of the Five Sisters ridge, hidden round a left-hand bend on the main road immediately after an old wood. There are birches around the rather damp course of the river, and no opportunity for a distant view ahead. A roadside monument near the loch was set up between the wars to a famous local shinty player.

Just after Loch Shiel is the start of the little settlement of Shiel Bridge, introduced by a petrol station, shop and tearoom run by Dochfour estate. Until fairly recently the main road kept left of the petrol station and over a metal bridge across a tributary of the River Shiel that comes down the slopes of the 3,314-ft peak of the Saddle, highest point on the south and west mountain boundary ridge of the glen; but the road improvements included a realignment along the other side. Now the main road sweeps over a new bridge through the haphazardly sited houses of Shiel Bridge, and comes to a junction that offers the first choice of route on this approach to Wester Ross. The main road keeps straight ahead towards Kyle of Lochalsh, but the turning to the left, which goes immediately over the old original Shiel bridge, leads towards a most attractive collection of mountain and loch-side byways that should certainly not be missed by anybody who isn't in a tearing hurry to get to Kyle.

CHAPTER 2

RATAGAN AND LETTERFEARN

ONCE OVER THE old Shiel bridge, there's a junction in front of Glenshiel Lodge, which is the lodge house for the deer stalking ground of the same name. For some years this building served as an inn, but it was closed down in 1907. This has been quoted many times as an example of the high-handed action typical of the sporting landlords of that time, who went to great lengths to make sure that no non-sporting visitors could interfere with the stalking. In fact, the reason was economic rather than feudal. An angling guide of the 1900s made it very clear how difficult it was to get from the Lowlands to Glenshiel in those days, advising visitors that the best way was by steamer to Glenelg and then over the difficult pass of Mam Ratagan. The guide remarked that the inn was comfortable but old-fashioned, having little accommodation to offer apart from the bedrooms. A local man still living nearby remembers that Miss Mackintosh, the last tenant of the place when it was an inn, closed it down because there just wasn't enough business; pressure from the estate owners had nothing to do with it.

The left turn in front of the lodge leads only to the river, although this was originally the main road; turning to the right leads very shortly past the entrance to Shiel House, now a private dwelling but for many years a much better known if little res-pected inn, established as a 'king's house' in the early eighteenth century, when the military road was built over the pass to Glenelg after the Jacobite risings of 1715 and 1719. If ever a hostelry had a miserable reputation, this was it. Just about every literate traveller who came this way exploded in print about its primitive lack of facilities.

One of them was the poet James Hogg, better known as the Ettrick Shepherd, who spent a night in it during his tour of the Highlands in 1803. His account of the place was included in a

1 Red deer are to be seen in most parts of Wester Ross, although rarely as close-up as this

2 The conical summit of Faochaig above Glen Shiel, with the serrated ridge of the Saddle to the right.   In the middle distance are mounds of old glacial debris

3 Road works at Shiel Bridge below the Five Sisters of Kintail

4 Looking out over Ratagan to the Five Sisters

series of letters describing his tour that he addressed to Sir Walter Scott, although they weren't published until about a hundred years later. In Hogg's time, the landlord was a low-country man called Johnston, from Annandale in Dumfriesshire, who had allowed the inn to go to rack and ruin. There was only one room available for guests, which was notable mainly for the shelter it offered to an appalling number and variety of bed bugs.

In the early hours of the morning there was an even more unwelcome intrusion, as Hogg noted with some exasperation: 'I was awakened during the night by a whole band of Highlanders, both male and female, who entered my room, and fell to drinking whisky with much freedom. They had much the appearance of a parcel of vagabonds, which they certainly were, but as the whole discourse was in Gaelic I knew nothing of what it was concerning, but it arose by degrees as the whisky operated, to an insufferable noise.'

The hullaballoo continued for something like two hours, throughout which time Hogg lay with his eyes closed and pretended, apparently with some success, to be fast asleep. Suddenly the solitary candle was snuffed out, and he heard a gentle rustling noise which he identified unerringly as the sound of somebody ransacking the pockets of his coat. Hogg bellowed for more light, prepared to lay about him with his stout Border walking stick, and had a top-of-his-voice interview with Mr Johnston, during which he made some highly unpoetic comments about the facilities and clientele of the inn.

Sixteen years later another poet, Robert Southey, in his diary of the tour he made with the great civil engineer Thomas Telford, recorded another chapter in the melancholy downfall of 'this inn built by Government solely for the accommodation of travellers in these western wilds. . . . The Laird into whose hands it has past, a certain Mr. Dick, quarrelled with the last tenant, got rid of him, and shut up the house, contrary to an express condition that it was to be kept open as an Inn. Owing to this, there is now no public house at which a traveller can lodge for the night, between the Western Sea and Glenmorriston.'

This same Mr Dick, who had a sheep farm at Ratagan on the west side of Loch Duich, quarrelled with many other people besides the tenant of the inn. His grazing lands extended far up the mountain side, and away over the summit of the pass in the

direction of Glenelg; to provide more and more grazing ground
for his sheep, he evicted many of the smaller crofting tenants from
his estate.   On the shores of Loch Duich he built walls and
embankments to keep the tide out of the lochside land, and he had
plans to establish a tweed mill; but no improvements of this kind
could sweeten relations between himself and the local people,
who utterly detested him.   The story of how one man got his
revenge on him has become a little bit confused after all this time,
but was the subject of a famous court case that was followed with
great interest in many of the surrounding parishes.

Two Glenshiel men were in a shepherd's bothy in Glen
Quoich, over the southern ridge of Glen Shiel, when one of them
decided to make a raid on Dick's house at Ratagan. Waiting until
his companion was asleep, he trekked over the hills to Glenshiel,
along an old path that still comes out beside a road metal quarry
a few miles up the glen, near the place where Prince Charlie spent
an anxious day hiding from the Redcoats in the valley below.
One version of the story mentions shots being fired at Ratagan
House, but the best-remembered one says that the Glen Quoich
man contented himself with stealing a couple of Dick's horses,
took them back up the mountain track, hamstrung them, and
threw them over the edge to be battered to death on the rocks
below. By early morning he was back in the Glen Quoich bothy,
and when his companion woke up, it was as if he'd never been
away. The case came to court, and the main detail common to
both versions of the plot is that the Sheriff dismissed it because
he refused to believe that anybody could make such a difficult
double journey over the mountains between sunset and dawn the
next day.

In the 1830s it was noted that there were three cattle fairs held
at Shiel House every year; although whisky was inclined to flow
like water on these occasions, the local minister admitted that
nobody got really drunk, and there was no fighting. These cattle
fairs were normally all-male occasions, but the minister had seen a
sinister development: 'The practice of exposing pedlar's wares at
these meetings, which has been lately introduced, threatens, by
attracting young females to them, to do injury to their morals.'

Beyond Shiel House the view is still restricted for a few
hundred yards, the road being bounded by a high stone wall to
the right and the rough grazing ground below the state forest of

Ratagan coming steeply down from the summits on the left. Ratagan Forest was first planted in the 1920s, and is one of the many forests whose ground isn't actually owned by the Forestry Commission. It is held on a ninety-nine year lease from Dochfour estate, which provided two and a half thousand acres, and later increased this by three thousand. The planted ground rises very sharply from the lochside, about a thousand feet in a vertical half-mile.

At the end of the roadside wall there suddenly comes the first view of Loch Duich, which is by any standards well worth the long wait. It's one of the genuine west coast fjords, surrounded by shapely peaks and ridges, and with only a narrow stretch of level ground down by the water's edge. The Mam Ratagan road begins its steep climb up through the forest, to the summit of the pass that leads it to Glenelg and the 'back door' car ferry to Skye, while a right turn down towards the lochside leads along one of the most beautiful roads on the west coast, towards the little hamlets of Ratagan and Letterfearn. At low tide there can be seen one of the old fish traps, where salmon were stranded on the ebb.

Ratagan, which is a scattered settlement beginning about half a mile along the lochside road, was at one time a village serving the local estate; but its old stone cottages are now outnumbered, if anything, by the timber houses built by the Forestry Commission after the second world war. They were bought in Scandinavia and shipped across to Scotland as kits of parts, which seems a rather odd operation by an organization dedicated to producing home grown timber. Because of their origin, they have the rather splendid postal address of Swedish Houses, Ratagan. From time to time during the summer a rather curious ritual can be observed here, as people steal out of the houses into their back gardens, and hurl buckets of water over their television aerials. It isn't a modern sacrifice to the ancient Celtic water spirits, but the only way to get reasonable television reception in dry weather; there's a lot of static from the Hydro Board power lines behind the village.

All the houses in the place are occupied by forestry workers, the only buildings with other connexions being the lochside youth hostel and Ratagan House, which used to be the headquarters of the local estate but was converted into a hotel some years ago. In 1970, however, it didn't open for the tourist season at all. The hostel is on the shore of the loch, just after the stone bridge across the little burn that comes down from the heights of the forest. Until 1969 it was run by Dom Capaldi, one of the great characters of the Scottish Youth Hostels Association, who had been there for more than thirty years and used to spend the close season travelling on the Continent.

Ratagan faces almost due east across the loch, and it's inclined to go out of the sun rather early in winter, although the forested mountain ridge behind it doesn't have the oppressive effect one might expect after looking at it on the one-inch map. In front of the Swedish houses there's a line of rowan trees planted along the roadside verge, and one of the most pleasant ways in Wester Ross to end a fine autumn day is to sit out on one of the porches and soak in the view. The trees are a warm mass of red rowan berries; behind them is the paler red of the sandstone pebbles on the rocky shore, with a scattering of seaweed on the margin of the loch, the colour of faded saffron. Loch Duich itself acts as a great blue mirror reflecting the majestic barrier of the Five Sisters and the curtain of hills beyond the narrow valley of Strath Croe directly opposite. In winter, too, there are few finer viewpoints than this, with the ermine peaks of Kintail vaguely seen through the enveloping cloud that seeps down through the great valley of Glen Shiel.

Beside the youth hostel is the local forestry office, and on the other side of the road stands Ratagan House, in the proper season almost invisible behind a splendid screen of oak, ash and beech trees. This is the same house in which James Hogg stayed the night in 1803 after his itchy experiences at Shiel Inn, as a guest of the hospitable sheep farmer Donald Macleod, with whom he chatted about the differences between sheep farming in Wester Ross and the way he had done it himself in his native Borders. There's a pleasant outlook to Inverinate, the long, scattered village on the far side of the loch, around which the steep forested hillside is interrupted by occasional fields and lines of cypress trees, with the mansion of Inverinate Lodge in a fine situation in a colourful garden at the edge of the water.

The road from Ratagan down through Letterfearn is one of the most attractive in Ross-shire, although fortunately ignored by most visitors because it doesn't lead anywhere in particular. The little whitewashed parish church of Glenshiel is along this way, and the narrow lochside road wanders quietly along past pleasantly situated cottages placed at civilized intervals. One of these in particular, just above the loch before the road takes a left-hand bend, occupies a position of almost unparalleled grandeur, with views in opposite directions of the peaks of the Five Sisters at the head of the loch, and of the restored castle of Eilean Donan where Loch Duich merges with Loch Alsh before becoming the open sea.

Letterfearn is a quiet and dreamy little hamlet of mostly old-fashioned cottages; several of them are the homes of retired forestry workers, but rather too many of the houses are opened only at holiday times or rented out for summer letting. The name Letterfearn means the Alder Slopes, while the district across the loch between Inverinate and Eilean Donan used to be known as Letterchoil, the Wooded Slopes. A hundred years ago and more, Letterfearn used to have wide expanses of alder and ash woods; the alder was used for making barrel staves, and the ash for boat building. Until 1970, Letterfearn had a daily influx of younger folk, because the primary school for the west side of the loch was in the village; but there has been centralization even here, and the school has been merged with a newer one at Inverinate.

Letterfearn used to have a Royal Pier, although there isn't much sign of it today. It was built in 1908 especially for Edward VII, who landed here during his sailing tour of the Western Isles. There used to be a lot of fishing done on this part of the loch, and even sixty years ago there were four or five Letterfearn boats involved in the Minch and Barra fishings; but now it is only a local and spare-time occupation. The nets and buoys and drying poles still make a pleasant, but hardly significant, addition to the lochside scene.

About a hundred and fifty years ago there was a much more secret trade in the village, when the Letterfearn estate was well known for the number of illicit whisky stills it supported. As in many west coast districts, the steep hillsides rising from the loch, with their woods of ash and alder and silver birch, and occasional outcrops of bare grey rock, were ideal camouflage for the wisps of smoke drifting away from the illegal stills.

This was after the evictions which started in the early years of the last century, when the old hill grazings were taken away from the crofting families who had used them for generations, and were turned over to southern sheep farmers who could pay much higher rents to the landowners. The old crofting tenants had to crowd into ramshackle settlements huddled at the edges of the sea lochs, on the narrow strips of ground that didn't offer much grazing for the invading sheep. There were three main occupations left to the landless people. Whisky smuggling, although illegal, was by far the most profitable. From thirty shillings worth of barley there could be distilled six or seven times that value of whisky. Eventually, of course, the excisemen stamped out the trade.

In the lochside settlements like Letterfearn, fishing was another possibility, but the erratic routes of the herring shoals took them away from the west coast just when they were most needed. Finally, there was the trade in kelp, which was for a short time an extremely lucrative business for the big landowners, and a means of survival for their dispossessed clansmen, although many of the 'lower orders' hated the dreary kelp-burning work. It was estimated, for example, that the chief of Clanranald made something like £30,000 from the trade, most of which went to pay off some of the gambling debts that eventually forced him to sell off his extensive and scattered family estates. At the height of the kelp boom, around fifty thousand people were supported by it.

The kelp trade was something of a fool's paradise, since it was kept going mainly because imports of Spanish barilla used in the making of soap, glass, iodine and bleaching materials were impossible during the Napoleonic Wars, and were taxed heavily for several years afterwards. In 1823 the tax was lifted, and about the same time chemists discovered how to produce the necessary alkalines artificially. When the bottom dropped out of the kelp market, it wasn't only the tenants and evicted smallholders who were affected; many of the west coast lairds found themselves in sadly reduced circumstances, and another wave of estate selling and renting began.

The minister of Glenshiel parish, which included Shiel Bridge, Ratagan and Letterfearn, wrote in 1836 about how his people were affected by the change to large-scale sheep farming: 'Though the change . . . produced an amazing increase of rent . . . the effect among the population was not so favourable. The valuable and respected class of "substantial tenants" has been entirely swept away; such of their number as did not emigrate to America, having sunk to the rank of lotters or cottars upon the large farms, are crowded along the shores of the loch, dependent for sustinence upon the laborious and uncertain pursuit of the herring fishing, or the still more fatiguing, precarious and pernicious practice of smuggling. Nor has the ruin thus brought on the tenantry been unattended with a corresponding reaction upon the landlords. Notwithstanding the incredibly rapid increase of the value of the lands, the expectations of this class, and the additional expenditure to which these led, rose in a progression still more rapid, and the result is apparent in the fact, that the whole lands of the parish were lately under trust or assignation, in consequence of pecuniary encumbrances. . . . It cannot be said with truth, that the class of people of which the majority of the population consists, enjoys the comforts of life in even a moderate degree. Poorly fed, scantily clothed, and miserably lodged, theirs is a life of penury and toil.'

Sir Walter Scott, who visited Loch Duich and spent the usual miserable night at Shiel Inn, didn't always see the Highlands through tartan-coloured spectacles, as his many modern detractors suggest: 'In too many instances the Highlands have been drained, not of their superfluity of population, but of the whole mass of the inhabitants, dispossessed by an unrelenting avarice, which will one day, be found to have been as short-sighted as it is unjust and selfish. Meantime, the Highlands may become the fairy ground for romance and poetry, or the subject of experiment for the professors of speculation, political and economical.' If ever there were an accurate prediction about the Highlands, that was it.

Letterfearn continued to be a fairly miserable settlement right through the rest of the nineteenth century. When the situation in the Highlands got so bad that a slow-moving government finally appointed a Royal Commission to investigate it, it was in 1883, by which time many of the local families, who had been at one time reasonably well-off cattle farmers, were in desperate straits. The Royal Commission held one of its enquiries in the village, when William Grant, one of the local tenants, explained that the people were starved of land: 'At present in Letterfearn one crofter has three acres, two others have two acres each, thirteen have one acre apiece, seven others have the eighth part of an acre each, fifteen families are without any lands whatever, and there are seven paupers, two of whom have one-eighth each. The reason why our part of the parish is so crowded is due to the evictions that took place in the other parts of it, in order to make room for large sheep farms even as far back as the times when the Earls of Seaforth were proprietors.' And the last Earl of Seaforth had died almost seventy years before. All the same, the Letterfearn people weren't in quite such a terrible condition as the recital of their land holdings suggested; they made a living of sorts from the Loch Duich fishing, which had improved slightly once again, and when their landlord offered them more land at a place called Nonach, some miles to the north-west near the head of Loch Long, they refused because the new place was too far from the sea.

Beyond Letterfearn village the road goes past Drudaig Lodge, the home of the present owner of the now much smaller estate, and winds its way into a kind of roller-coaster tree-lined avenue hacked out of the rocky hillside towards the end of the road at Totaig. There's a wall to stop over-adventurous motorists from driving off the edge into the water, and over it are pleasant views of the little inlets on the near side of the loch, and of the grander hillsides opposite where the main Kyle of Lochalsh road continues on its way towards the village of Dornie.

Totaig is nothing more than an old jetty and a tiny ferry house that has recently been renovated and rented out during the summer season. The ferry has had a rather interrupted history; at one time it made valiant efforts to carry light cars across from Dornie, but now it's for passengers only. Its occasional but regular crossing times should be found out in advance. In previous years the ferry house was licensed, but this amenity has long since gone.

At the beginning of this century the great west coast transport firm of David MacBrayne Limited, in which the government now has a controlling interest, used to have its coasting steamers call here on the way from Glasgow. The Glasgow steamer would arrive off Totaig about three o'clock every Friday morning to unload supplies and passengers for the settlements from Glenshiel to Letterfearn. Boats would be rowed out to meet it, and older people still remember that a dozen horses and carts would spend the rest of the morning delivering the goods to the various lochside hamlets. In those days the steerage fare from Glasgow to Loch Duich was only five shillings.

About the time of the first world war, three local men invested in a boat called the *Isa Reid*, and began to do good business along the lochside, collecting all the food and farming supplies from Kyle and landing them directly onto the smaller piers which MacBraynes' bigger steamer couldn't reach. Within a short time the MacBrayne boats stopped calling at Loch Duich, and after the *Isa Reid* went out of business the district was forced to rely solely on land transport.

From Totaig there's a fine view of the steep hillsides at the meeting of Loch Duich, Loch Alsh and Loch Long, and of the village of Dornie, connected with Ardelve across Loch Long by a long road bridge. The most famous feature of Dornie, the restored castle of Eilean Donan, is seen at a most attractive angle.

The sheltered bays around Totaig are favourite summer anchorages for cruising yachts, and beside one of them, beyond the end of the public road, there's a mysterious cache of rusty metal lifeboats. They got there during the second world war, when the lands of Ardintoul, a Department of Agriculture farm that could be reached only by sea or by a footpath round the roadless coast from Totaig to Glenelg, were occupied by a series of naval oil tanks. As luck would have it, the war was over before the oil installations were completed, but the monster tanks remained an eyesore at Ardintoul until they were dismantled only a couple of years ago.

During the war, the meeting of Loch Duich and Loch Alsh was used as a Royal Navy service and repair depot. One day a fire broke out aboard the *Port Napier*, one of the Navy's fastest minelayers, and there was a great panic that her highly explosive cargo might blow up, taking most of the lochside with it. The greatest fear was that if she blew up, there might be a 'sympathetic detonation' of the enormous store of mines held near Kyle of Lochalsh. The *Port Napier* was rushed out into the middle of the channel between Ardintoul and Skye, where water was pumped into her in an effort to douse the flames. Not surprisingly, perhaps, the ship sank somewhere near the Skye shore, and various bits of equipment and rigging drifted ashore, like the lifeboats at Totaig. Now and again, frogmen go down to keep an eye on the old hulk.

The footpath beyond Totaig, along which the cattle from Ardintoul used to be driven to lorries waiting by the slipway, goes through another patch of forestry planting and then above some older woodlands, towards the old farmhouse, which the Forestry Commission have recently offered for sale. James Hogg came this way too, and he fell like a ton of bricks for Flora Macrae, a daughter of the house of Ardintoul. On the day he was to be ferried across the loch to continue his journey northwards, he was delighted to find that she was to be one of his fellow-passengers: 'Miss Flora was tall, young and handsome, and being in a dark riding habit, with a black helmet and red feather, made a most noble figure.' The four passengers sat in the stern of the boat, and Mr Macrae spread his greatcoat over himself and his elderly sister. 'This was exactly as I wished, and I immediately wrapped Miss Flora in my shepherd's plaid, and though I was averse to sailing, I could willingly have proceeded in this position for at least a week.' He was supposed to meet her once more, but an illness at home forced her to return to Ardintoul. The bold James took a philosophical view of the separation: 'Considering of what inflammable materials my frame is composed, it was probably very fortunate that I was disappointed of ever seeing Miss Macrae again, as I might have felt the inconvenience of falling in love with an object in that remote country.'

Ardintoul's greatest claim to fame, however, may be in its musical rather than literary connexions. It was James Malcolm Macrae of Ardintoul who, while a surgeon with Hastings in India, introduced the bagpipes to Nepal and laid the foundations for the Gurkha pipe bands of the present day.

CHAPTER 3

MAM RATAGAN AND GLENELG

BEHIND RATAGAN IS THE famous hill road over to Glenelg, across the magnificent pass of Mam Ratagan. Although not much more than half the height of the Pass of the Cattle to Applecross farther up the Ross-shire coast, this is perhaps the most Alpine-like of Scotland's mountain roads, in construction if not in outlook. It was originally a military route, built to connect the government headquarters at Fort Augustus on Loch Ness-side with the barracks at Glenelg, which were designed to keep an eye on the Skye crossing during the Jacobite days. It was never a very good road, because the private contractors who were engaged to put up the bridges developed the habit of building them, not to suit the line of the road that was to connect them, but at places where the stone and timber used in their construction were closest at hand; the military road builders who came later had a devil of a job threading the roadway between them.

Telford planned the line of the modern road, the first version of which was finished in 1819 and proved to be, as he had suspected, far from a paying proposition for the contractor. At that time too, Telford surveyed the apparently more obvious route from Ratagan to Glenelg, round the coast by Letterfearn and Ardintoul, but rejected it as being too much in danger of rockfalls and avalanches.

Mam Ratagan is a narrow but well surfaced road that winds steeply uphill for about three miles, from near sea level at Loch Duich to the summit not far short of twelve hundred feet; the Ordnance Survey spot height at 1,116 ft appears to be a little way below the highest point. For most of the way it clambers through the forest, with many sharp corners and near-hairpin bends over bridges. At one or two places there are breaks in the trees, with great swooping views down to the loch; until late in the spring, there are some wider views through patches of road-side larch that haven't yet come out in full summer leaf. People who knew Mam Ratagan before it was engulfed in the forest bemoan the fact that the outlook is now so restricted; but this modern concentration on the confined forest view ahead is a fine preparation for the summit area, which the Forestry Commission have left unplanted. Before the foresters came, this ground was often rented out as a grouse moor, along with the Glenshiel deer stalking.

Almost at the top, after the steepest section of the climb, the road comes out into an open space which offers one of the half-dozen finest loch and mountain scenes in the whole of Scotland. It is a superb eagle's-eye view away down over the forest to the head of Loch Duich and into the steeply guarded valley of Strath Croe that faces Ratagan across the water. Some idea of the effect may be given by the bald statistic that the lochside is less than a mile away, but eleven hundred feet lower down. Little more than two miles to the east is the first of the soaring summits of the Five Sisters of Kintail, and, a little way to the south of there, the more ragged tops that mark the end of the western mountain wall of Glen Shiel. A short climb up from the road can be very rewarding to photographers, especially as most people are content to brandish their cameras from the roadside. That 'eagle's-eye view' remark is not just poetic licence; there have been several sightings of eagles from here, notably on one occasion in 1949 when a golden eagle was seen flying high above the summit of the pass, holding in its talons a fiercely struggling wildcat, which was soon dropped to its death on the rocky hillside below.

A short distance farther on comes the top of the pass, which also marks the boundary between the counties of Ross-shire and Inverness; all the country from here on is in Inverness-shire, although there is no road access to this virtually detached portion without going through another county. It's for this reason that the postal address of all the places over this way is Ross-shire. This county boundary is the northern limit of the vast parish of Glenelg, which stretches miles away to the south and east across Loch Hourn and as far away as Loch Nevis, most of it empty land given over to deer forests. Glenelg itself is an odd name, spelling the same way backwards as forwards; derivations of it range from Glen of the Deer and Glen of the Hunting to Glen of the Irish, since Elg was a name sometimes given to Ireland in Celtic poetry.

At one time it is also said to have been part of the territory of the Kings of Man.

The gradient isn't quite so steep as the road sweeps down out of Ratagan Forest into the fertile valley of Glenmore. From the descent, it's possible to get a first look across to the mountains of Skye, which seem from here to be just another range of mainland hills. As the road passes out of the forest at a cattle grid, it potters along the edge of the rough grazing ground, dotted with bracken, that makes up the northern hillside of Glenmore. It's a pleasant view, with the river winding along through the farmlands in the floor of the glen. Although the Ordnance Survey give the river the same name as the glen, it is usually called the Glenelg River. Back over the high edge of the forest, the Five Sisters still dominate the eastern skyline.

The road is narrow with passing places, but on this side of the pass it's much more straight and open, and there are longer views to show up oncoming traffic. At one point it goes over a stone bridge, with a fleeting glimpse of a heavy waterfall pounding down to join the main river below. The neat arable farms down to the left of the road are on land that was taken over between the wars from a private estate, and rented out by the Department of Agriculture to families who came over from Skye. There are still signs here and there of the old strip cultivation, showing that this was once a crofting stronghold; how its people were bundled off the land is one of the saddest stories of the Highland Clearances.

In the late eighteenth century the whole district of Glenelg proper, which is the part north of Loch Hourn, was the property of the chiefs of Macleod from Dunvegan in Skye. Leod, the founder of the family, seems to have been the son of a twelfth-century King of Man and the Isles. They were enlightened landowners, often pointed out for their wise system of encouraging their tenants to improve the land by granting them unusually long leases, sometimes for as many as forty years. Unfortunately the Macleods, like most of the hereditary clan chiefs, were forced to sell off the greater part of their estates. As a later writer remarked, 'the condition of the people did not improve under Macleod's successors.'

Glenelg had various owners in the early part of the nineteenth century, most notable of them being Charles Grant, a barrister and career politician who bought the estate for £85,000. Born in India, Grant entered Parliament in 1811 as member for the Inverness Burghs and then, from 1818 to 1835, represented the county. He held various high government posts, including those of Chairman of the East India Company, President of the Board of Trade, and Treasurer of the Navy. The Rev. Alexander Beith, writing about Glenelg in 1836, seems to have been in two minds about him. At one point, in a rather syrupy passage, he describes Grant as 'eminent no less for his literary taste than for his talents and success as a statesman, both being graced and sanctified by his unostentatious and unfeigned piety'. Later on, while admitting that the great emigrations of the turn of the century took place 'before the time of the present race of proprietors', Mr Beith made it clear that 'the large farm system has come more fully into operation, and its evils have been developed. By it the country has become bereaved of her worthiest children, and, in the exaltation of a few individuals, thousands are doomed to poverty. The ease of the landowner in securing the returns of his property can be no compensation for this evil.'

Mr Beith's high opinion of Grant as a politician didn't quite square with the facts. Mrs Elizabeth Grant of Rothiemurchus, in her splendidly catty *Memoirs of a Highland Lady*, blew the gaff about one of the Inverness elections in which her father stood against Charles Grant: 'To secure his seat, he promised my father unlimited Indian appointments if he would give in. This was the secret of my father's Indian patronage, which he provided ultimately for so many poor cadets.'

Charles Grant was a fairly good constituency member, but after the Reform Act, which opened up voting to tenants paying more than £50 in rent, the various underhanded arrangements by which he kept his seat wouldn't have been enough; in 1835 he was created Baron Glenelg of Glenelg, and shifted to the House of Lords. He then became Secretary of State for the Colonies.

In this job he was really out of his depth, although admitted to be an 'amiable, pious, worthy man, and a capable parliamentary speaker'. Lord Melbourne dismissed him in a crushing phrase as 'too late and never ready', while the King, who was exasperated with his indecision, called him 'vacillating and procrastinating'. The end of his parliamentary career came in 1838 after the rebellion in Canada, and he was forced to resign, with a golden handshake of £2,000 per year and a minor appointment as a land-tax commissioner. A later judgement of him was that he was 'irresolute and of no very decided political views, and somewhat lethargic and dilatory in the conduct of business. The somnolent expression on his long, drawn features led to his being habitually represented, in the caricatures of the period, as asleep.'

During Grant's ownership, the emigration that had been going on from Glenelg ever since the Macleods sold up continued steadily, and his factor James Stavert simply added the emigrants' crofts to his own large farm. Through the early parts of the nineteenth century, as the Highland landowners began to turn over the smallholders' cattle grounds to Lowland sheep farmers who could pay higher rents, Glenelg did not escape this general trend. At first, the emigrants were people of some substance, having been successful cattle farmers; then, more and more people from Glenelg, having been turned off onto smaller holdings along the coast, 'having tried to content themselves with sadly reduced possessions, until, finding that thus they were losing their all, and induced by the flattering tidings which reached them from the western continent, they too, though in different circumstances from their predecessors, bade farewell to a country, to which they had clung till they could do so no longer.' There was, in fact, a new settlement called Glenelg across the Atlantic.

Throughout all these troubles, the crofters in the twelve townships in the rich valley of Glenmore held onto their land, despite a potato famine in the 1830s and the failure of the west coast herring fishing, on which so many of the settlements depended. When Charles Grant went into a rather sour retirement—he died at Cannes in 1866—he sold the estate to Baillie of Dochfour, which must have seemed a hopeful move for many of his tenants. The Baillies were in the process of building up a vast property centred on Loch Ness-side, stretching all the way from Strathspey to the Atlantic. Evan Baillie, the third laird of Dochfour, had made a fortune in Bristol from the West Indian trade. At the beginning of the nineteenth century, the Baillies had been applauded as model landlords, always interested in agricultural and social improvements.

During the terrible years of 1846 and 1847, when there was an even more disastrous failure of the potato crop, Baillie was one of the landowners who petitioned the government for help for the starving people; not for the first or last time, the remote legislators were uninterested. By this time the Glenmore tenants were badly in need of assistance. They sent a letter to Baillie, who had visited them only once but was considered a good landlord, asking him to provide means of existence at home by allowing them extra land, or at worst to help them to emigrate to Canada.

Baillie's reply, given through his factor, was that he would help to pay their passages on an emigrant ship, or let them sit rent free until the years of the potato famine were over. However, his factor kept quiet about the possibility of the rents being waived, and let the tenants understand that they would have to clear off. Baillie put up £2,000, to which the recently formed Highland Destitution Committee added another £500. Money could always be found to get rid of people.

A ship was chartered, but it was only at the last moment that the five hundred 'assisted' emigrants from all corners of the extensive Glenelg property discovered that there was neither doctor nor food supply on board. It was left to one of the main sheep-farming tenants on the estate, a Mr Stewart from Eilanreach a little way down the coast, to come to their help. As soon as the people left, the cottages in Glenmore were demolished, and the land added to the sheep farm of a man called Mitchell, who also rented Ratagan. Forty or fifty families who couldn't find accommodation on the *Liscard* were left behind to exist in hovels on the shore. Most of the crofters left Glenmore in 1849, and within a year or two most of the improvements for which they had appealed were put under way—dyke-building and draining schemes that now helped only a handful of shepherds and a few thousand sheep.

Alexander Mackenzie's *History of the Highland Clearances* pointed out that, although many parts of the Highlands were desperately overpopulated and needed most of the people to leave so that the others could make a living from the available land, this certainly did not apply to Glenmore: 'On the whole, Mr. Baillie behaved liberally, but, considering the suitability of the beautiful valley of Glenelg for arable and food-producing purposes, it is to be regretted that he did not decide upon utilising the labour of the natives in bringing the district into a state of cultivation, rather than have paid so much to banish them to a foreign land. That they themselves would have preferred this is beyond question. . . . If a judicious system had been applied of cultivating excellent

5 The gaunt remains of the barracks at Glenelg

6 Highland garrons barring the way up Glenmore; hills of Skye in the background

7 Looking down the lonely middle reaches of Loch Hourn

land, capable of producing food in abundance, in Glenelg, there was not another property in the Highlands on which it was less necessary to send the people away than in that beautiful and fertile valley.'

A little way down the Glenmore road there's a sharp turning off to the left towards Moyle, one of the Department of Agriculture farms down beside the river; its name is almost the only reminder left of the twelve crofting villages that flourished here before the clearances. The Moyle road goes through the arable land, with bits of undrained boggy ground here and there. From a telephone box beside the first of the farms there's a good view of the waterfall that comes tumbling down the north side of the glen. The main river is fast-flowing here, with a scattering of birch trees alongside: a very pleasant place for a quiet picnic. The public road ends beside Moyle farm, at the entrance to the Ratagan Forest plantations. This whole valley is of great geological interest, and it's quite usual to see Land Rovers from universities and other seats of learning whisking miniature expeditions about the district. Away above the trees, once again, are the summits on the county boundary that stretches southwards from the top of Mam Ratagan. It's a view of substantial mountain country, the steep-sided peaks getting steadily higher towards the skyline, until they go out of sight at just over three thousand feet.

High up on a little pass due south of Moyle is John MacInnes's Loch, where a crofter of that name is said once upon a time to have captured a water horse. All went well until one day when MacInnes decided to ride the horse, which was always a most unwise thing to do with these magic creatures; it rushed down into the depths of the loch, taking the poor man with it, and the only trace ever found thereafter of John MacInnes was his lungs, which were discovered floating on the surface.

Continuing down the Glenmore road after the Moyle junction, the valley gradually swings round to the right, although the sea is still completely out of sight. As the valley opens out a little, there are more farms and houses, some of them with well drained fields, although much of the ground has gone sadly back to its original boggy condition. Up on the hillside to the right of the road there are stretches of bare rock, often like miniature craggy faces, among the rough grass and bracken. As the glen narrows again, there are patches of old woodland on the far side, not quite hiding a long narrow waterfall.

Johnson and Boswell came this way, almost at the end of their exhausting day's trek from Glen Moriston. By this time the good doctor was becoming very irritable indeed. It had been a hard day for a man in his sixties, especially one who wasn't by any means used to clambering up and down wild mountainsides. His dignity and temper hadn't been mollified by the bothers about deciding which of the locally hired horses would be strong enough to take his weight, or by the owner's capering attempts to cheer him up. When Boswell made to go ahead to see if their accommodation was ready, Johnson gave him the rough edge of his tongue for behaving in such a clod-like manner as to leave him unaccompanied at this late stage in the journey.

The final arrival into the very scattered village of Glenelg comes at a tree-shaded road junction, where the left turn leads into the main part of the village and the right turn goes past Galder and Bernera towards the Skye ferry that sails to Kylerhea. Among the fields straight on from the junction stand the considerable remains of the barracks of Bernera, built after the Jacobite rising of 1719 to provide a permanent base for government troops in this largely rebel area. Beyond them, at last, is the sea, with the sharply rising east coast of Skye over the waters of Glenelg Bay.

Boswell looked rather longingly at the barracks from the road which, in his day, went closer to the sea: 'As we passed the barracks at Bernera, I would fain have put up there; at least I looked at them wishfully, as soldiers have always everything in the best order. But there was only a sergeant and a few men there. We came on to the inn at Glenelg. . . . A lass showed us upstairs into a room raw and dirty; bare walls, variety of bad smells, a coarse black fir greasy table, forms of the same kind, and from a wretched bed started a fellow from his sleep. . . . They had no bread, no eggs, no wine, no spirits but whisky, no sugar but brown grown black. They prepared some mutton-chops, but we would not have them. They killed two hens. I made Joseph broil me a bit of one till it was black, and I tasted it. Mr. Johnson would take nothing but a bit of bread, which we had luckily remaining, and some lemonade. . . . I took some rum and water and sugar, and grew better; for after my last bad night I hoped much to be well this, and being disappointed I was uneasy and almost fretful. Mr. Johnson was calm. I said he was so from vanity. "No," said he, "'tis from philosophy." '

Luck was against the two travellers that night, because Macleod's factor would have been happy to put them up in his own house if he'd known that they had passed by; but he sent them a bottle of what the connoisseur Boswell described as 'excellent rum' as a consolation. In fact, the pair of them might not have needed to go over Mam Ratagan at all, because their Skye host had had a boat waiting for them back at Shiel Inn, but the boatman had given it up as a bad job and sailed back home at the very time they were wandering down past Cluanie.

Present-day Glenelg is a very pleasant and airy place scattered round the wide sweep of Glenelg Bay, an inlet of the Sound of Sleat and not much more than a mile from the almost empty north-east coast of Skye. Turning right at the junction near the entrance to the village leads along the road towards the Kylerhea ferry; round about here there used to be small-scale lead and silver mines, but their products weren't of very high quality. Beside the junction is the Free Church, built in the 1840s after the great split in the established Church of Scotland. The Rev. Alexander Beith, quoted earlier, had been the established minister of the parish; he left in 1839 to join the Free Church, and in August 1845 had the honour of preaching the first sermon in the new building. He too was going over to Skye, and recalled in a book how the ferry road came to be built:

'The walk from the Clachan to the boathouse, from which point we were to embark, reminded me that the road along which we moved, as well as the boathouse, was the result of the people's industry in 1837, the year of famine. A considerable share of the provisions sent on that occasion in aid to the Highlands, fell to our parish. On my suggesting to the people that they might fairly earn their meal by doing work for it—work of a public kind— work which might be useful to themselves afterwards, instead of accepting the gratuity as a dole to paupers, they immediately consented, and the work then constructed remains till this day, a memorial of an independent and manly feeling, which, at the time, greatly rejoiced me.'

It's a very pleasant road towards the ferry, although it doesn't actually go to Kylerhea as a signpost suggests, since that is the corresponding settlement over in Skye. Beyond the roadside gorse there are green flats where the river from Glenmore flows finally to the sea. There are pleasant cottages on both sides of the road, with some rebuildable ruins among them, a hill rising sharply to the right, and a wide stretch of grazing ground going over to the water's edge on the left. When the wind is whipping up the Sound of Sleat, it would be difficult to imagine a fresher or more healthy spot.

West Highland villages are rarely as monolithic as they appear on small-scale maps, and this part of Glenelg is really called Galder or Galltair. The crofters here suffered in the same way as their neighbours in Glenmore at the time of the great emigration in 1849; some of them were able to stay, and a few of the old Glenmore tenants joined them in this tiny coastal township that shouldn't have been of much interest to the sheep farmers. However, only two years after the emigrations, when he had been able to add the whole of Glenmore to his sheep grazings, Mitchell asked Baillie's factor, who was a friend of his, if he could take over the Galder land too. Although the tenants said that that would leave them with practically no land at all, the factor wouldn't listen and, although their rents for the land had been paid, it was added to Mitchell's already massive holding.

Even then the factor wasn't finished with the people of Galder, because some of them were evicted from their houses, and had to squat in the road with all their furniture and belongings about them, until they agreed to give up their land. It's notable in all this that the tenants were sure that their landlord knew nothing of what was going on—curiously, they didn't seem to be too concerned that he visited them only once in his lifetime—and that these things were done by the factor without the laird's knowledge; sometimes, indeed, against the laird's instructions. It wasn't until 1883 that the estate gave the Galder crofters a little land, and that was probably only because the great government enquiry into crofting conditions was imminent.

After some way, the hillside to the right of the road opens out at the sheltering plantation guarding the entrance to Glen Bernera against the wild prevailing winds. This is a smaller individual property belonging to the Ellice family, who in the middle of the last century bought over tens of thousands of acres of mountain country in Glen Garry, miles away to the east. For many years there was a market stance beside the entrance to the glen, well placed to meet the great cattle drives from Skye. The little river that comes down Glen Bernera is the Eilg burn, its name connected in some way with the name of the whole district.

At the head of the glen is a hill called Glas Bheinn, on the summit of which is a cairn to the MacCrimmon clan. Its name recalls an old punch-up when a party of MacCrimmons from Glenelg were hurrying home after misbehaving themselves in the territory of the Mathesons of Lochalsh. When they got this far, almost in sight of home, the MacCrimmons relaxed and bedded down for the night; but the Mathesons had been stealthily following them, and few of the MacCrimmons survived their sudden midnight attack.

The county boundary runs over the top of Glas Bheinn, and where it runs down to the sea, a little way north round the coast towards Ardintoul, is a strip of 'debateable land' called Teanga na Comhstri, the Tongue of Contention. It got its name because the counties of Inverness and Ross used to argue away about which of them had the better legal title to it; why it was so important is not very clear.

Leaving Galder and Glen Bernera behind, the road climbs narrowly over the shoulder of a low hill, protected from the drop into the sea by a stout retaining wall. There's a splendid view down the coast from here, with the tiny Sandaig Islands scattered casually at the foot of the steep eastern hills of the Sound of Sleat. Then comes a short stretch of rough rocky country towards the ferry slipway. The only building beside the slipway is now a private house, although it served until a year or two ago as the Glenelg youth hostel. It is sometimes identified as being on the site of the inn that Johnson and Boswell visited, but there is little real evidence about where that miserable hostelry was situated; understandably, neither of them was at any pains to advertise its exact location. The general opinion, however, among people who have delved in the old maps and records, is that it was in the Kirkton of Glenelg, the main part of the village some way south of the barracks.

From the landing stage the view is directly across to the isolated little settlement of Kylerhea over in Skye. Up the glen behind it can be seen the snake of the enterprising little hill road that goes doggedly over a pass towards the interior of the island. The township takes its name from Kyle Rhea, the narrow strait separating Skye from the mainland. This used to be the place where drovers brought the island cattle across to the mainland, at the start of the long haul to the markets of Muir of Ord, Crieff or Falkirk. The beasts were tied behind boats in batches of half a dozen, their mouths roped almost shut with the tongues protruding, so that they wouldn't take too much salt water aboard. Three to four hundred beasts could be taken across in this way in a single hour, and it has been estimated that five to eight thousand used to make the journey in a busy season. Most of the hill tracks inland from Glenelg started as drove roads, and before the railway came to Kyle of Lochalsh this was the main crossing place to Skye.

The Kylerhea car and passenger ferry does not run on Sundays, and the service stops altogether in winter. It has had rather a chequered history. Once or twice in this century the ferry-boat has been swept from its moorings away into Loch Alsh. The service was suspended during the war, restarted in 1946, closed down again a year or two later, but has been well established ever since.

The legendary origin of the name Kyle Rhea concerns one of the giants who reputedly infested the coasts of Scotland and Ireland in earlier days; he is supposed to have been drowned while attempting a massive pole-vault across from Skye to the mainland. There's another reminder of him in the point and lighthouse of Rudha Reidh on the Ross-shire coast north of Gairloch. Not far from the ferry is a place that was traditionally regarded as a giants' burial ground, long guarded by one of those predictions about 'wrath from above' if it should ever be disturbed. In the early days of the last century some local gentry decided to investigate and started digging. They discovered two very large skeletons with jawbones twelve inches across, but the remains crumbled into dust soon after being exposed to the air. The excavations ended hurriedly when a furious thunderstorm sprang up, forcing the party to run for shelter; but not before they had cautiously re-interred the remains. Some years later the site was ploughed over.

Back at the junction at the foot of Glenmore, the other road leads into the main part of the village. Glenelg is a rather bigger place than might be expected from its fairly isolated situation, although some of the houses are just for holiday use and there's a fairly high proportion of retired people. A sign of the only recently introduced industry is the settlement of Forestry Commission houses over to the left, after the lately rebuilt bridge across the Glenelg River, before the modern primary school and village hall.

Older Gaelic-speaking local people still refer to the land on the other side of the road, around the ruins of the barracks, as Grunnd nan Righ, the King's Ground. Work began on them just after the Jacobite Attempt of 1719, although there's a certain amount of argument about precisely which year they were completed. When they were built, Glenelg was still part of the Macleod properties. The chief himself was in London when he agreed to sell the government a fair amount of ground for the purpose; in this parcel of ground, however, was accidentally included the glebe of the Glenelg manse. The Presbytery of Lochcarron did a very shrewd deal by which a complete neighbouring farm was handed over to form the new glebe. It came to a total of three hundred and sixty acres, far bigger than was usual, and as land values appreciated through the years, the rent from it made a significant increase in the minister's income.

Not long after the Jacobite rebellion of 1745 a group of soldiers brought an epidemic of smallpox to the district. However, four years later, an English visitor claimed that the local people welcomed the garrison and were 'much civilised by the barracks of Bernera', as if a military fortress designed to keep them under the thumb of an unpopular central government were ever greatly welcomed by any local population.

The people of Glenelg had a fine opportunity for some hilarity at the garrison's expense one day in June 1745. The whole idea of having a barracks there was to guard against any recurrence of the old Jacobite troubles of 1715 and 1719. Although the presence of the barracks and the fact that Macleod of Macleod didn't throw in his lot with Bonnie Prince Charlie made it difficult for the local people to offer much support, there isn't much doubt that their sympathies lay with the Young Pretender. Imagine their reaction when the French ship that had just landed the Prince safely down the coast in Moidart sailed up the Sound of Sleat and through Kyle Rhea, right under the noses of the Redcoat garrison, captured four English supply ships and sent them back under prize crews to add to the Prince's provisions. The incident was noted rather shamefacedly in the garrison's report, but they were unable to do anything about it; although the original plans for the building allowed for gun emplacements, a recent researcher considers it unlikely that the guns were ever actually mounted.

During the Forty-five, one of the most hated men in the Highlands spent much of his time at the barracks. This was Sir Alexander Macdonald of Sleat, a clan chieftain from Skye who was known to be a Jacobite at heart, but because he reckoned the latest rebellion to be a lost cause even before it started, offered his support to the House of Hanover. Among thousands of Jacobites who took no thought of the consequences, but joined their young Prince as soon as they were called to arms, his very name was execrated. He died at the barracks in 1746, after an attack of pneumonia, and one of his enemies penned an epitaph which has never been equalled for Highland contempt:

> If Heaven be pleased when sinners cease to sin,
> If Hell be pleased when sinners enter in,
> If Earth be pleased to quit a truckling knave,
> Then all are pleased—Macdonald's in his grave!

The great traveller Thomas Pennant came to the barracks just a year before Johnson and Boswell took the ferry over to Skye. In his day the garrison, which had once been manned by one or two companies of foot, was reduced to a corporal and six privates. It was soon to be abandoned altogether. Pennant too went on about how much the local people loved the military presence, saying that they lamented the reduction in manpower: 'They are now quite sensible of the good effects of the military, by introducing peace and security: they fear lest the evil days should return, and the antient thefts be renewed, as soon as the *Banditti* find this protection of the people removed.' It was removed, in fact, only a few years later, and the only thefts that followed were committed by the landlords.

In 1831 it was reported that 'some of those in receipt of Kirk Session Poor Relief are staying there'; but during the evictions and emigrations that followed, Baillie's factor is said to have turned them out again and again, finally burning the roof off so that there wouldn't be proper shelter. There is still one active relic of the days of the military occupation: in Glenelg funerals the army custom is followed, and the mourners walk in front of the coffin.

One of these Glenelg funerals was once the occasion for an infamous local row. In December 1814 the wife of Macdonell of Barrisdale died. Barrisdale is in Knoydart, several miles to the south and separated from Glenelg proper by the difficult crossing of Loch Hourn; but it is within the bounds of the vast parish of Glenelg, and the funeral was held in the village church. Several of the mourners came by boat from Lochalsh. Some minor argument started, Glenelg tempers flared, and before the Lochalsh visitors could gather themselves together they were the victims of a 'bloody assault', with the local men laying into them with fists, sticks and boathooks. John Matheson of Attadale in Lochalsh, no doubt still nursing his bruises, wrote to a friend a couple of weeks later that the people of Glenelg 'from time immemorial were notorious amongst the rest of the neighbourhood for their savage deeds'.

The old Kirkton of Glenelg, along what might be called the main street, is not exactly the most cheerful looking of West Highland settlements, although there are some modern council houses based on traditional designs among the older ones. In the 1830s the place looked rather brighter: 'The Kirkton of Glenelg can boast of being a village of some extent, having the principal street of slated houses, and displaying the attractions of some well-stocked shops. . . . The whole appearance of Kirkton is truly picturesque, including, as it does, the church, factor's residence, and street already alluded to, with its numerous train of straw-covered cottages, interspersed with various kinds of ornamental trees, surmounted by a thriving plantation of fir that towers majestically over it, and having lines of trees along the various roads that lead from it.' Nowadays, perhaps the most notable feature of the Kirkton is the fine avenue of trees leading to it from the bridge.

In those days the immediate district of Glenelg had a population of around eleven hundred, and the village was very much the centre of its vast parish, in effect if not in strict geographical arrangement. The parish school was near the road junction at the entrance to the village, in a most unsuitable position for the outlying districts. Scholars from Knoydart, the middle part of the parish, had to come eighteen miles by land and cross a broad ferry; from North Morar, the southernmost limit of the parish, they travelled twenty miles and crossed two ferries. It was indeed an 'immense deficiency'.

In present-day Glenelg another deficiency is that there isn't a hotel, which makes it probably the only West Highland settlement of its size where visitors have to rely on private houses for accommodation. There was a hotel here until the 1950s, when it was burned down. It was replaced by a bar run by the Glenmore Trading Company, which was formed by some of the landowners round about, to operate a few of the essential services; one point of view is that they should have left these affairs to individual local men, since the opportunities for making an independent living are few enough anyway.

After this the road goes through a rock cutting, with some of the old pine trees and clumps of rhododendron above the local church, and then comes out beside the coast again, before the war memorial. Over to the right of the road is the Glenelg jetty, but it doesn't make much contribution to the local way of life, if the county council notice pointing out that all use of it is prohibited because of its dangerous condition is to be taken at face value.

Around here is the last of the individual bits and pieces that go to make up the conglomerate village of Glenelg; there's a row of older cottages, including the cottage police station that was given up only in 1970, a couple of new bungalows and then the open road again. There are usually several boats and sailing dinghies moored in the bay hereabouts. The shoreline is very stony, at times separated from the roadside by banks of gorse that also act as a screen for a small rubbish dump. A pleasant hour or two can be had examining the beach for a collection of the delicately veined and tinted pebbles that are spread around it.

There's plenty of fresh air here as the wind comes smartly up the Sound of Sleat, and attractive surroundings of seascape and mountain, with the east-coast hills of Skye dipping unrelieved to the water across the Sound, and a high wooded cliff falling down to the sea a little way to the south along the mainland coast. The road curves left to avoid the mouth of a river, hugging the foot of a hill before coming to the bridge at Eilanreach, beyond which an even more adventurous road wanders high above the Sound of Sleat on the way to the infinitely more remote community of Arnisdale.

CHAPTER 4

GLEN BEAG AND ARNISDALE

THE ROAD BEYOND GLENELG, as far as tourist traffic is concerned, is one of the loneliest on the west coast of Scotland. It goes on for nearly ten miles of narrow, twisting single-track, plunging and rising with magnificent coastal scenery always in front and to the west. It turns right over the river bridge at Eilanreach; but the road straight ahead from the bridge, up the narrow valley of Glen Beag, should on no account be ignored by anybody who has penetrated as far as this.

Glen Beag is the Little Glen, in comparison with the Great Glen of Glenmore over the hills to the north. Recently widened and resurfaced, the road along it runs for about three miles up to the farm of Balvraid. In its early stages it is quite unlike any other road for miles around, winding alongside the sparkling river and shaded by old woodlands of birch, hazel and alder. The birch-smothered hillside to the left, however, shows some signs of tree-clearing; it would be rather unfortunate if forestry activities were to remove much more of the old natural woodland. At the moment, the lower part of the glen can't have changed much since the last of the great MacCrimmons, hereditary pipers to the chiefs of Macleod, came to farm here after a disagreement with the chief had closed the family's famous piping college at Boreraig over in Skye.

Soon the hills on the far side of the glen are occupied by the climbing plantations of Eilanreach Forest, on ground that was leased to the Forestry Commission by Lord Dulverton's Eilan-reach estate. Lord Dulverton is head of one of the wealthy and bewilderingly numerous Wills families, of Imperial Tobacco Company fame, who own hundreds of thousands of acres in the Highlands: in Perthshire, Speyside, Inverness-shire, Kintail, Glen Torridon and Applecross.

The Dulverton Trust is a substantial charity that provides

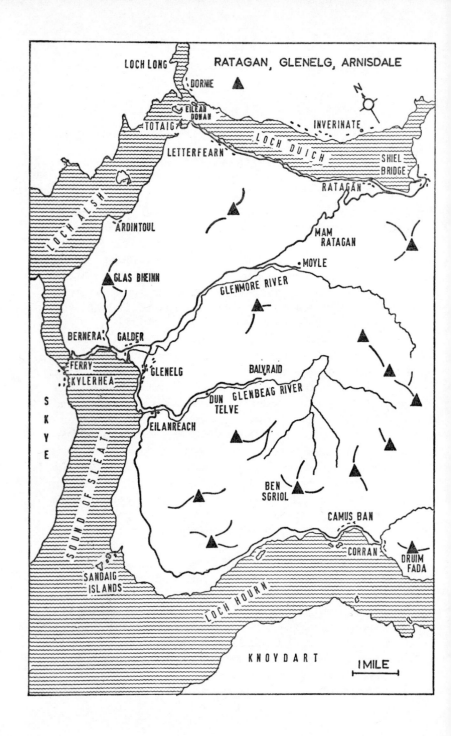

RATAGAN, GLENELG, ARNISDALE

LOCH LONG
DORNIE
EILEAN DONAN
TOTAIG
INVERINATE
LETTERFEARN
LOCH DUICH
SHIEL BRIDGE
RATAGAN
LOCH ALSH
ARDINTOUL
MAM RATAGAN
MOYLE
GLAS BHEINN
GLENMORE RIVER
BERNERA
GALDER
FERRY
KYLERHEA
GLENELG
BALVRAID
DUN TELVE
GLENBEAG RIVER
EILANREACH
SKYE
SOUND OF SLEAT
BEN SGRIOL
CAMUS BAN
CORRAN
DRUIM FADA
SANDAIG ISLANDS
LOCH HOURN
KNOYDART

1 MILE

finance for various educational, social and nature projects. It was founded in 1949, and by the middle of the 1960s it had a home and foreign income of something like £200,000. Many of the projects it supports are based in Scotland, two of the most recent being a sail training ship and a nature reserve. Recently, Lord Dulverton has been connected with a project called *Highland Village 1970*, which involved a number of Highland schools in schemes to improve particular local sites, set up museums or renovate old buildings. It started with a grant of £5,000 that was intended to promote a study of how West Highland crofters might best become involved in forestry; but when it was discovered that crofting law did not in fact allow crofters to plant woodlands on their rented land, it was agreed that the grant should be turned over to the schools project. Much of Lord Dulverton's interests lie in forestry: Eilanreach estate is actually owned by a firm called West Highland Woodlands Ltd., and he is involved in various timber projects in Lochaber, where he has his Scottish home.

Over on the far side, the forest all but hides a rather fine waterfall, the second, in fact, on the south side of the glen; in summer it's a delicate spidery thing, but after heavy rain it takes on a much grander aspect, with the water filling the gully and hardly taking time to bounce from one rocky landing to the next. There's arable ground on the valley floor, which provides good grazing for cattle and sheep; but the most notable things in Glenelg are the ancient Pictish towers for which this out-of-the-way valley is archaeologically famous.

The first of them is called Dun Telve, just to the right of the road among the riverside fields. It is one of the best preserved of the five hundred or so examples that remain in Scotland of the Pictish broch. The brochs were tall beehive-shaped buildings designed about two thousand years ago as fortified homes for groups of families. There is another example, Dun Troddan, a little way farther on to the left of the road, but Dun Telve is the one on which most work has been done; it was cleared of rubble in 1914. Celtic folklore suggests that the brochs of Glen Beag were the home of some of the old Fingalian giants, and they have sometimes been called the Castles of Teilba.

Thomas Pennant, who visited Glen Beag in 1772, was the first person to bring them to the general notice, although they had been briefly written about before, by a man called Gordon who came here in the 1720s. In his *Voyage to the Hebrides* Pennant noted: 'Some Goth purloined from the top seven feet and a half under the pretence of applying the material to certain public buildings.' It seems very likely that there was no pretence; the stones went into the building of the Bernera barracks whose presence he so much admired.

Because of the depradations he mentioned, the walls of Dun Telve are now little more than thirty-three feet high. The circular courtyard, for many centuries open to the elements, but once completely enclosed, is a similar distance in diameter. This broch, like its neighbour, is now in the care of the Ministry of Public Building and Works, which has added one or two metal bars here and there to support the aged structure. They are very discreetly positioned, and in general it's difficult to realize that this fairly intricate and sophisticated design has survived for something like twenty centuries.

There are various little rooms and compartments built into the broader parts of the double wall near the base, and it doesn't take much imagination to see what an ideal site Glen Beag must have been for such a building. The broch is on level fertile ground conveniently close to the river and only a mile and a half from the sea, but at the same time hidden away in a steep-sided valley unlikely to be discovered by seaborne raiders or casual passers-by. In any case, the key to the design is a very narrow and constricted entrance; unwelcome visitors would have been unable to enter the building, if they managed to get close enough, any way except in single file, and the occupants would have had plenty of time to dispose of them one by one as they emerged crouching from the low-slung doorway.

Perhaps because Dun Telve is still in a perfect situation two thousand years later, there is a slightly eerie atmosphere about the place, even in broad daylight. It's easy to get the uncomfortable feeling that this is a house whose occupants had just stepped out for a short while, and may at that very moment be looking on disapprovingly from a dark corner. There are few records of anyone having spent a night alone in this austere relic of the days before history.

From the first broch, the view up the narrowing part of the glen is towards the tangle of peaks south and east of the Mam

Ratagan summit. Beyond the entrance road to the forest on the far side of the valley, the long ridge of Beinn a'Chapuill stretches rather grandly above the plantations on its lower flanks. Soon the road gets closer down by the river again, and the glen unexpectedly opens out into much barer sheep country before coming to the final turning place at the farmhouse of Balvraid.

Back down at the Eilanreach bridge, the Arnisdale road goes immediately through some houses, sheep pens and sawmills connected with the Eilanreach estate. Soon after leasing ground to the Forestry Commission, the estate began to go into the timber-growing business on its own account. There's a fair amount of planting down the Arnisdale road; generally speaking, the older plantations are in the state forest of Eilanreach and the newly forested ground is run by West Highland Woodlands. Eilanreach Lodge is set a little way back to the right of the road, a rather haphazard kind of building that seems to have been constructed at various times as different kinds of building material came to hand. It has recently been replaced by the New Lodge, which is actually a splendidly situated bungalow some way behind it, just above the waters of the Sound of Sleat and seen to its best advantage from the rocky shore at the south side of Glenelg Bay.

Eilanreach began as one of the big sheep farms leased out by the owners of Glenelg in the days when sheep rentals were far higher than anything the crofters could produce. Even eighty years ago it was still owned by the Dochfour estate, covering a total area of 33,000 acres for which the rent worked out at 10½d per acre; crofters at Arnisdale, farther along the coast road, thought it hard that they should be paying £2 for the single miserable acre that was all they were allowed. Some years later it was sold off, and it included the lands of Glenmore which were taken over by the Department of Agriculture during Sir Henry Scott's ownership.

After Eilanreach the Arnisdale road begins climbing in earnest to fight its way above the wooded cliff that's such a feature of the view from Galder and the north side of Glenelg Bay. Anyone who can spare a glance backwards down the narrow and high-banked road can just see through the trees a splendid view of the opening of the river below Eilanreach, with a gravelly bar across the mouth, and the graceful sweep of Glenelg Bay stretching away beyond. This outlook is particularly impressive because of the height the road manages to climb, in such a short distance, above the sea. It does seem unfortunate that the plantations along this road, for the first part at any rate, are on the seaward side, effectively blocking off a very fine high-level view of the Sound of Sleat and the coastline of Skye. What appear to be equally suitable heathery moorlands on the landward side are at the moment reserved for sheep.

Once it was sold by the Dochfour estate, Eilanreach was cleared of sheep for a while about 1900 and turned into exclusively deer ground. Now, with the development of public and private forestry, deer and sheep are having to take second place, even the old deer sanctuary higher up the inland hills being part of the Forestry Commission land. Eilanreach is therefore a perfect example of the crofters-deer-sheep-trees progression that has affected large areas of the Highlands and is moving fast into its fourth stage thanks to the death-duty advantages from owning woodland.

There's a fair tarmac surface on the narrow road as it winds and dips high above the coast, with more plantations and ground being made ready for trees on both sides. Across the water there are many fine views to the Black Cuillin of Skye, the lonely peaks of the Nature Conservancy island of Rum, and the bizarre aircraft-carrier silhouette of the island of Eigg. There's an accidental-looking little lochan to the right of the road, and then the isolated cottage of Upper Sandaig, just about the only occupied dwelling in the whole distance from Eilanreach to Arnisdale. Opposite the cottage, and going down through more freshly-forested country towards the coast, is a track leading to the remote house of Sandaig, itself invisible from any point on the public road.

Sandaig was the 'Camusfearna' of Gavin Maxwell's otter books, and it was around here that most of the action in *Ring of Bright Water* and the rest took place. Idyllic as it was to begin with, Camusfearna seemed at the end to turn against Maxwell. The house was burned out one January night when the nearest fire engine, based almost forty miles away at Kyle of Lochalsh, couldn't battle its way over the pass in time to control the blaze; Maxwell's personal affairs became tangled; his last book *Raven Seek Thy Brother* had a terrible foreknowledge of disaster about it, and he died not long afterwards in hospital in Inverness.

It's a very steep, rugged and exposed coastline as far as the eye can see towards the south, as the Arnisdale road begins to climb again over the shoulder of a hill, turning the corner from the open water of the Sound of Sleat into the fjord country of Loch Hourn. The wild country ahead, on the south side of the loch, is the Rough Bounds of Knoydart, an almost deserted deer-stalking preserve of something like 100,000 acres that belongs to Sir Oliver Crosthwaite-Eyre, publisher and Member of Parliament. In a series of long left-hand bends, the road fights its way across the high, lumpy, heathery country above the entrance to Loch Hourn, always with the almost overpowering sight of the mountains of Knoydart ahead and to the right. Through a patch of country where the old indigenous birch woods have survived, and then it plunges deep into the second of the major sections of the state forest of Eilanreach.

There are several places along this part of the road where a driver might have some trouble seeing over the bonnet of his car, as it sweeps up over blind crests that don't give much clue about which way the road goes immediately afterwards. For much of this way the road is simply a ledge hacked out of the hillside that soars steeply up from the loch. In the forest, the surface has gone back to what rally drivers call three-ply: two tarmac strips with grass growing up the middle. The telephone wires to Arnisdale could hardly be in a more vulnerable position, in places practically draped through the branches of the trees, which must be very frustrating during the stiff gales with which this exposed coastline is often afflicted. It's a little ironic to read in early nineteenth-century accounts that what Arnisdale needed, almost above anything else, was a telegraph office at the disposal of the many fishing boat skippers who operated in Loch Hourn.

Out of the forest, and the road is now firmly away from the Sound of Sleat, running high above Loch Hourn across a steep grassy mountainside made more pleasant by the old birch woods that seem to have been shaken casually over its gully-scarred face. This long mountain is the 3,196-ft Ben Sgriol or Screel, the Hill of the Screes; the scree-runs themselves can be clearly seen along its higher reaches. Over Loch Hourn are the great Knoydart peaks, and there's a group of rocky, heathery, brackeny islands just off the northern shore; but the oddest thing in this view from the start of the sporting and sheep-farming estate of Arnisdale is a few miles ahead, where the great south-eastern buttress of Ben Sgriol teeters down to the water's edge in a series of humps and depressions. To put it fancifully, it looks as if some giant ridge-backed prehistoric monster, with its hind feet paddling about in Loch Hourn, has been petrified while stretching to its fullest extent in an attempt to browse on whatever gastronomic delights lie waiting at the towering summit.

Down on the lochside is a succession of rocky and pebbly bays, with some sheep-grazing land and a deserted-looking steading at Rarsaidh. The apparently interminable run from Glenelg—this is one of the slowest, if most spectacular twelve miles in the Highlands—comes suddenly almost to its end after a one-in-five drop down from a minor summit, at the foot of which lies the first part of the little village of Arnisdale, one of the most away-from-it-all settlements on the whole of Scotland's Atlantic coast.

Arnisdale, whose name is a reminder of the days when the Norse sea-rovers controlled this coast, is really in two separate parts; the first is known locally as Camus Ban, from the 'white bay' that gave it its name, while the other, some distance farther on at the very end of the public road, is called Corran. Camus Ban is a line of little cottages set back behind some garden ground, with only one modern house in the place; as the layout of the settlement shows, it was primarily a fishing village.

For many years, in fact, the Loch Hourn fishing was about the finest on the west coast, and the loch was on occasions almost packed with fishing boats from local villages and from places much farther afield. The best early description comes once again from Thomas Pennant, who came here on 6 August 1772 with his friends the Rev. John Lightfoot of Uxbridge and the Rev. John Stuart of Killin:

'Land on the North side, three miles distant from our ship, and visit Mr. Macleod, of Arnisdale: I shall never forget the hospitality of the house: before I could utter a denial, three glasses of rum, cordialized with jelly of bilberries, were poured into me by the irresistible hand of good Madam Macleod. Messrs. Lightfoot and Stuart sallied out in high spirits to botanize: I descended to my boat, to make the voyage of the lake.

'Steer S. East. After a small space the water widens into a large bay, bending to the South, which bears the name of Barrisdale;

turn suddenly to the East, and pass through a very narrow strait, with several little isles on the outside; the water of a great depth, and the tide violent. For four miles before us the loch was strait, but of an oval form; then suddenly contracts a second time. Beyond that was another reach, and an instantaneous and agreeable view of a great fleet of busses, and all the busy apparatus of the herring industry; with multitudes of little occasional hovels and tents on the shore, for the accommodation of the crews, and of the country people, who resort here at this season to take and sell herrings to the strangers. An unexpected sight, at the distance of thirteen miles from the sea, amidst the wildest scene in nature.

'A little farther the loch suddenly turns due South, and has a very narrow inlet to a third reach; this strait is so shallow as to be fordable at the ebb of spring tides; yet has within, the depth of ten and seventeen fathom: the length is about a mile; the breadth a quarter. About seven years ago it was so filled with herrings, that had crowded in, that the boats could not force their way, and thousands lay dead on the ebb.

'The scenery that surrounds the whole of this lake has an Alpine wildness and magnificence; the hills of an enormous height, and for the most part cloathed with extensive forests of oak and birch, often to the very summits. In many places are extensive tracts of open space, verdant, and only varied with a few trees scattered over them: amidst the thickest woods aspire vast grey rocks, a noble contrast! nor are the lofty headlands a less embellishment; for through the trees that wave on their summit, is an awful sight of sky, and spiring summits of vast mountains. . . .

'In our return from the extremity of this sequestered spot, am most agreeably amused with meeting at least a hundred boats, rowing to the place we were leaving, to lay their nets; while the persons on shore were busied in lighting fires, and preparing a repast for their companions, against their return from their toilsome work.

'So unexpected a prospect of the busy haunt of men and ships in this wild and romantic tract, afforded this agreeable reflection: that there is no part of our dominions so remote, so inhospitable, and so unprofitable, as to deny employ and livelihood to thousands; and that there are no parts so polished, so improved, and so fertile, but which must stoop to receive advantage from the dreary spots they so affectedly despise; and must be obliged to acknowlege the mutual dependency of part on part, however remotely placed, and however different in modes or manner of living.' And with that, he returned to Arnisdale, where he and his friends spent 'a most cheerful evening'.

In Pennant's time, of course, all this part of Glenelg proper was part of the estates of the Macleod chiefs. Towards the end of their ownership, it was noted that the herring season, which lasted from July to mid-autumn, attracted boats from the Firth of Clyde as well as from the north-west coastal villages, and something like 30,000 barrels of herring were caught every year. At this time, and for many years afterwards, the salt tax laws made curing and preserving the catch very difficult.

Thomas Telford's *Survey and Report of the Coasts and Central Highlands of Scotland*, written in 1803, recommended the setting up of government-sponsored fishing villages along the west coast 'on the principle laid down and practised so successfully by Mr. Hugh Stevenson, of Oban, at Arnisdale, on Loch Hourn'. Contemporary drawings show the loch crowded with fishing boats, and the fishing was so successful and dependable that Telford had loads of Arnisdale herring taken overland to add to the rations of his workmen on the Caledonian Canal and road-building projects.

The Arnisdale people had crofts, but they didn't pay too much attention to them because of their successful stake in the herring fishing; stock rearing was much less important to them than the planting of some patches of potatoes for their own use. Often there was a glut of herring, as at so many of the fishing villages in Inverness-shire and Wester Ross; what with the operation of the salt tax laws, the lack of a really good distribution system, and the uncontrolled over-fishing, there were times when mounds of stinking fish were left to rot away on the shore. All the over-fishing and the mysterious movements of the herring shoals culminated in the disastrous time when the sea suddenly seemed to empty of fish. In 1836 there were still six hundred people living at Arnisdale, but many had already begun to emigrate, even before the enforced clearances began. In that year the parish minister wrote: 'The sea and sea-lochs were famed for the number and quantity of herrings frequenting them, but of late years the herring fishing has failed, as on all the west coast, to the impoverishment of a large population who subsisted by it.'

The potato blight of the 1840s played its mournful part, but Arnisdale had an extra misery visited on it about that time, when many of the remaining villagers died in an epidemic of typhus brought to the district by a sailor home on leave from a foreign station.

The Arnisdale people had nothing to turn to when the fishing failed, because the only ground they had was a single acre each. Most of them left the place during the emigrations in the time of Lord Glenelg and the first of the Baillies, when almost all the land round about was turned into a single rented-out sheep farm. The Loch Hourn fishing picked up again, but it is really something of a mystery how the few families left in the village managed to hang on in this remote outpost. Archibald McGillivray represented the people of Camus Ban in the government enquiry of 1883, the local hearing of which was in Glenelg on 4 August. He said that there was so little grazing ground available to the tenants that there was only one cow among the twenty-six families in the township. He also spoke harshly of Baillie and of his local factor, an unpleasant character called George France, when describing the state of the houses at Camus Ban: 'They are built on the shore. We built them ourselves, for the proprietor gave us no assistance. We had to pay for the wood which we got from him for the purpose. We spoke to the factor about a change of site for the houses, and as an answer he asked us whether the sea was coming over the roofs of them. We said it sometimes did; and he told us that we should put back doors upon them, and when the sea came in that we could run away. I should like to see himself flopping in the midst of them.' This France also had a neat little corner in the selling of salt and barrels, both of which were essential to the fishermen; he charged extortionate prices for second-hand barrels, which they had to pay because there was no other local supply.

What outside work was available at Arnisdale in those days, said the tenants, didn't come from Baillie of Dochfour, who took no personal interest in this out-of-the-way part of his vast domain. It was provided by Sir Michael Arthur Bass, head of the Bass brewing firm, one of the original southern business tycoons who came to realize about the third quarter of the last century that a great thing to do with their money would be to rent Highland deer forests, which were then becoming available since the bottom had dropped out of the wool market, and the Highland landlords couldn't get the same high rents out of the sheep farmers. He rented from the Baillies the deer-stalking grounds of Glen Quoich and Cluanie, and others in the wild mountain country around Loch Hourn. Since overland access was difficult, he used to sail his yacht to the head of the loch and then have only a short journey through the hills to the stalking grounds. One day he sailed into Arnisdale, and happened to see an old man thatching his cottage roof. Bass asked him how often the job had to be done, and the old man said it might be every two years or every three months; it all depended on how wild the weather might be. At this, Bass said that in another year the whole village would have slated roofs. Sure enough, next year he sent boatloads of building materials to Arnisdale, and the work was done.

In 1866 Bass was created Lord Burton. Some time before this, his daughter married one of the Baillies of Dochfour, founding a joint family line of great wealth and property. She succeeded as Baroness Burton in 1909, and the present Lord Burton, owner of the still extensive Dochfour estates, is her grandson.

Nowadays there isn't any commercial fishing or much in the way of crofting done at Arnisdale, and most of the people living there are retired or semi-retired. Camus Ban, much reduced in size, is a pleasant little township, but it seems a pity that most of the cottages still have untreated stone walls. If they were all whitewashed, what a transformation there would be; but then, the outward face a place shows to visitors is not particularly important.

The recent history of Camus Ban is rather complicated. In 1890 the Dochfour estate sold off its Arnisdale and Loch Hourn properties—the second of these stretches along the north shore from Corran to the head of the loch—to Robert Birkbeck from Norfolk. He immediately cleared off the sheep which fed on the hill grazings, and turned both properties into strictly preserved stalking grounds. The Loch Hourn section was kept in the Birkbecks' own hands, while Arnisdale was usually rented out to shooting tenants. About twenty years later, the Birkbecks sold off the Arnisdale estate to Valentine Fleming, member of a London banking family; he was the father of Ian Fleming of James Bond fame, and of Peter Fleming, well known as a traveller, explorer, writer and *Spectator* columnist, who must be the only person with Arnisdale connexions to be a member of the Order of the Cloud and Banner of pre-Communist China.

Valentine Fleming built the present Arnisdale House and farmhouse, arranged for many improvements on the estate, and was locally very popular. He was killed during the first world war, and Arnisdale was sold off. The Fleming family's present Scottish properties are concentrated in a great mountainous area of deer forests in Argyll, around the Black Mount and the shores of Loch Etive.

Arnisdale was bought by Sir John Sutherland Harmood-Banner, head of a great auditing and accounting firm. He was Lord Mayor of Liverpool for a while, and sat in Parliament for almost twenty years as the member for Everton. In the 1920s the estate was sold again, this time to the Kidston family. Glen Kidston was a well known racing driver and pilot, one of the 'Bentley Boys' who were so successful in the great Le Mans twenty-four hour race in the twenties. An occasional shooting guest at Arnisdale during that time was the South African diamond millionaire Woolf Barnato, whose money kept the Bentley firm going until it was bought by Rolls Royce during the slump. Glen Kidston himself was killed in an aeroplane crash in the Drakensberg Mountains, shortly after arriving in South Africa on a record-breaking flight from England early in 1931.

Now the Arnisdale estate is owned by R. N. Richmond-Watson, who farms in Northamptonshire; it is kept as a sheep-farming and sporting property. During all the changes of ownership, the village of Camus Ban itself remained in the hands of the Dochfour estate, who made occasional efforts to get rid of it. It was a long way by road from their other estate centres, rather cut off even from Glenelg, which is still their property, and impossible to reach from the estates they control beyond the head of Loch Hourn. The rents did little more than cover the cost of collecting them: the twenty-odd Arnisdale tenants each paid £1 per year for their house, grazing land for two cows, and a share of the hill pasture for a few sheep. An estate representative was sent to offer to sell the crofters their land and houses; but the tenants would have none of it, ownership of their own land, which is not what crofters are after anyway, being a poor bargain compared with the controlled rents and security offered by the modern laws

of crofting tenure. After half a dozen enquiries, the Dochfour
man gave up. When Arnisdale estate came into its present
ownership, the new landlord agreed to buy over the village as
well.

What followed was a unique incident in the history of West
Highland sporting estates. The tenants were told that if they
were ever short of meat or fish, they should enquire at the home
farm to see if the estate store had any to spare. If not, they were
to go to the river or the hill and try for a salmon or a deer themselves. This is a jealously guarded agreement, quite unheard-of
in the general run of sporting estates, which the local people
respect by not overdoing things. To make sure that no incomer
upsets the arrangement by poaching, they keep a casual but very
close eye on any visitors; elsewhere in the district it's said of
Arnisdale that 'they're all gamekeepers over there!'

There's a fine row of old-established trees along the roadside
beyond the cottages set round the bay at Camus Ban, on the way
to the unpretentious mansion of Arnisdale House, which is set
back a little behind some grazing land. A private estate road off
to the left a short distance beyond the house leads over a patch of
level ground to the mountains of the deer forest; the steep foothills are slashed by a most dramatic ravine where the Arnisdale
River comes plunging down towards sea level, and there's a
particularly fine wooded pinnacle towering over the deep-cut
gully.

The separated eastern division of the village at Corran is quite
different from the line of cottages along the bay at Camus Ban.
It's a compact collection of more substantial houses, close-packed
under the looming bulk of the five-mile ridge of Druim Fada that
goes towards the head of the loch, and right at the rocky mouth
of the Arnisdale River. There's no room in the little township for
visitors' cars, which should be left at a parking place before the
bridge.

Back in the days of Lord Glenelg, Corran too had suffered from
the activities of James Stavert the factor, who seemed to want to
depopulate the whole district and gather more and more land for
his own sheep farm. The Corran people were starved of land
during the Baillies' time. John McCuaig, one of the Corran
tenants, said in 1883 that nobody in the place had more than an
acre of ground. 'We would be indebted to our proprietor or any

person who would give us more, because there is land that might be given to us. . . . We have no hill pasture or anything beyond that one acre of land.' Their arable land was often flooded by the very high tides that also washed into the houses at Camus Ban, and all they could grow was a few potatoes, which had had to be sown in the same plots every season for the past sixty years. As at other townships in Glenelg, they had to pay the big farmer for the privilege of grazing their few cows on the pasture land that had previously been taken away from their own holdings.

There was, however, another side to the story of the Arnisdale tenants, although it didn't get much of a hearing during the Royal Commission's enquiry at Glenelg. James Mollison, who was the factor for the whole of Baillie of Dochfour's estate, went to Inverness in October to put before the Commission the estate's point of view, which hadn't been heard during the original sitting at Glenelg in August.

He said, first of all, that the tenants who had complained about the £2 rent for their croft lands hadn't said that the house rent was included in that figure. In some detail, he then went on to suggest that the Arnisdale tenants were a pretty idle lot: 'A number of the houses occupied by these people are miserably poor, many comparatively unthatched, and otherwise greatly neglected; there is, however, an abundance of thatch to be had at no inconvenient distance . . . (it) could be carried—if not in carts, in the fishermen's boats, to the very door of every cottage in Arnisdale, so that not one need be without thatch; many are, however, in a deplorable condition, necessitating the removal of roofing every other year; yet young and able-bodied men may be seen on any day throughout the year, in groups at the end of each other's houses, keenly discussing imaginary grievances, rather than attending to the improvement of their cottages or crofts, or the performance of any kind of regular labour whatsoever.'

Mollison said that he considered the Arnisdale people had a nerve to complain about not having land of their own for cows, because grazing was offered to them at reasonable rates on the bigger farms. It was also untrue that there was no work for local people on the estate: on the very day that statement had been made to the Commission at Glenelg, there were twenty-seven local tenants regularly employed by the factor. In the previous year a total of fifty local men had been given work on the estate, but not a single Camus Ban or Corran tenant had asked for any. Mollison's opinion of them was that they were just plain lazy.

He was rather annoyed about their claim that they'd had to pay for timber to repair their houses after the storm tide of 1881, dismissing it as completely untrue. In that gale, many of the fishermen on the Glenelg estate had had their boats badly damaged. Baillie had offered to supply them with larch from the woodlands at Ratagan and Letterfearn, and said he would pay fifteen shillings a week to any fisherman who would go there to cut the timber into suitable lengths so that it could be taken easily to Glenelg. They had said no; the wage would have to be twenty shillings.

Money from public funds had paid for floating the rafts of timber from Loch Duich round past Totaig and Ardintoul to Glenelg Bay. There were horses ready to haul the timber ashore, but not a single man from Glenelg would help with the work of bringing the wood onto the beach unless a suitable wage were offered. When the timber finally got ashore, Mollison said that much of it had lain outside the houses for months without being put to sensible use. He had no patience with the tenants on the Glenelg estate, saying they were so idle it was small wonder they had a poorer standard of living than the east coast people. It has to be remembered, of course, that the crofting and fishing tenants on many west coast estates had had the spirit squeezed out of them over eighty years by then.

Mollison suggested that it might be a good idea if the government sponsored deep sea fishing from the west coast villages; the locals seemed to think of nothing but the herring that could be caught very easily almost on their doorsteps, and made no attempt to fish offshore or for other kinds of fish. All they did was wait for the herring shoals, and if they didn't come, complain about the estate owner. When the herring shoals did arrive, so did the much more professional east coast fishermen; the locals were left with little but the gleanings.

To confuse an earlier issue even more, Corran is not part of the Arnisdale property, but belongs to the Birkbecks' Loch Hourn estate. This begins at the bridge, and includes the whole long hill of Druim Fada that makes up the north side of the great lonely fjord of upper Loch Hourn, towards the shooting lodge and farm at Kinlochhourn, which is the headquarters of the estate.

There used to be an inn at Corran, which must in its day have had a fair amount of passing trade. Most of its customers would be fishermen, because the Hebridean cattle drovers rarely came this way. The Skye cattle that were swum across the narrows of Kyle Rhea followed an old route through the hills to the north and east of Arnisdale, behind Ben Sgriol and across an inland pass to Kinlochhourn. Corran is only six miles in a straight line from Kinlochhourn, but to get there by road involves a journey of nearly twelve times that distance, away round by Shiel Bridge, Cluanie and Glen Garry. An ever-present feeling of remoteness is an added attraction—to the casual visitor. Without question, this is one of the most splendid situations on the wild west coast, surrounded by sheer-rising mountains and with fine clear views out through the mouth of Loch Hourn to the spiky peaks of Skye. W. H. Murray, a connoisseur of Highland landscape, has written that the view of the Black Cuillin from Corran is perhaps the best on the whole mainland coast.

Except for a hill-walker or climber, the best view of the Knoydart peaks across the loch is from a little hill on the seaward side of the road, immediately before the steep plunge down the one-in-five gradient into Arnisdale from Eilanreach and Glenelg. It's a good place too for a grandstand seat at the porpoise Olympics that sometimes spill over from the Sound of Sleat. The chances of having a really clear view into the mountain country to the south and east are, to be honest, not very great. Knoydart is often obscured by clouds or rain. Its high mountain ridges, rising without hesitation from the sea into a jumble of three thousand foot peaks, rip the bottom out of any rain clouds coming in from the Atlantic. Loch Hourn is often raked by squalls described even in the understated prose of the sailing guides as erratic and extremely fierce.

However, on any kind of clear day—and it would be mischievous to suggest that Loch Hourn is never quietly bathed in warm sunlight—the outlook from this little roadside knoll is quite unforgettable. Knoydart's mountains are shapely, individual, no-nonsense *peaks*; to the outsider there is no pretence that they are either homely or hospitable. Due south across the loch is the long high ridge of Ladhar Bheinn or Larven, farthest west of all the three thousand foot peaks on the Scottish mainland. Slightly to the east, straining up utterly remote in the farthest background, is the very tip of the sharp and regular summit cone of Sgurr na Ciche, nearly three and a half thousand feet high and towering over the head of Loch Nevis.

There's an air of unapproachable mystery about this Empty Quarter of the West Highlands. Knoydart was part of the territory of the Macdonells of Glengarry, whose clan chiefs were among the first in the Highlands to encourage emigrations and evictions. It was in the 1770s that the first people began to emigrate from Knoydart, which until about a hundred and seventy years ago was spelled with its middle consonants the other way round: Knodyart, Knodiart and then the gradual change to Knowdort; the initial letter has remained silent throughout. From 1770 to 1793 around eight hundred people left the wooded glens and the hills that gave good grazing, which even then were being rented out to incoming sheep farmers. The Rev. Colin Maciver, who wrote about the district in 1793, mentioned that 'the inhabitants dwell in villages bordering on the sea, along the sides of Lochurn and Lochneavis; here the soil is in general light, yielding crops of barley, oats, and potatoes. The hills, though high, are mostly green to the top, and afford excellent pasture for all kinds of cattle.'

There was no reason why the people who remained in Knoydart shouldn't have been able to live comfortably; but the ruling family of the Macdonells of Glengarry were a miserable crew, and when their stupid extravagances forced them to sell off this part of the clan territory, they did it in a particularly odious way. The buyer was one of the wealthy kings of the Industrial Revolution, the Lowland ironmaster James Baird of Gartsherrie and Cambusdoon. In an infamous contract, he agreed to buy over Knoydart if the Macdonells would guarantee to evict all the crofters from the district. In the most brutal clearances outside of Sutherland, the people were chased and burned out of their homes and holdings, and the well documented history of the affair makes harrowing reading.

Today the population of the whole of Knoydart, about a hundred square miles, can be counted in dozens. There is only one village, at Inverie on the north shore of Loch Nevis, whose only lifeline with the outside world is a ferry from Mallaig. From the estate's point of view, arable farming is virtually neglected in favour of deer stalking and ten thousand sheep on the hills;

visitors are not encouraged during the stalking season, although the situation has eased since the day in 1968 when one visitor stood up very firmly for his rights in a confrontation with an estate representative. However, anybody wanting to visit the interior of Knoydart must be a sturdy mountaineer, travel in a party and carry his own supplies. There are right-of-way tracks through the district, which make exploration possible for rough-country cyclists.

Looking towards Sgurr na Ciche seems to take the eye towards the head of Loch Hourn, about four miles from the viewpoint at Arnisdale. In fact, as Pennant's account made clear, this is only the wide sweep of Barrisdale Bay on the far shore. Upper Loch Hourn turns out of sight to the left, ploughing through a narrow trough in the mountains, sometimes only two or three hundred yards wide, heading eastwards for another five miles to the lonely hemmed-in settlement of Kinlochhourn, by which point the waters of the loch are so far inland that they take on little of the movement of the open sea.

Barrisdale is another deer-stalking estate, outside the limits of the much larger Knoydart property; Inverness County Council have to employ a teacher especially for the three children who live at this lonely and roadless outpost. The estate recently changed hands, and is now owned by Major Gordon from Lude, near Blair Atholl.

In the middle of the eighteenth century, Coll Macdonell of Barrisdale was one of the most notorious characters north of the Highland Line. He controlled most of the country of Knoydart, making a great deal of his fairly substantial fortune by extorting money from prosperous landowners in many parts of the Highlands, in return for promising not to remove their cattle. He was one of the earliest exponents of the protection racket; blackmail was originally 'black meal', so called because the fee for guaranteed protection was usually so many bolls of meal or grain. Barrisdale gathered payments from estates many miles away from his own, and even had the President of the Court of Session, Scotland's most important legal dignitary, 'on his books'.

Scattered references to him in history books show just how perfidious a Highland gentleman could be if he put his mind to it; and Coll Macdonell was on the surface a perfect gentleman, 'a man of polished behaviour, fine address, and fine person'. He was also well known as the inventor of a useful instrument of torture, which came to be known after him as the barrisdale. It was a device into which a victim was tied, and which then pushed his body closer and closer to a sharpened iron spike. Small wonder that few people whom Coll Macdonell interviewed for business or political reasons were able to withstand the argument of twenty inches of cold steel being forced inexorably towards their throats.

During the rebellion of 1745, Barrisdale played a dangerous double game. Nominally on the Jacobite side, there is little doubt that he was also in the pay of the government; the suspicion grew almost to a certainty when the Redcoats destroyed his fine new house, which had 'eighteen fire-rooms and many others without fires, beautifully covered with blue slates', but left severely alone the great herds of cattle which were the real outward show of his wealth. He was absent from Culloden, because he and his men were on a private raid to the north coast of Sutherland to look for £12,000 of Prince Charlie's gold hidden there; and it was believed that his local knowledge contrived the chain of Redcoat outposts that were strung along the eastern border of Knoydart, to catch the Prince in his break-out northwards to Glenshiel.

After the rebellion failed, the Jacobites held Barrisdale a prisoner on the Continent, until he returned to Scotland in 1749. Then the government arrested him, being by no means convinced of his protested loyalty to the House of Hanover. He tried to exchange his freedom for a complete account of all his double-agent work for them during the rebellion; but he was still in a cell in Edinburgh Castle when he died.

The hill country around the upper part of the loch used to be terrorized at least by the thought of the Beast of Barrisdale. A few generations ago there were gruesome tales of a great, malodorous flying monster like a pterodactyl, which lived in the mountains to the north-east and used to come screeching for human prey over the little hamlets huddled nervously by the lochside.

A last lingering memory of this strange outlook from the rise of ground near Arnisdale is of the inscrutable waters of the loch, great silent mountains on every side, and the old white house of Barrisdale caught in a splash of sunlight through the clouds, brooding quietly to itself about these half-forgotten tales of the older days, far away among the empty hills. That tiny flicker of human life on the fringes of what might just as well be the mountains of the moon: surely it must be nothing more than a trick of the light?

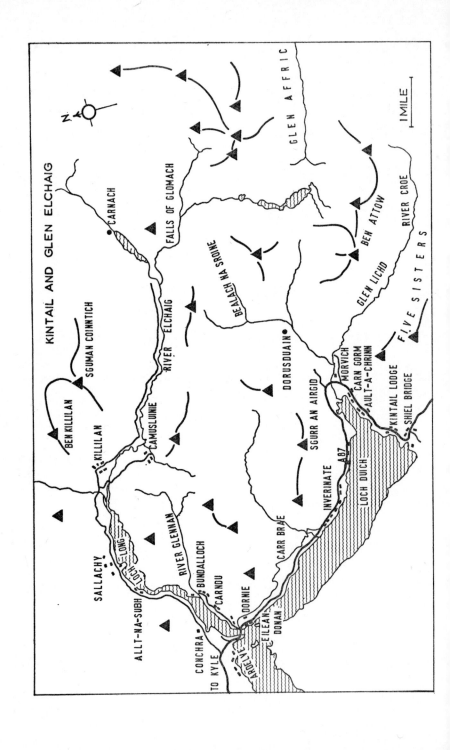

KINTAIL AND GLEN ELCHAIG

8 Dornie from the bridge across Loch Long to Ardelve

9 The rumpled mountains of Knoydart seen from Isleornsay, across the Sound of Sleat in Skye

10 The Falls of Glomach, in the heart of the mountains of Kintail

CHAPTER 5

KINTAIL

WHILE THE RATAGAN, GLENELG AND ARNISDALE districts are all
on dead-end minor roads, the way from Shiel Bridge along the
north-east side of Loch Duich is by the main road to Kyle of
Lochalsh. Going beyond the Ratagan turning, the main road
swings right through a rock cutting, between the first slopes of
the Five Sisters and the head of Loch Duich. From here the full
length of the loch is seen in all its glory, steep mountainsides,
often carpeted in forestry plantations, rising grandly from the
water's edge. From here on, the Kyle road goes for several miles
along the edge of the country of Kintail, scenically one of the
most superb districts in the whole of Wester Ross.

There are some cottages to the right of the road, making up the
hamlet of Invershiel, backed by the sweeping hillside that forms
the west end of the Five Sisters. One of them is rented out for
holiday use by the National Trust for Scotland, which owns the
Five Sisters themselves and a spill of ground in some of the other
valleys. On the left, as the main road climbs uphill for a short way
before dipping down again towards the lochside, is Kintail Lodge
Hotel. In a district whose proprietors were for many years totally
inhospitable to visitors, even to the extent of warning their
tenants that they were liable to be evicted if they took in paying
guests, it's something like poetic justice that the old shooting
lodge should have been turned into a hotel. After the National
Trust took over the estate in 1944, they ran the hotel themselves,
but since this was not by any stretch of the imagination their real
business, they soon handed it over to professionals. During the
summer, a tourist information caravan is parked on a slip road
beside the hotel.

To the right of the road just before the hotel, there's a village
hall that serves most of the communities around the head of the
loch, and an old cottage that has provided accommodation for the
adventure camps run by the Trust.

The modern Kintail road, from Shiel Bridge to Dornie, was originally based on the one planned by Telford, although great changes are being made to the old route. Telford reported that the estimates for building this road were so great that the contractors invited tenders for ten-foot and twelve-foot widths as well as the more normal fifteen, but that they decided at last to accept the original width.

Coming back down towards loch level after the tiny hill beyond the hotel, the road goes between a great spread of crags on the hillside to the right and a rather damp patch of ground that stretches over to the waterside. On this level ground the Trust have laid out sets of their picnic furniture, with chairs cut out of one piece of timber, and a sliced-off bit of trunk for a table. This isn't as twee as it sounds, but it would be rather helpful if the damp ground were drained a bit, and the chairs and tables occasionally renewed. For all that, it's a pleasant spot, with a fine outlook over the loch and the chance of catching a glimpse of the eagles that are said to have an eyrie on the rocky slopes above; either that, or they're buzzards, often confused by visitors with the more majestic bird. Unfortunately, the lochside and the narrow glens that come down through the mountains seem to be a favourite training area for jet fighters, and the nerves are often set jangling by the blare of noise that follows an unnoticed low-level approach. A correspondent to a national newspaper recently suggested that these flights should be promoted as some kind of tourist attraction, because of the sudden contrast with the lonely mountain scene. Let's hope the man was only joking.

The road gets right down alongside the loch again at the square-edged bay that marks where the River Croe comes down to the sea, then through the haphazard little hamlet of Ault-a-chrinn, with a fine view north-east into the mountain country above Strath Croe. Narrowly above the lochside again, and it runs into the jumble of old cottages at Carn Gorm, last of the four townships round the head of Loch Duich. The present main road follows the indentation of the lochside, but is not by any means up to the standard of the improvements being made throughout the whole length of the Glen Moriston to Kyle of Lochalsh route. County engineers did their sums and came to the conclusion that to rebuild the road from Ault-a-chrinn past the entrance to Strath Croe, rebuilding one substantial bridge on the way, would be a lot more expensive than building a causeway to cut right across the water towards the old graveyard seen on the other side. One early scheme was for a watertight dam, which would have cost too much money, and the tidal waters of the bay will now ebb and flow almost unhindered. The latest Bartholomew's half-inch map of the district has already taken the plunge, and showed the line of the causeway road even before it had been approved; these Bartholomew maps are kept smartly if unobtrusively up to date, but there are three places on the *Skye and Torridon* sheet where they got in very early with road alterations that were little more than gleams in the planners' eyes.

Carn Gorm, although you wouldn't think so to look at the tiny cottages of which it is composed, was almost within living memory a place of very great significance in the story of the West Highlands; it was here that the incredible intolerance of the great sporting landlords grew to such lunatic proportions that the law of the land finally creaked into action to offer protection to the humble crofting tenants. The government enquiry of 1883, mentioned many a time in this book, led by gradual stages to the Crofters Holdings Act of 1886 which finally gave the smallholders a fair deal and recourse to a court of law if they felt they were being swindled. By that time, the worst days of the clearances were long since over, and the tenants who had been in the way of the great landlords and sheep farmers had been safely shovelled into tiny coastal holdings; but the oppressed crofters who remained all over the West Highlands and islands benefited from the national publicity given to the affair at Carn Gorm. The whole storm, oddly enough, centred on nothing more significant than what has come to be known as the Pet Lamb of Kintail.

The Mackenzie Earls of Seaforth who controlled the lands of Kintail were unlike many of the clan chiefs whose power and influence the government was determined to crush after the Forty-five; in 1786 one of the Earls, offered twice and three times the existing rent for some of his hill grazings by southern sheep farmers, retorted that he would never turn his lands into sheep runs, nor 'turn out his people upon any consideration, or for any rent that could be offered'. When the crofters' leases ran out, he renewed them at 'a pretty moderate augmentation'. In the early part of the nineteenth century, however, the last of the Earls of Seaforth died, and his successors in Kintail didn't have the same scruples about the hereditary tenants. Throughout the nine-teenth century, sheep farming was the only source of income that mattered.

The reign of the sheep farmers, however, was not to last for ever. In the 1870s there was a drastic fall in the price of wool. It was so crippling that when the leases of the big sheep farms expired the flockmasters decided not to renew them, even though some of the landowners slashed the rents in an effort to induce them to stay. Since the land had long since been cleared of the original tenants, many of whom had been substantial cattlemen in their own right, the proprietors could think of only one other way to make money from their estates; the great day of the deer forest arrived.

Deer forests, of course, had been a prominent feature of the Highland scene for hundreds of years. It was only at the begin-ning of the nineteenth century, however, that the habit of lending or leasing the forests to outsiders had come into fashion, at first as a favour to other landed gentry, or because the local laird was too old or frail to enjoy a day's stalking himself. The rents were very low in the early years, but as more and more rich southern sportsmen began to come north, prices rose substantially and the whole thing became very much a business venture. To the land-owners of Kintail and Glenshiel, owners of estates that had been cleared of people and in some parts almost denuded of trees to make way for the sheep farms that now lay vacant, deer forests were the only hope of financial salvation. The interests of the crofters were almost completely ignored, and the whole effort of the estates was concentrated on attracting wealthy shooting tenants. By the 1880s there were so many deer forests, and they had become so enormous in extent, that it was difficult to let them to the tobacco, whisky, brewing and industrial millionaires who were attracted to them. To improve the grazing for deer, so that the 'bags' would be of better quality and that there would therefore be more chance of attracting a stalking tenant, some proprietors cleared their estates completely even of their own sheep. Since human intrusions into the stalking preserves upset the deer, visitors were very much unwelcome. At one time the north of Scotland deer forests numbered over two hundred, and extended over an area of more than three and a half million acres; although that figure included a great amount of otherwise useless land, it represented a sixth of the total area of the whole of Scotland. The county councils were generally unconcerned about this basically unhealthy state of affairs, because they claimed very high county rates from sporting land.

In the 1880s, two hundred thousand acres of deer forest, stretching right across Inverness and Ross-shire from the Moray Firth to the Atlantic, were leased or bought by a tremendously rich but obviously unbalanced American railway millionaire called Louis Winans. The Winans family were of Dutch extraction, and they were no more than comfortably off until one day in 1828 when Ross Winans arrived in Baltimore to try to sell some horses to the Baltimore and Ohio Railroad. Instead, he became fascinated by the working of the railway. The following year, the Baltimore and Ohio sent him to Britain to study railway operation here; when he got back to America he developed the first of a long and lucrative series of inventions and developments concerned with locomotives and carriage design.

Ross Winans was invited to Russia to advise on the organization and construction of the state railway network there; but he decided not to go personally, and one of his sons made the journey instead. The American consortium of Harrison, Winans and Eastwick managed to outbid everybody else in an international struggle for the contract to equip the whole of the new Russian railway system with locomotives and rolling stock; one thing led to another, and by the time they had gathered in more and more subsidiary contracts, even for bridges over some of the great rivers, the consortium came out with something like seven million dollars. And that was only the Russian end of the Winans operation.

Louis Winans, then, was not short of a dollar or two when he decided to make a hobby of gathering deer forests. Like many another character with far too much money and nothing in particular to occupy his attention, he came to behave in a way that would have caused anybody with a slimmer bank balance to be reckoned completely off his head. It seemed to be his sole interest in life, in Scotland at any rate, to buy or rent as many deer forests as he could lay his hands on, and then devote his ingenuity to making life as miserable as possible for everybody connected with them. To make the whole business more bizarre, he himself had no interest in stalking; now and again he would have as many as possible of the deer in his two hundred thousand acres moved into the forest of Braulen, in Strathfarrar some miles north-east of Kintail, and take pot shots at a few dozen as they were driven in front of him. His son Walter, who had a lifelong obsession with firearms, was rather more businesslike about it; more than once, in the Strathfarrar deer drives, he shot a hundred or so stags in a season.

Louis Winans, if he had an interest in history, may have been aware of an old Privy Council order dated 6 February 1610, commissioning Mackenzie of Kintail 'to apprehend all and sundry who shall thereafter shoot or slay deer within his bounds'; because in Kintail, which he rented from later Mackenzie owners, and in the rest of his forests, his keepers had strict instructions to watch and follow anybody who set foot on the hallowed ground. Sir Hugh Munro of Lindertis, an Angus landowner who was one of Scotland's pioneer mountaineers, recalled one of his expeditions between Glen Affric and Kintail; every few miles, he wrote in an article in the *Scottish Mountaineering Club Journal*, one of Winans's sentries would pop up and ask him, quite civilly, where he was from and where he was going. Acting on his boss's instructions, one of these keepers followed Sir Hugh all the way over one of the mountains.

About the same time, the parish minister of Kintail sounded off about the situation: 'Glen after glen is being cleared of its shepherd families, who are replaced by one or two solitary game watchers, or "stoppers", as they are popularly called, who are usually the idlest of people pretending to earn a living, and the best customers of the adjacent public houses and shebeens.' To be forced to accept work as one of Winans's sentries, of course, was enough to drive any previously proud Highlander to drink.

The whole thing came to a head in the episode of the pet lamb, which has been told in considerable detail elsewhere, notably in Wilfred Taylor's *Scot Easy*. Briefly, there was a cobbler called Murdo Macrae, who was tenant of one of the cottages at Carn Gorm. His family 'adopted' a stray lamb that his son had found wandering at the side of the road. One day the lamb was observed by one of Winans's keepers, who must have been infected by his master's monumental stupidity, grazing a few feet off the public road that ran through the deer forest. The keeper reported this outrage to the American, who always tended to forget that he only rented the land and didn't own it. Winans decided to take Macrae to court, on the grounds that he had allowed a lamb under his control to commit trespass. Unlikely though this may sound, it was quite typical of the man; when he wasn't cornering the market in deer forests, he was up to his ears in interminable lawsuits.

The case came up before the Sheriff-Substitute at Dingwall in December 1884, and he found in favour of Murdo Macrae. Winans appealed to the Sheriff-Principal of the county, who can't have had an iota of humour in his body, because he reversed the original decision. By this time, Murdo Macrae had a great deal of support, legal, moral and financial, throughout the length and breadth of Scotland, and was able to appeal to the Court of Session in Edinburgh, pinnacle of the Scottish legal system, which heard the case in June of the following year. This time there was a unanimous decision against Winans, and the Lord Justice-Clerk was at no great pains in his written judgment to disguise the court's opinion of the American's action. There was a suggestion that Winans might go so far as to make a final appeal to the House of Lords, but nothing came of it. After the verdict, he is said to have remarked to Macrae that he would have found it cheaper to present him with a model of the lamb in solid gold. The story of the pet lamb of Kintail passed into Highland folklore, and certainly helped the crofters' supporters in Parliament in their struggle to pass the Crofters Holdings Act, even if the landowning interests in the House managed to side-step many of the commission of enquiry's recommendations.

Winans almost made a final monumental bloomer by offering to give every tenant on the Kintail estate £5 to forget the whole affair. He was warned off this miserable expedient just in time. As some kind of revenge, he had all the deer in Kintail driven miles away to the eastern part of his domain. Within a week they were all back again, while the men of Loch Duich went about their business as if it had nothing to do with them.

After the break-up of the great deer forest empire his father had created, Walter Winans didn't forget his obsession with guns; the family's good reputation in Russia didn't pass him by, either, and he must have been the only president of the Ashford (Kent) Rifle Club who also had the distinction of being a Chevalier of the Imperial Order of St Stanislaus of Russia. As vice-president of the National Rifle Association of Great Britain, he was the author of a series of books with no-nonsense titles like *The Art of Revolver Shooting, Hints on Revolver Shooting* and *The Sporting Rifle*.

The opening words of *Practical Rifle Shooting*, published in 1906, are as good a summing-up of the man as any: 'In my first book on Revolver Shooting, I drew attention to the dangerous consequences which a nation may incur when excessive devotion to such games as cricket, golf and football, leads its men to ignore the art of handling firearms. Many partisans of these games were indignant at my remarks, but two regrettable wars have had a salutary influence in this respect. Public opinion now endorses my doctrine of the absolute necessity that every able-bodied man should be able to bring at least as much skill to the handling of a rifle as he evinces with the cricket bat or golf club.'

Later in the book, he made it clear how much he disliked the expression 'deer-drive' when applied to the kind of shooting he and his father had enjoyed on their Highland estates. He suggested 'coining a word in the German manner, Deceiving deer-into-going-where-you-want-them-to'. It was all a far cry from Ross Winans, whose main literary endeavour, apart from railway contracts, was a work of the 1880s entitled *One Religion: Many Creeds*, which upset several orthodox churchmen with some stinging criticisms of the fragmentation of the Christian faith.

Beyond Carn Gorm the road begins to double back on itself to follow the curve of the bay at the entrance to Strath Croe. A side road to the right leads through the farmlands of Morvich, which is the headquarters of the National Trust for Scotland's estate; during the holiday season there are camping and caravanning pitches available here. Beyond the farmhouse the narrow tarmac road keeps alongside the tree-screened River Croe, with the view into the glen that's such a prominent feature from Ratagan changing gradually as the road gets closer to it. There are some substantial gullies on the flanks of the mountains, and the whole place looks very grand indeed under snow. A tributary river comes down from the north-east, through the valley on whose steep slopes the eastern, detached portion of Inverinate Forest is planted; the River Croe itself flows down the even steeper-sided valley of Glen Lichd, which comes from the south-east, behind the Five Sisters ridge. The upper slopes on both sides of Glen Lichd are part of the Trust property.

The public road comes to an end at a little bridge over the Croe just after a newly-built NTS adventure camp headquarters that is taking the place of the old one near Kintail Lodge Hotel. The track that goes over the bridge is a good hill route over to the famous Falls of Glomach. There's an old right of way up Glen Lichd on the south bank of the river, a relic of the days when these passes over to Glen Affric were the usual way into Kintail. As you might expect from the precipitous hillsides, Glen Lichd has had more than its fair share of avalanches in the past, especially on the steep slopes of Ben Attow that make up the northern wall.

It was also a great place for poaching, in the days when one notorious Kintail poacher was said to keep three barrels permanently filled: one with the laird's venison, one with the laird's mutton, and the third with the laird's salmon. In the time of the Seaforths, one of the Earl's hunters once went missing after a hill-shooting expedition in the glen. His body was found in the snow a fortnight later. It turned out that he had discovered somebody trying to steal his goats, and was leading the thief along one of the narrow hillside paths when the man saw his chance, pushed him off the edge and made off over the mountains. For many generations, local writers complained of the state of the pathways through the hills; on many of them there were dangerous places where two men could barely walk abreast. These high valleys weren't always the empty places they are today. In days gone by, when the crofters of the district had access to the high-level pastures for their summer grazing grounds, so many cattle were kept here that the whole district was known in Gaelic as Kintail of the Cows.

Back down at the main road, a little way after the Morvich road-end, is the rather narrow Croe Bridge. This is the one that would be too expensive to replace by a more modern effort, one of the reasons why there is going to be a causeway built over the loch from Ault-a-chrinn. After the bridge, the main road keeps swinging round to the left, under the flanks of Sgurr an Airgid, the mountain that keeps trying to push Inverinate into the loch. The western part of Inverinate Forest begins some way farther along the main road, while the eastern part in Glen Croe can be reached by a minor road turning sharp back right towards Dorusduain. It stays public as far as the farm of Lienassie, guarded by a screen of rhododendrons and looking over the grazing ground below it that reaches down to the river.

In the 1950s Lienassie was one of the farms 'adopted' by London schools, under a scheme set up by the Association of Agriculture. Regular bulletins were sent south about how the work was going on at Lienassie, with photographs to show the city children about planting and draining and looking after stock. In the middle of the last century, Lienassie was best known for a murder attempt there during the worst days of the clearances. Two men of Kintail, who were never identified despite strenuous efforts by the authorities, laid an ambush for a Lowland sheep farmer called Laidlaw, who rented thousands of acres of hill grazings around the borders of Inverness and Ross-shire, from which the crofters had been barred. Their plan was to shoot him as he rode over the much-used hill track from Glen Affric to Dorusduain, higher up the glen. However, their nerve failed them as he came into their sights, and they contented themselves with firing a few shots through his bedroom window after he'd settled down for the night at Lienassie.

The track through this glen and up by Dorusduain to Glen Affric was one of the old coffin roads, over which funeral parties used to come on their way to the burial ground of Kintail. Another branch of it went from Dorusduain by the Falls of Glomach into Glen Elchaig, the next main valley to the north, over a pass known as the Bealach na Sroine. Frank Smythe, the famous mountaineer, once described in a book how he came over the pass and saw a ghostly funeral party moving slowly along in front of him.

Looking down over the river from Lienassie, the view is to two great valleys in the mountains. One is Glen Lichd, seen from here at its most dramatic; the other, into which the road beyond Lienassie disappears, has its lower slopes covered by the eastern part of the state forest. Down by the river, in a clearing of the forest at the foot of a great ring of mountains, is the pleasant white lodge of Dorusduain. In the early 1920s, when the Inverinate estate was owned by Sir Keith Fraser, an MP who lived mostly in Leicestershire, Dorusduain was reported to be unsurpassed as stalking ground; but much of the southern part of the property is now planted by the Forestry Commission.

Going back down to the main road, there's a good view to the

fine wedge-shaped summit above the Mam Ratagan pass on the
far side of the loch. Much nearer is Clachan Duich, the old burial
ground of Kintail, set on a little hill to the left of the main road as
it goes round the north side of the bay towards Inverinate village;
crowning the hill is the local war memorial. The graveyard is
around the ruins of the old parish church of Kintail, which was
destroyed by Wightman's troops in 1719 during his rampage
through the district after the Battle of Glenshiel. By the side of
little Loch nan Corr, a short way west of the church, the Jacobites
had set up an ammunition dump, which the Spanish soldiers
guarding it blew up as soon as the government warships came
sailing up to the head of the loch.

Most of the gravestones bear the name Macrae, this family
having been settled in the district for five or six hundred years.
Originally from farther east, they soon became the fighting men
of the Mackenzie chiefs. It happened that many of the early chiefs
of that clan died without leaving any sons, which meant that they
were unusually short of friendly relatives to help them in their
various inevitable disagreements with neighbouring lairds. The
Macraes took over the job, and came to be known as 'Mackenzie's
shirt of mail'. The other main family who settled in Kintail were
the Maclennans, and the local minister, who was himself a
Macrae, noted in 1836 that there was not only a geographical
dividing line between the two family groups, but even a noticeable difference in the way they spoke Gaelic. He allowed himself
some stiff remarks about 'the unworthy invention which an
individual of a neighbouring district palmed upon the credulity
of Dr. Johnson, and to which the weight of that great name has
given currency; viz. that the Macraes only attained to consequence
by marrying the widows of the Maclennans slain at the Battle of
Auldearn'. It was enough to give a decent Macrae a fit of the
vapours.

The connexion between the Macraes and the Earls of Seaforth
lasted for a very long time, and one of the last manifestations of it
led to a troublesome incident that came to be known in military
circles as the Affair of the Macraes. For their support of the
Jacobite cause, the Earls of Seaforth found their title forfeited
over two or three generations. Eventually, the authorities
relented and one of the Mackenzies of Kintail was elevated again
to the peerage. In 1778 he raised a regiment to show his gratitude;

this was a fashionable thing to do in those days, especially as it was a handy way of getting rid of unwanted tenants, although this was not likely to have been uppermost in Seaforth's mind. Naturally, considering the Earl's circle of influence, most of the soldiers were Macraes of Kintail. The Earl himself was appointed Lieutenant-Colonel in command of the new regiment, which set off in August 1779 to march to Leith, before taking ship for the East Indies.

It was not, however, a very happy regiment. The men were discontented, and several reasons were given for their notable lack of enthusiasm. The military discipline was said to be irksome, especially as the adjutant 'had one panacea for all the ills of life—drill, drill and more drill'. There was some complaint that they were well behind in their pay. Finally, Seaforth in person didn't measure up to the gallant, dignified and sympathetic chief they had expected. It was said that he 'incurred their absolute contempt'.

Obviously, it wouldn't take much to push the new 78th Regiment over the edge to mutiny. A rumour arose, perhaps spread by parties unsympathetic to the government, that the regiment had been sold to the East India Company, and that they were bound for a climate from which not one man in a hundred would come back alive. On the very day on which they were supposed to embark for the East Indies, those members of the regiment who were billeted at Edinburgh Castle refused point-blank to go on board ship. Led by their NCOs and pipers, and preceded by two standard-bearers with tartan plaids fixed to poles to represent the regimental colours, they marched up to Arthur's Seat and settled down for a long wait.

They were supplied with food and drink by the citizens of Edinburgh, some of them supporters, but others more worried about what the 'wild' Highlanders might do if they had to scour the city for provisions; it wasn't so long, after all, since the Jacobite days when nervous Lowlanders were solemnly assured by Redcoat propaganda that the Highland hordes who supported Prince Charlie had a taste for raw human flesh. The mutiny ended peaceably enough, with a government guarantee that the 78th would in no circumstances be posted to the Indies. Wisely, no official action was taken against the men, but the affair did eventually reach a tragic conclusion.

The regiment went to the Channel Islands for a few months, and then in April 1781 sailed from Portsmouth for India. As was not unusual in those days, the voyage was a terrible one. Seaforth himself died as the ships were nearing St Helena, and by the time they reached Madras nearly two hundred and fifty men had died of scurvy. Many of those who survived needed a long convalescence, and there were only three hundred and seventy anything like fit for immediate service.

As one of the plaques in the ruined church makes clear, there has been a long legal tussle about the chieftainship of Clan Macrae. In 1909 the head of the Macraes of Inverinate, one of the two main branches of the clan, petitioned the Lyon Court for recognition as chief of the whole clan; but his claim failed because he couldn't offer enough evidence. His grandson Kenneth Macrae, a writer on Highland affairs, became chief of the Macraes of Inverinate in 1970, and is reopening the claim. The other main family of the clan spell their name MacRae, and their hereditary seat is at Eilean Donan Castle farther down the lochside. Although in modern terms a dispute like this may not seem particularly vital, especially as there's nothing but the honour involved, there's no denying that here, by the lochside and the mountains where Macraes and MacRaes have lived and died for five or six hundred years, it assumes a significance of its own.

Beyond the old graveyard, after passing the point where the causeway is to reach over the loch to Ault-a-chrinn, the main road passes below the western plantation of Inverinate Forest and into the long drawn-out village of the same name. The road through Inverinate has recently been improved out of all recognition, in many places blasted out of the hillside to give a better line. Inverinate is a mixture of older cottages, Forestry Commission timber houses, bungalows, and some magnificently situated council houses right down on the lochside, on a little road that runs past the church, which stands beside some old pine trees. There is also a fine new primary school replacing one that served a small local district; the new one takes pupils from Ratagan and Letterfearn as well. When the school was built, it was on ground that was formerly part of the church glebe. Nobody complained about that, but when the county council took over more of the ten-acre glebe for the council houses, many local people thought it rather curious, to put it no higher, that the tiny church property should be rifled again, instead of the very extensive private estate and institutional land that makes up almost the whole of Kintail.

There's a fine view out over the loch from Inverinate, in one direction back into the spiky entrance to Glen Shiel and in another to the green gullied hillside between Ratagan and Letterfearn. It's easy to see from here how the planted area of Ratagan Forest has been extended down the lochside, from the 'uncut moquette' effect of the more recently forested areas over towards Letterfearn. Back up the nearside hill a little, the main road pursues its new line, a little farther away than it used to be from the main driveway to Inverinate Lodge. Like all the other properties round about here, Inverinate has had a succession of owners in the last hundred and seventy years since the Seaforth estates began to be sold off. Sir Keith Fraser disposed of it in 1929 to the Portman family, who built the lodge in a splendidly bright and airy situation almost on the water's edge. It gets the sun for almost all of the day, and the gardens, seen from the Letterfearn road across the loch, are a fine splash of colour with azaleas, rhododendrons and broom. When the seventh Viscount Portman died, the property passed to his daughter, who lives most of the time near Grimsby and married, incidentally, into the Bowlby family who bought Knoydart when it was sold by the Bairds of Cambusdoon. Nowadays, Inverinate estate is interested mainly in sheep farming and in its sporting rights.

About halfway between the lodge and the church is an old jetty. In the days when road transport was rather difficult, which means right up to the early years of this century, funeral parties going to the church often sailed along the loch, and it's for this reason that the jetty is still sometimes referred to as the coffin pier.

The lodge entrance is only halfway through the long settlement of Inverinate, from the second part of which there's a much more open view across the loch. The hillside is still pretty steep here, and various retaining walls have been built along the high side of the new road to stop great lumps of Inverinate Forest from sliding across it. Soon there's a brand new junction, where the old road follows a very exciting line high above the loch to the summit of the Carr Brae, and the modern one, opened only in 1969, skirts the lochside on the way to the next village at Dornie.

Although the new road is far superior to the old one, it loses the Carr Brae's remarkable elevated view. Not far from the start, it goes over a bridge across the Leth-allt burn, which comes rollicking down a rocky and wooded ravine. Beyond the bridge the new road gets right down to the point where a high tide makes menacing noises at it, and it's not for nothing that there are signs warning of falling rocks. The road is just a ledge blasted out of the foot of the steep hillside coming down from the Carr Brae, and rockfalls and even avalanches are not unknown; one tree came down in the early months of 1970 like something out of a caber-tossing contest, flattening part of the lochside guard rail.

The low road follows exactly the lines of the different bays and inlets along the coast, which means that there are one or two very long corners to catch the unwary. Originally, there was a plan to fill in at least one of these bays with rubble from the blasting, so that a straighter line of road could be followed; but this notion was reportedly abandoned because it would have altered the sailing charts of Loch Duich too drastically. Another idea that came to nothing was to have a ramp leading from the road into the loch, so that the old unwanted cars that are such an eyesore in parts of the Highlands, because there just isn't anywhere legal and unobtrusive to dump them, could be simply slid down to disappear forever under the water.

Altogether, the new road, though a tribute to modern civil engineering, just doesn't seem to have the character of the hairy old affair farther up the hill; on wild days, however, when the grey waters of the loch are slapping angrily across the shore, it has a certain atmosphere of its own.

Farther along the new road, the view ahead is to the meeting of Loch Duich, Loch Alsh and Loch Long, although, because of the lack of elevation, a first-time visitor has no means of telling that there are so many different bits of waterway in that direction. Across the loch, there are older woodlands of birch, ash and alder enveloping the hillsides above Drudaig Lodge and Totaig; the skyline above them is a rough, knobbly shoulder rising directly from the entrance to Loch Duich. The green hills above Letterfearn are streaked with little burns, although more and more of them are being hidden as the forest marches closer to the open sea.

Round a right-hand bend, through a small rock cutting, and suddenly there's a view that couldn't be seen from the old high road: the magnificent restored castle of Eilean Donan, seen from here on its island with a modern bridge connecting it over the tiny stretch of tidal water with the mainland. From the high road, the only view was a steep downhill one, which has become rather mournfully familiar over the years from its constant repetition on biscuit tins and table mats. From here, too, under a hillside that is almost cleared of the trees that used to cover it, there's a fine outlook to the mountains of Skye and round the mainland corner from Totaig, where more Forestry Commission plantations are heading for the isolated house of Ardintoul.

Although it may have become a rather hackneyed feature of the Highland scene, even this cannot take much away from the essential grandeur of Eilean Donan. The early history of the place is rather hazy, although it is said to have taken its name from the early St Donnan, who worked nearby. There was a fortress here from the early years of the thirteenth century, when Alexander II of Scotland was building strongholds on his western coast against the activities of the Norsemen who controlled the Hebrides. Traditionally, Alexander III appointed one Colin Fitzgerald as governor of the castle sometime after the Battle of Largs in 1263, which effectively removed the Norse menace, and Fitzgerald is supposed to have been the founder of the Mackenzie family; Mackenzie historians, however, tend to regard this tale with little more than a curl of the lip.

For many years Eilean Donan had a very stormy history, thanks to the strategic position guarding the coastal routes that made it a much-prized pawn in the political and military struggles of the Highlands and Western Isles. About 1330 a group of rebels in the castle were attacked by Thomas Randolph, Earl of Moray and nephew of Robert the Bruce. Once the castle was taken, so the story goes, Randolph beheaded all fifty of the rebel garrison and had their heads exhibited on spikes round the outer walls, as a gentle hint to anybody with similar ideas.

The castle was involved in many of the later disputes about the Lordship of the Isles and the Earldom of Ross. In 1539, a few years after it had been visited by James V, it was attacked by the Macdonalds of Sleat in Skye, who had ambitions about extending their territory in the north-west. The leader of this expedition, which is mentioned in every account of the castle, is almost always said to have been Donald Gorm Macdonald, a notoriously troublesome character who spent most of his time sailing up and

11 Ben Killilan and Sguman Coinntich from Allt-nan-Subh

12 The wooded cliffs at the head of Loch Long

13 Sunset over Loch Duich and Loch Alsh, with the mountains of Skye in the background

down the Western Isles making life unpleasant for his neighbours. A more painstaking historian pointed out some years ago that the Macdonald of Sleat who led the attack wasn't Donald Gorm, but his kinsman Donald Grumach. This technical point doesn't make much difference, because, although the names are not the same, the belligerent tendencies of the two men were identical.

When the Macdonalds' fighting galleys sailed into Loch Alsh, Eilean Donan had for some reason been left in the hands of only three or four defenders. One of them was killed, and then, by a lucky chance, another got a clear sight of the Macdonald chief as he stood around deciding where to make the main attack, and shot an arrow into his leg. The wounded chief was taken over to the curious low-lying island of Glas Eilean off Ardintoul. When the arrow was eased out of his wound, the barb severed an artery, the flow of blood couldn't be staunched, and Macdonald died soon afterwards. His clansmen withdrew, and for the economic removal of a public menace, Mackenzie of Kintail was granted extra lands by a grateful central government. What is perhaps most interesting about the story is that the Ordnance Survey still show on Glas Eilean a spot called Larach Tigh Mhic Domhnuill—the Site of Macdonald's House.

Since Kintail and the rest of the Seaforth country had always been attached to the Stuarts, Eilean Donan was garrisoned by government troops after the execution of Charles I; the same thing happened during the first Jacobite rebellion of 1715, when the locals regained possession of the castle by a neat piece of trickery. A Kintail farmer came to the garrison commander, spun him a yarn about how his rheumatism told him there was soon going to be a violent storm, and asked for help in gathering his harvest before the rains came. Most of the soldiers in the castle were detailed to go out into the fields, whereupon Seaforth's men, who were hiding nearby, rushed the stronghold and took it easily from the skeleton force left behind.

Eilean Donan's role as a fortress, of course, came to a sudden end in 1719 when the bombardment by the *Worcester*, *Enterprise* and *Flamborough* practically blew it apart. It stayed that way until 1912, when it came into the possession of Lt.-Col. John MacRae-Gilstrap, a descendant of the family who had once provided the Constables of Eilean Donan. He had married a rich American, and they decided to rebuild the castle—outwardly, at

W.R.—7

least—exactly as it had been in its heyday. The work went on for twenty years, at the staggering cost of a quarter of a million pounds. During the rebuilding, evidence was found of the remains of a Pictish fort, and of a deep-sunk well which had provided fresh water for the inmates of the castle in times of siege. Most of the rock for the rebuilding was quarried locally, just as the original material had been. In the renovation, the MacRae-Gilstraps were helped by a local man called Farquhar MacRae, who had had a dream revealing the appearance of the castle in the days of its greatness, when a contemporary account described it as 'a strong and fair Dungeon upon a rock, with another tower compased with a fair Barnkin wall, with orchard and trees, all within ane yland of the length of twa pairs of butts, almost round'.

Although interrupted by the first world war, the work continued steadily. Not everybody who saw it in progress, however, was enthusiastic about the final outcome. M. E. M. Donaldson, gathering material for her exhaustive book *Wanderings in the Western Highlands and Islands*, was enraged when she passed this way in the early 1920s. The operations at Eilean Donan roused one of her great passions, which was that almost everybody who built or restored a house in the West Highlands was, from an architectural point of view, nothing more than a lout:

'I was horrified and repelled by the ruined picture which obtruded itself on the outraged surroundings, the remains of the castle being in the throes of a rebuilding which must permanently disfigure the landscape. In any modern rebuilding operations, the end no less than the means to the end are alike hideous. From start to finish of the proceedings, everything is ugly; and one can only marvel at a taste which finds any satisfaction in transforming a picturesque ruin which harmonizes so completely with its surroundings into a permanent blot on the landscape. For a modern mansion-house must in the nature of things be aggressive in its pretentiousness, and especially if it is to be connected with the mainland by a bridge, as is reported. How any one identified with the country by reason of his clan can thus choose to identify himself with a proceeding usually connected with Americans or vulgarians, passes comprehension.'

Good claymore-swinging stuff; but she hadn't stopped long enough to let the real scope of the operation penetrate her disgruntlement at Americans and bridges. When the project was finished, with the castle a correct and dignified replica of what had stood there more than two hundred years before, she had to eat humble pie in the columns of the *Scots Magazine*.

Nowadays open to the public, Eilean Donan has been restored in a particularly magnificent style. Most splendid part, perhaps, is the banqueting hall, complete with a collection of trophies and relics of the old Jacobite days, the Black Watch regiment with which the MacRaes were so much concerned, family heirlooms and all the rest. Although it's used for all kinds of local affairs and celebrations, Eilean Donan isn't the usual home of its present owner; Mr John MacRae lives beyond Inverness, oddly enough not far from the field of Culloden, where Jacobite hopes were dashed for ever.

It's not far along the main road from the Eilean Donan car park to the start of the village of Dornie; but taking the low road all the way from Inverinate to Dornie, and ignoring the old high route over the Carr Brae, would be to miss one of the finest viewpoints in the whole of Wester Ross. Taking the Carr Brae road, sometimes referred to as the Keppoch Hill or just simply as 'the Dornie', means going back to the north-western edge of Inverinate and attacking the narrow hill up to a higher crossing of the Leth-allt burn. It's astonishing how restricted and difficult the old road looks compared with the coast one, although only two or three years ago it was the regular route, not only for local and holiday traffic, but for most of the heavy lorries that make for Kyle of Lochalsh and the crossing to Skye. It's still a single-track affair with a moderate supply of passing places, although some of the higher reaches have been resurfaced fairly recently.

Climbing the first part of the road, with bits of Inverinate Forest on the hillside to the right, leads up to a hairpin bridge over the rough gully of the Leth-allt; straight ahead is the only moderately high, but from this angle rather impressive wedge-shaped top of Boc Beag. Going higher up, there are traces of old arable land, although it's only rough sheep grazing nowadays. Now and again there are derisory strips of crash barrier on the outside edge of the road. All this steep climb is worth the effort, because of the superb panorama from the highest point overlooking the loch.

Looking southwards, there is one of the best views available from any public road of the Five Sisters and the other majestic mountains of Glenshiel at the head of the loch. North-west the view is of the very pleasant indented coastline around Totaig, with the bays and inlets that offer such good anchorage for yachts showing up very well. Slightly to the right of that is the meeting place of the three lochs at Dornie, all of them seen to be really steep-sided mountainous inlets of the sea.

For hundreds of years, almost the whole of the country that can be seen from the top of the Carr Brae was part of the extensive territory of the Mackenzies of Kintail. They had already ruled the district for many generations when Kenneth Mackenzie was created Lord Mackenzie of Kintail in 1609. His son Colin became the first Earl of Seaforth fourteen years later; the title came from a loch in the Outer Isles. The Seaforths controlled wide-ranging tracts of land in Easter as well as Wester Ross, and had been involved in national politics at least since John Mackenzie supported Robert the Bruce, whom he is supposed to have entertained at Eilean Donan. The trouble with the Seaforths was that they rarely supported the winning side, since they were mostly enthusiastic adherents to the House of Stuart.

George Mackenzie, the second Earl, was originally a Covenanter, but changed over to the losing side, for which he was excommunicated by the General Assembly of the Church of Scotland. His successor Kenneth threw in his lot with Charles II at the Battle of Worcester, and ended up in prison, with all his estates confiscated; Cromwell thought so ill of him that he was excluded from the Act of Grace and Pardon in 1654. Even in private life poor old Kenneth didn't have the best of luck; he married the sister of the Earl of Cromartie, an alliance which brought him, according to an old account, 'neither beauty, parts, portion nor relation'.

Another Kenneth, the fourth Earl, was one of the original Knights of the Thistle when that Scottish order was founded in 1687, and soon afterwards followed the deposed James VII to exile in France and later in Ireland. In 1690 he was one of the Jacobite chiefs who were defeated by General Mackay, to whom Seaforth surrendered in person. He was imprisoned for the next seven years in Edinburgh Castle, which wasn't as bad as it might have been, because the Countess was allowed to move in with him.

It was William, the fifth Earl, who was wounded at the Battle of Glenshiel. He supported the Old Chevalier in the rebellion of 1715, being granted the rather empty title of Lieutenant-General of the Northern Counties after the Battle of Sheriffmuir. With all his estates and titles forfeited, William might have had a hard job making ends meet during his years of exile, although how he managed to lay his hands on the rents from his tenants in Kintail is a story that can be told later. By October 1718 he was complaining that his allowance from James Stuart was five months overdue; but there were rumblings from the Jacobite court that he hadn't paid back some of their funds that he'd been given during the rebellion. Captain Stratton, James Stuart's agent in Edinburgh, wrote to the exiled court that he was 'truly amazed at Lord Seaforth's shameful conduct about money matters, and have inquired about his affairs here and, by all I can learn, his effects here cannot be reached either by his old or his new creditors'.

The Earl survived the troubles after the 1719 rebellion and all these financial bothers, to gain a personal pardon seven years later. However, it wasn't until well after the Forty-five that Kenneth Mackenzie of Kintail, who had taken no part in it, came back into full official favour. He regained the full title only in 1771.

The eighth Earl of Seaforth was Francis Humberston Mackenzie, in whose time the famous prophecy of the Brahan Seer came true—the Doom of the House of Seaforth. Exhaustive details of this affair and other prophecies of the Brahan Seer are available in many other sources, including a 1970 edition of Alexander Mackenzie's book on the subject. The basis of the Seaforth prophecy, which was well known in the Highlands and was mentioned in print years before it was fulfilled, was that, apart from all the other details, there would come a time when one of the Earls of Seaforth would find that four of his neighbouring lairds were suffering from noticeable disabilities: one would be buck-toothed, the second hare-lipped, the third half-witted and the fourth a stammerer. Seaforth would then know that all his sons would die before him, that the great line of the Seaforths would come to an end, and that the Seaforth lands would pass into strangers' hands.

At first, it didn't seem as if Francis Mackenzie had much to worry about. By his time, the Seaforth estates had spread to the

West Indies, and he was Governor of Barbados from 1800–06. During that time he provided a glimmer of humanity in the evilly exploited area by talking the assembly into passing a law 'whereby any one wilfully and maliciously killing a slave, whether the owner of such slave or not, was to suffer death on being convicted on the evidence of white witnesses, instead of being fined, as previously'.

Despite all his apparently successful local and colonial interests, and his political work far away from his ancestral home, the old prophecy was working against the last of the Seaforths. Financially, he was in deep water. To pay off his many substantial debts, caused by business losses and his early extravagances in London society, where he had been a gambling partner of the Prince Regent, he had to sell off parts of his estate, and the great dispersal of the Seaforths' lands began. He was a little hard of hearing, after an attack of scarlet fever during his schooldays; this and the 'corresponding taciturnity' which he adopted came to be noticed as an approximation of the old prophecy that the last of the Seaforths would be deaf and dumb. Then, people began to realize that there were four great Highland chiefs—Mackenzie of Gairloch, the Chisholm, Grant and Raasay—suffering from the disabilities predicted all those long years ago.

Within a few years two of Seaforth's three surviving sons took ill and died. The last, who was MP for Ross-shire, also went into poor health, and was packed off to the south coast of England by his now seriously worried family. Every day, messages were sent to the Earl about his son's progress; but the old prophecy was not to be denied, and the young man died in August 1814. His father survived him by only a few months, and the once-proud line of the Seaforths came to an end in January of the following year. Another Earl of Seaforth was granted the title some years later, although he wasn't of the direct line and didn't control any of the great estates. It was only a very brief renaissance, because he too died without leaving a family, and the title lapsed, apparently for ever.

Although there has undoubtedly been a great deal of invention about other prophecies attributed to the seventeenth-century Brahan Seer, and some recent authorities have argued that he was really two separate men mistaken for the same one, there is a great fascination about the Doom of the Seaforths; many other details fitted, apart from the handful mentioned here. Perhaps the attraction is that it is an old-style story that came true in more or less modern times, in the days of sober, well documented history; only a few months, in fact, before the Battle of Waterloo.

Getting back to the present day, it's a steep and sharp-cornered run down the far side of the old Carr Brae to Dornie, a road that still bears watching even if the traffic on it is now very light. Towards the foot of the hill is the old familiar view over Eilean Donan Castle, better than it used to be, because of the tree clearing that's been taking place on the intervening slopes. There is also a good outlook over Dornie and the bridge from it across the narrow mouth of Loch Long, which is seen here really for the first time. A few yards from the bridge the old and the low-level roads come together, before a bit of modern civil engineering which aroused so many local passions that it came to be known as the Berlin Wall.

CHAPTER 6

LOCH LONG AND GLEN ELCHAIG

DORNIE'S 'BERLIN WALL' is nothing remotely like the grim barrier of the original. When the new coast road was built, it had to come through Dornie on a line that would provide a fairly gentle curve onto the bridge across Loch Long. It follows the line of the old road between two rows of houses, but several feet higher. Despite the fears of the local people, what the new road has done is make Dornie a safer place for pedestrians, because the rather dangerous crossroads just before the bridge has been replaced, from their point of view, by a short tunnel under the new main road.

Like many of the settlements along the shores of Loch Long, Dornie is the result of the clearances which forced the old smallholders off their inland ground and into villages and hamlets beside the sea. It was laid out by Sir Hugh Innes in 1802. The main road cuts the village into two main parts; turning left leads down past a line of pleasant houses towards Eilean Donan Castle, and right, following a signpost to Bundalloch, along the front of Dornie Hotel and on for a short distance up the east side of Loch Long. Both parts of the village have a fine outlook over the meeting of the lochs, and of the stiff hillsides out towards the open sea.

The Bundalloch road (the accent is on the first syllable, which is long) is a very pleasant dead-end. At the hotel, they may remember the patronizing attitude of the *Round Britain Quiz* teams a few years ago, when a question sent in from the hotel stumped the experts completely, and they got their revenge by nattering on for a couple of minutes about how incredible it was that such a difficult question should have come from such an obviously remote and uneducated outpost. Beyond the hotel, the road goes between the loch and the single line of houses, many of them once fishermen's homes. As is often the case in West Highland coastal villages, many of the houses have their gardens on the far side of the road, closer to the water.

Going along this Bundalloch road doesn't give an idea of how attractive Loch Long really is, because the road is so close to the water and it is, in any case, the upper reaches of the loch that are the finest. At the edge of Dornie, near the Roman Catholic church—this part of the district has been a Roman Catholic stronghold for many generations—there are some of the typically neat modern council houses that fit in so well with the general appearance of these Ross-shire villages.

This is still crofting country, although there isn't as much as there used to be of the loch fishing by which the people had to support themselves in the proper season. Towards the end of the eighteenth century, when the old rights of the Highlanders to take a stag from the hill and a fish from the river were gradually eroded under the new social order, passions ran fairly high around Loch Long-side. The loch and its feeder rivers were famous for their salmon, and when the old tenants were forbidden to fish them once their lairds rented the lucrative salmon rights to the highest bidders, the newcomers' nets were more than once torn out of the water overnight. There were great tales about how much poaching was carried on, but the fishing survived and the Loch Long salmon rights are still rented out every year.

After a Z-bend, the narrow road goes into the crofting hamlet of Carndu, from which there's a good view across the loch to the mansion house of Conchra, sheltering on the facing hillside in a great spread of woodland. There are several caravans round about on individual sites.

In the 1880s the crofting tenants of Carndu and the next township of Bundalloch were simply desperate for more land or work on the great local estate. They complained that work on the estate, which they could have done as well as anybody, and which would have given them some kind of wage, was always given to outsiders. They had only tiny strips of land alongside their cottages, and could raise very little in the way of crops or stock. In bad times, which came round very regularly, they went behind in their rent. Those who had nothing that they could sell to make up the deficiency were often evicted; others had their sheep valued at trifling prices and confiscated by the factor in place of the rent. It was a common complaint that some of the so-called arrears of rent had been going for two hundred years, passed on from proprietor to proprietor without being called in until the factor wanted to make trouble. In fact, more than £2,000 in rent arrears had been cancelled by one of the proprietors during the potato famine of the 1840s, but forty years later the factor pretended not to remember.

After another little gap, the road reaches the final settlement of Bundalloch, a very pleasant crofting village with a fair number of houses set in a double curve ending up in a little bay at the foot of the River Glennan, which comes down through a sweeping valley on the hill ground of the Inverinate estate.

In many ways Bundalloch is a real old-world Highland crofting township, white cottages looking out over the loch, ruins of older houses dotted occasionally here and there, sometimes with the old low outside walls containing vegetable patches for the houses nearby. There is arable land on the gently sloping ground behind the village, before the steeper hillsides take over, and a fair amount of grazing for cattle and sheep. The road ends at a little bridge over the River Glennan, which leads to two or three cottages at the very edge of the village on the other side. There are steep grassy hillsides all around, a rocky shore fringed with damp bright seaweed, which has often been sold to make alginates that go into jams, ice cream, fruit jellies and so on, and a view of Loch Long curving to the left as it seems to come to a dead-end in the hills; but the loch has a long way to go yet, and what appears to be the narrow final notch is really only the restricted approach to its very pleasant upper reaches, which can be approached by road only along the other shore.

During the government enquiry in 1883, the representative of the Bundalloch crofters had many direct remarks to make about the landlord and his factors. At that time there were three hundred people living on the east side of Loch Long in Dornie, Carndu and Bundalloch, and most of them were in very sore straits. The factor, a man called Finlayson, had the name of taking over crofts all over the district to add to his own farm. The Bundalloch representative said that once he had lost all his potato crop after a severe frost; that was most of his family's basic food ration for the next year completely destroyed. 'I went to the authorities for assistance and wanted work on the road, which is in a disgraceful state between Bundalloch and Dornie, but I was refused. The reply I got from the factor was that, although myself and all I had should die of starvation I would get no work. This is our grievance. What we want is a little land to help us live. After that we met with the factor at the schoolhouse, Dornie, but all he did was to make fun of us, telling us to take crops out of the rocks, and to imitate the earthworms who were splendid drainers. . . . A vessel was sent to the country loaded with potatoes by the proprietor, but the factor went amongst the better class of people to give them a supply, and kept from the poorer classes all knowledge of it; and had it not been for the parish minister, who through charity and kindness got a supply for us, we should have been in a very bad state indeed.' At a later hearing, the factor hotly denied using the form of words ascribed to him.

Getting across to the far side of the loch means returning to Dornie and driving over the narrow bridge into Ardelve; the west side of the loch is in the district of Lochalsh. Until 1940 there was a ferry here, which meant that Lochalsh was the only mainland parish in Britain to which there was no uninterrupted road access at all, since the way in from the north was over another ferry at Strome. Local people, however, were dismayed to find that after all the years of waiting for a bridge, the government put a toll on it when it was finally opened. The charge was removed in 1946. The centre span was made to open, to accommodate not only the coasting puffers that used to unload cargoes in the lower part of Loch Long, but also the yacht belonging to another branch of the Wills family who owned an estate at the head of the loch.

Although the village across the bridge is Ardelve, the Dornie village hall is on that side too, just to the left beside a car park. From the nearby pier the little passenger ferry runs occasionally to Totaig on the Letterfearn shore. When the crossing of Loch Long from Dornie was also by ferry, Ardelve was a fairly important place. Its original pier, like the one at Dornie, was built at the time of Telford's great engineering works in the district. Ardelve market was held twice a year, when cattle from all parts of Kintail, Lochalsh and the other parishes round about, were auctioned to buyers who came from the Lowlands. After 1870, when the railway came within reach at Strome, the cattle were driven over the hills to the railhead. The market continued until a few years before the second world war, when it became easier to take the cattle in vans to the bigger markets in the east and south.

Beyond Ardelve the main road improvements continue; even the existing bridge has only fifteen or so years to go, because the plan is to replace it with a wider one from the point beside Eilean Donan Castle to the car park at Dornie hall. Ardelve itself is too scattered and haphazard a place to be very attractive; its air of having been casually dumped in position is understandable, because when the last Earl of Seaforth sold Lochalsh to Sir Hugh Innes in 1801, Innes's first move was to evict crofters from much of the best grazing land, and many of the ones who didn't emigrate had to build themselves houses here on the poor coastal ground that was all they were allowed. That Ardelve had previously been an important part of the Seaforth territory is shown from the story of Kenneth Mackenzie of Kintail, the one who kept out of trouble during the Forty-five. The first step in his rehabilitation towards the earldom was his creation as Baron Ardelve, and it was a few years after that that he regained the title Earl of Seaforth.

Most of Ardelve is a collection of old cottages round the head of a double bay on the north shore of Loch Alsh. Some way offshore, not far from Ardelve Point, which is the landing stage for the Totaig ferry, is the weirdly shaped Eilean Tioram or Dry Island. Shaped like a thin letter C, almost in the form of a coral atoll, it is said to have been often dug into for ballast in the days of the sailing ships. It was an old tradition to have cattle swum across to graze on the island.

Turning right off the main road there's a short dead-end towards Camuslongart. This was one of the places where crofters evicted by Sir Hugh Innes, who turned most of the hill and valley land between here and Strome into rented sheep farms, built themselves houses when they had to turn to the sea-lochs for a living. Nowadays it's a line of very bright modernized cottages looking happily out over Loch Long to Dornie, Carndu and the mountains of Kintail.

The long road up the west side of the loch towards Killilan begins a little way beyond the Camuslongart entrance. Just after the start of the road is the original Free Church of Lochalsh, with its well situated manse at the end of a long driveway at the foot of the hillside behind. Financed by Isaac Lillingston, Sir Hugh

Innes's successor as laird of Lochalsh, it was described not long after its building in the 1840s as 'an immense fabric', which was true only by the Highland church standards of those days. The laird's design ideas, oddly enough, led to the church having the reputation of being the most malodorous place of worship in Wester Ross. A contemporary writer explained:

'Built at a spot where violent tornadoes occasionally come sweeping down from the neighbouring mountains, he conceived that to give it a roof elevated in the least would be to expose it to risk. So the roof was entirely flat, except that the smallest possible incline to one side was provided for, that the rain should run off, and not lodge anywhere on the vast flat. It was covered with felt, which was periodically pitched with boiled tar. In summer the rays of the sun produced their proper effect, which was by no means pleasant to many of the worshippers. The great bulk being fishermen, and accustomed to such flavour as abounded there, were not disturbed by it.' Although it has been altered a little since those early days, the rather gloomy church building is soon to be replaced.

Going on alongside a well trimmed beech hedge, which is rather unusual in this part of the country, the Killilan road soon passes below the wooded grounds of the mansion house of Conchra. Earlier this century, Conchra was the first foothold in his ancestral lands bought by John MacRae-Gilstrap, before he acquired and set about rebuilding Eilean Donan. Now it and the Ardelve estate are owned by his daughter, Miss Dorothy MacRae; but it's another part of the family which deals with the castle.

From Conchra, where the public road runs very close to the lochside along the shore of a seaweed-trimmed bay, there are pleasant reflections in the narrow waterway and a splendid view over to the crofting lands of Bundalloch, behind which the steep valley of the River Glennan shows up very well. Road and loch bend left here for a while, and it seems that neither is likely to be able to force a way through the narrow defile beyond. Up over the brow of a hill, and suddenly the view is to the narrowest, rocky-sided part of this long thin loch as it goes into an S-bend to reach the wider, gentler upper reaches.

There's a bank of trees on the steep slopes above the road, and then a handful of cottages at Allt-na-Subh, the Burn of the Raspberries, all that's left of an old village that isn't even named any longer on the one-inch map. In the last century, after the sheep clearances that moved them from better land at Sallachy a little way farther up the loch, Allt-na-Subh was the home of several families who made a rather precarious living fishing the loch and trying to farm the inhospitably steep and rocky hillside above. The hills were so steep that the arable land had to be worked in terraces.

Road and loch swing right into the broader valley ahead, past the pleasant and scattered village of Sallachy, where the willows which gave it its name are no longer very apparent. Because of the stiffly guarded route along the narrows of Loch Long, this most attractive place has the air of being some kind of secret valley among the mountains. Many of the old houses are just ruins on the hillside, but there are several modern ones here and there, with plenty of elbow-room among them all. There's some crofting done, with a share of the common hill grazing, but there are many older people living here nowadays. After being in the hands of the Earls of Seaforth, Sir Hugh Innes and Isaac Lilling-ston, this side of the loch beyond Conchra became part of the Attadale estate, which stretches away over the hills to the north, and is based on the house of the same name over on Loch Carron. Years after having their hill grazings taken over by Sir Hugh Innes, the Sallachy crofters were given some of them back in the 1880s by the Mathesons of Attadale.

From Sallachy, as the road passes some newly planted private forest land, the view ahead is to the twin rounded mountains of Ben Killilan and Sguman Coinntich in the deer forest of Killilan, with a long deep valley separating the two. On the slopes of Sguman Coinntich, to the right, there's a little patch of woodland. The head of the loch beyond Sallachy leaves great tidal flats when the water is low, and there's a rough rocky hillside on the far shore. As the road continues, the outlook is dominated by Ben Killilan, which, under snow, must be one of the most impressive hills in the district, and the great cliff of Creag a'Chaisil right at the head of the loch, where it is fed by the River Elchaig and the River Ling; years ago the loch itself was called Loch Ling, and the modern name, though appropriate, seems to have been just a misreading. The cliff looks quite substantial, with a knobbly ridge rising from its right, but is really towered over by the bulk of Sguman Coinntich beyond.

Soon there's a view up the valley of the Ling, with the steep slopes of Creag Mhor standing rather dramatically behind the main mass of Ben Killilan. Looking back down the loch, there's a much better view of the rocky buttresses on the far side from Creag a'Chaisil to the narrows, which seem much grander than they did on the way up. The grassy tidal ground through which the Ling and the Elchaig feed the loch has several channels winding through it, and it's from here that the mountains round the head of the loch are seen at their very best. Almost at the head of the loch, the most recent one-inch map still shows a public house at a place called Ceann-an-Oba, which is a cottage at the roadside just after a very sharp left-hand bend. In fact, although this house on the old drovers' road into the mountains had a licence for many years to sell beer, porter and ale, the licence was withdrawn during the 1960s, when the old building just couldn't keep up to modern requirements. While it lasted, Lochlonghead Inn was a very popular pub; but the old cottage and new bungalow alongside nowadays have nothing to offer the drouthy traveller.

Ben Killilan looms larger and larger in the view as the road reaches the head of the loch and soon passes a rough private road off to the left towards Nonach Lodge, headquarters of this part of the Attadale estate. That track goes off to follow the valley of the Ling, which runs to the north and east of Ben Killilan; the other main feeder of Loch Long, the River Elchaig, comes down from the south-east, below the slopes of Sguman Coinntich. Now there can be seen, at the foot of the tumbling valley that separates the two mountains, a plantation that temporarily hides the little settlement of Killilan, centre of the estate of the same name which occupies the high ground between the two rivers. The valley of the Ling is rather obscured from view, but the course of the Elchaig is seen as a steeply flanked ravine guarded by interlocking ridges and independent summits on both sides.

Going over a flatter piece of land and aiming straight at the entrance to Glen Elchaig, the public road crosses a wooden bridge over the Ling and then a cattle grid beside a little primary school. The grid is for the Killilan estate cattle which graze inside a deer fence on good arable land in the angle between the two rivers; the school is for the younger children of the district around the head of the loch, and is noted for its handsome record in Gaelic and other local competitions. At the bridge, Lochalsh is left behind and the road comes back into the parish of Kintail.

Just before the gate at the start of the private road to Killilan, the public road turns right over the level riverside ground, to make a sharp bend to the left before the Elchaig, and then go right over a bridge to the steeper far bank of the river on the way to the faraway little hamlet of Camusluinie. That last syllable is pronounced 'liney'. Camusluinie was much harder of access before the bridge was built about ten years ago, because the only way of crossing the river was then by a rather rough but shallow ford. Once over the bridge, the road hugs the west side of Glen Elchaig, often on an embankment at the edge of the rather damp grazing ground across which the river meanders from side to side. The hamlet and mansion of Killilan are seen clearly for the first time, in their grand situation among the woodlands at the foot of the steep valley between the two rounded hills. There are wilder hillsides farther up the glen, with some scrubby patches of trees, and over on the far side, upriver from Killilan, one or two deep-scarred gullies leading mountain burns helter-skelter down to the glen.

Camusluinie itself is a small collection of cottages in a pretty dramatic situation, below a great hillside to the west and south which keeps much of the sunlight away from the place in winter. It's a rough stretch of hill, with gullies, crags and rock faces, and a fine narrow waterfall; it can be especially forbidding under snow, and the usual foreshortening effect tends to make it look rather more vertical than it actually is.

The nineteenth-century history of the place is much the same as usual; when the Camusluinie tenants had their summer grazings taken away from them they simply couldn't make enough money to pay their rents, even the slightly reduced ones that their landlord allowed. In the 1870s he offered timber, lime and slates to the value of £80, and £20 in cash, to any of the crofters who would build a new house; but for some reason only two of them took advantage of the offer. Asked why the estate wouldn't build a bridge over the Elchaig for the benefit of the Camusluinie people, the factor said that it would cost far too much, because the river was at least seven hundred yards wide— an exaggeration of something like seven thousand per cent.

The houses in this old-fashioned wee place are on a rise of

ground looking up the wild Elchaig valley. There are one or two thatched roofs, and a rather Austrian Alpine atmosphere of pleasant isolation and self-sufficiency. Crofting is carried on in a fairly big way here, and there are plenty of cattle down on the rather boggy alluvial ground on the valley floor. About ten years ago, BBC Television made a documentary about life in Camusluinie, and it wasn't a bad choice to give the programme the title of *The Back of the Sun.*

Back on the main line of the Glen Elchaig road, immediately after the Camusluinie junction there's a well surfaced tree-lined avenue leading pleasantly up to Killilan. At the foot of the burn that comes down into the little settlement is a bridge with a 'No Motor Vehicles Allowed' sign beside it; but a glance at a smaller notice underneath reveals that Killilan estate will allow strangers' cars to use most of the private road up Glen Elchaig in return for a signature in the visitors' book normally kept beside the gate into the courtyard of the big house.

Killilan is a very neat and well tended private estate village. Among the trees are various estate workers' houses, and the whole place is pretty well self-contained, having its own water and electricity supplies, the latter provided by a small hydro electric generator in times when the mountain burn is full, and at others by a diesel plant. There is also a small post office.

Killilan takes its name from an old chapel that was established here more than a thousand years ago, and dedicated to St Fillan. There's a traditional tale that St Fillan himself established a cell here, and that when he died far away from this place, his coffin was solemnly rowed up the loch to its final resting place in this valley he knew so well; but nobody seems to know if this was the Fillan who is well known for his missionary work farther south, or some even more shadowy figure about whom practically nothing is known at all.

To the left of the road almost opposite the big house is an old walled graveyard, unused these many years. In it are headstones to Macraes and MacRaes, Camerons and McKerlichs, from farms and settlements all the way up Loch Long-side from Allt-na-Subh, and from lonely places in the glens of which even the names are now forgotten.

Killilan had several owners after the Seaforth days, coming at the turn of this century into the hands of yet another branch of the Wills family. For many years its thirty-odd thousand acres of deer forest were stalked very thoroughly, having been given over almost entirely to deer in 1901. In the change, none of the estate workers lost their jobs. There was a deer sanctuary of around three thousand acres at a place called Coire-Domhain, still marked on the map beyond Creag Mhor on the south bank of the River Ling, which is the march between the Killilan and Attadale estates. The deer were of very high quality, since the hillsides and corries were covered more in grass than in heather, and the grazing was excellent; Killilan stags were able to find plenty of feeding on their home ground right through the year, which could not be said of many other stalking grounds round about. The big house used to be noted for a series of deer forest frescoes painted on its inside walls, but these were later papered over.

Since the second world war, there has been less interest in stalking on this estate, and more in sheep and cattle farming; a famous herd of Highland cattle was built up. Nowadays it isn't really a sporting estate at all. Mrs Douglas, the present owner, is a daughter of the last Wills proprietor.

The private road, on which visitors' cars are allowed to drive as far as the car park beside the track to the Falls of Glomach, continues away up Glen Elchaig, following the North bank of the river. Beyond the old kennels house it becomes untarred, often with unavoidable potholes in the narrow wheeltracks, but generally in quite fair condition. To begin with, it runs between great banks of rhododendrons, with fir trees behind to the left, and an old stone dyke protecting it from the ill-drained rough ground down towards the river. For most of this first stretch, the view ahead is filled by the steep craggy ridge on the far side of the glen above Camusluinie. It's important to remember that this is a farm and estate road, and that there may well be sheep or estate vehicles hidden over a brow or round a corner. There's a good view of Camusluinie as the road gets down to the water at the side of one of the Elchaig's meanders, through scatterings of alder trees close to the river's edge.

There are one or two neat estate houses along this way; but there was, of course, a time when Glen Elchaig supported many times the handful of people who live in it today. Even before the last Earl of Seaforth had to sell off his ancestral lands of Kintail, there were some particularly odious clearances here. The Earl's

factor, one Duncan Mor Macrae, evicted dozens of tenants who
had held lands in the glen for generations, not on the Earl's
behalf, but simply to add the rich Glen Elchaig grazings onto the
already over-large sheep farms run by himself and his father. Not
long afterwards, he performed the same service for fifty families
on the lands of Letterfearn. Most of the evicted tenants had to
emigrate to Canada, and local historians have rarely been able to
hide their satisfaction that Macrae's fortunes finally turned sour,
and that he died in poverty and ruin.

The district around Loch Long was a Roman Catholic stronghold during its most populous days, and this influence has
remained into modern times down at Dornie. The Protestant
persuasion, in fact, was a long time being established in Wester
Ross, and the early ministers of the kirk used to go to great
lengths to vilify the priests and adherents of the older way. In
1793, in the first Statistical Account of Kintail, the Rev. Roderick
Morison let fly in a footnote concerning Glen Elchaig about 'the
reasons for the growth of Popery':

'1st, The Presbytery of Lochcarron in 1778 entered into a
resolution, and passed an act obliging every member thereof to
keep regular registers of baptism. And that, instead of the usual
due, one shilling should in future be exacted, to enable the
schoolmasters to keep up and preserve the registers. — Many of
the most ignorant in Glenelchaig hearing of the new act, considered it as a heavy grievance; and, to avoid its consequence,
applied to Roman Catholic priests for baptism, and in the heat of
passion dragged whole families after them. . . . It is to be regretted
that the people are subject to low and melancholy fits, which (as is
conjectured) arises from too much hazy and damp weather; on
these occasions a priest, with whom the art of exorcism is supposed to be found, attends for relief to the distressed. If it happens
that a kind providence thereafter removes the malady, the glory
of the cure redounds to human frailty, and the pretended miracle
becomes the ground and ostensible reason of conversion.

'Lastly, the people in the district of Glenelchaig . . . are extremely ignorant, and easily become the dupes of trafficking
priests. — In the last century, there were no established schools
in the place; as yet few, if any at all, of the tenants in this glen,
read or understand the holy scriptures. There are however
grounds to believe, that the Society for Propagating Christian

Knowledge will soon appoint a school, whereby the blessings of
knowledge may be more liberally diffused through this valley,
which is in the near neighbourhood of a Popish district.'

All this rhetoric has to be approached with some caution, since
it's a fact that Presbyterianism was more or less forced on many
of the districts in Wester Ross; the first ministers from the Church
of Scotland were so unpopular that there was one famous
occasion when the ministers of the extensive presbytery of
Lochcarron were 'rabbled' on their home ground, and had to
meet in more peaceful territory over the Inverness-shire border.
The Society for Propagating Christian Knowledge, although it
established many much-needed schools and solved many social
problems, was sometimes inclined to act in a very sectarian way.
According to Calum Maclean's book *The Highlands*, it was responsible for the nasty technique in some areas during the potato
famine of the 1840s, of doling out relief supplies to half-starved
Roman Catholics only if they would renounce the Pope.

Level with Camusluinie on the far side, the glen bends round to
the left and narrows substantially. There are sheep pens here and
there, steeper hillsides and a great deal of bare rock on the slopes
on the far side of the river. A track leads across the river to the
farmhouse of Coille-Righ, which is actually on Inverinate ground,
since the boundary between the two estates follows the river
exactly. In Sir Keith Fraser's day, when the Elchaig fishing used
to be rented out, anglers would put up overnight at Coille-Righ.

Although the road is entirely on Killilan ground, it is also used
by Inverinate estate to reach the higher deer stalking grounds of
Benula, at the west end of Loch Mullardoch. It's a good example
of the rather bewildering qualities of Gaelic spelling that Benula
is the approximate pronunciation of the mountain whose name is
usually written Beinn Fhionnlaidh; however, southern types
would be well advised to swot up on the basic rules of Gaelic
speech before complaining, since Gaels are quick to point out
that they have more logical rules than the English.

Coille-Righ means the King's Wood, and there used to be a
large forest in the area, the most obvious relic of it being a patch
of woodland on the south side of the glen between Coille-Righ
and Camusluinie. When the forest was cut, the timber was
floated down to Bundalloch.

Beyond the track over the river to Coille-Righ the road goes through a gate in a deer fence, which must not, of course, be left open; the local sheep often congregate near the gate, and are strangely adept at slipping through when a car driver walks back to close it. From here the track takes on more and more of the atmosphere of a road to nowhere. Uphill from the gate, a round tower summit that's been in view for some time across the glen is matched by a sharper top on the north side; this is the high-angled escarpment of Carn Tarsuinn, linked to the hill nearer Killilan by a saddle down which a burn tumbles from the little hidden tarn of Loch nan Ealachan, the Loch of the Swans.

As the road gets higher above the river, splashing through a tree-lined curve over its rock-spattered bed, the way ahead once again seems to be blocked by a great circle of ridges; but valley and road continue winding relentlessly through the bare and open landscape, heather and grass with boulders scattered over the hillsides, especially on the lower slopes of Carn Tarsuinn, whose middle reaches are made up of a series of miniature rock faces. Then, instead of getting wilder, the valley suddenly softens a little, with a patch of grazing ground down by the river's edge. The lower slopes of Carn Tarsuinn become even more smothered in boulders and great blocks of rock piled carelessly on top of one another. This is splendid cover for the red deer, which can often be seen right down at the roadside.

Now the road begins to climb more steeply above the river, roughening up in places as it makes great sweeps across the hillside. Although it may seem like the road to nowhere, there's an old milestone near the top of the climb to serve as a useful reminder that this used to be one of the main routes through the tangled glens, to the lochs and summer grazing grounds in the high wild borderland of Inverness and Ross, and on through the eastern valleys to the softer lands of the Moray Firth.

The steeper parts of Glen Elchaig used to be noted for the fierce rockfalls and landslides that made living here occasionally precarious. A late eighteenth-century account devoted some space to the problem: 'The farms which are bases to high mountains, as in Kintail, suffer great losses from what is called *Scriddan*, or "mountain torrent". After heavy rains, the summit of the hills are so impregnated, that the mountains may be said to be in labour, till an aperture is made by chance somewhere on their sides; the explosion which then succeeds is loud and alarming.

Gravel and massy stones roll together, and desolate the fields beneath. The farm of Auchuirn, in Glenelchaig, once a populous town, was, in 1745, rendered uninhabitable, and is since converted to a grazing, by an awful *Scriddan*. The traces of these eruptions have, to the eye of a traveller, all the appearance of a military road, in the face of the steep ascent of the mountain.'

There's a natural birchwood above the edge of the road, in a wider stretch just after the point where the Glomach Burn comes diagonally down from a steep ravine on the other side. Deer can often be seen on the rough, heathery, rocky slopes around the valley floor. This is as far as visitors can take their cars along the private road, and there's a little parking place for those who want to climb up the exposed flanks of the Glomach Burn to the famous Falls of Glomach; as the notice down at Killilan points out, anybody who wants to make the climb should be in good physical condition, well shod and accustomed to this kind of expedition.

The falls are invisible from the road, high up the curving gully. About the time the National Trust for Scotland took over the Kintail estate, which lies due south from here over an intervening ridge, the proprietors of Killilan and Inverinate presented it with a tongue of land that took in the Falls of Glomach and the whole extent of the gully down to the point where it joins the Elchaig. This is the shortest climb to the falls, which can otherwise be reached only by walking over a pass from Morvich in Strath Croe. These are not the highest falls in Scotland, that honour going to the Eas-Coul-Aulin near Kylesku Ferry in Sutherland, which are higher than any falls in Norway; but for steepness and difficulty of access, Glomach is enough for most people.

Getting to the far side of the Elchaig was made much easier in 1960 when the Scottish Rights of Way Society built a footbridge in memory of the Rev. A. E. Robertson, a former president of the society and of the Scottish Mountaineering Club. Robertson was one of the pioneers of Scottish climbing, and the first man ever to climb all the two hundred and seventy-seven peaks in Scotland over three thousand feet, usually known as Munros after the man who first catalogued them; this was the same Sir Hugh Munro who fell foul of Louis Winans's guards in a mountain pass only a little way south of here. Robertson wrote many fine accounts of his pioneering travels, which included one journey of exploration into Knoydart when he was ferried across by a boatman from Arnisdale; looking carefully at his passenger's ice-axe, and remembering his own round-the-world travels as a merchant seaman, the Arnisdale man could not be convinced that it wasn't a tomahawk.

Many climbers have now managed to stand on the summits of all the Munros, and there are even one or two intrepid souls who have completed the whole circuit twice over.   Recently, an English mountaineer invented a whole new category of 'Corbetts', which are summits more than two and a half thousand feet above the sea; it's more than likely that these classifications will survive even in these decimal days.

This is as far as the motorist can go, but Glen Elchaig is not by any means finished yet. Not far beyond the parking place, there's a point where the river widens into a little loch. At the head of it is a house called Carnoch, which used to be the shooting box for Glomach when that part of Kintail was a separate deer forest on its own. Fifty years ago, it was noted as the haunt of eagles, falcons, buzzards and wild cats. Louis Winans got his hands on the Glomach deer forest in a rather indirect way; it and three others in the deserted mountains round about were owned by the substantial landowner Sir Kenneth Matheson but rented out to Lord Lovat, who sub-let them to the American.

Beyond Carnoch is another slightly more open part of the glen, reputed to be the scene of one of those unlikely supernatural folk tales with which the Highlands abound. As was often the case, almost identical yarns were told about several different districts; only the names were altered. The Glen Elchaig version concerned one Donald Macrae, who rented grazing ground here and over at Ardintoul. One morning he was out early herding cattle when he saw a crowd of the 'fairy people' flying through the air. They were carrying a kind of basket which they threw around with gales of wicked laughter, all of which was highly uncomfortable for the woman who was inside it. Macrae shouted at them to leave her alone, at which the whole cackling crew disappeared in a cloud of yellow smoke, leaving the woman bewildered but safe on the braes of Glen Elchaig.

Macrae took her home and looked after her, but in two years she never managed to remember who she was or where she came from. After that time, he went through the hills to the great St Mary Fair in Inverness, carrying her scarlet plaid with him.

Somebody at the fair recognized the plaid as his wife's, and after what must have been initially a rather tense conversation, Macrae explained the situation, and the newcomer went back to Glen Elchaig to claim his long-lost wife. Every year after that she sent a new suit of clothes to Donald Macrae, in thanks for the kindly way he had looked after her.

The private estate road comes to an end a little way farther on, at a place called Iron Lodge, which got its name from its corrugated iron construction, although there is some talk of an old chalybeate well nearby. Old stalkers' tracks continue in three directions: to the Benula deer ground at Loch Mullardoch, to the very isolated Patt Lodge at the west end of Loch Monar—both these lochs having been greatly extended as a result of hydro electric workings—and to the now derelict house of Maolbhuidhe or Millbuie, beside a little loch at the headwaters of the River Ling which marks the boundary between Killilan and Attadale. It isn't very long since Millbuie was occupied; in those days it was the farthest-out house in the Kyle of Lochalsh doctor's practice, and Dr MacRae used to have to make a long and difficult journey by motor-cycle through the wilds of the deer forest to reach his patients there. In the great days of the deer forests, the keeper used to spend six months at Millbuie and six months at Patt. Many of the deer forests in that remote mountain country used to be part of the empire of the unspeakable Winans.

During that time in the 1890s, a young boy called Alexander Renwick, descendant of a famous Covenanter, used to walk through the hills from his home at Millbuie to the little school down at Killilan—a distance, depending on the route he took, of at least nine or ten miles. Years later, in 1931, he was appointed Moderator of the General Assembly of the Free Church of Scotland; but by then he had to come home from Peru to take up the position.

After a spell as a civil servant in Manchester, he had graduated from Edinburgh University and become a minister of the Free Church. It was in 1926, after war service in France and charges in Aberdeen and Dumbarton, that he went to South America as principal of the Anglo-Peruvian College in Lima. For much of the second world war he was head of the British Chilean Institute, and then in 1944 he came back to Scotland to occupy the Chair of History at the Free Church College. He was

Moderator again in 1960. Dr Renwick was known mostly for his writings on church history, but the list of his publications includes such varied titles as *The Story of the Church* and *Wanderings in the Peruvian Andes*. He died in 1965 at Lochgilphead in Argyll.

Until a hundred and fifty years ago, the rich grazings round about Loch Monar used to be where many of the crofters of Lochalsh took their cattle for the summer. When the idea arose of renting the old clan territories as sheep farms and deer forests, the Monar grazings were among the first to be barred to tenants whose families had had the grazing rights there for generations. Much earlier than that, Monar was one of the favourite hunting grounds of the Earls of Seaforth; in the seventeenth century, the Earl would annually visit 'his deer forest of Monar, where they had a great and most solemn hunting day'.

The Wardlaw MS gives an account of one of these hunts that took place in 1655, when the Earl was joined by the Master of Lovat, whose father had extensive lands on the eastern side of the mountains: 'We got sight of six or seven hundred deer, and sport of hunting fitter for kings than country gentlemen. The four days we tarried here, what is it that could cheer and renovate men's spirits but was gone about? Jumping, archery, shooting, throwing the bar, the stone, and all manner of manly exercises imaginable. And for entertainment, our baggage was well furnished of beef, mutton, fowls, fishes, fat venison—a very princely camp—and all manner of liquors. . . . Masters Hill and Man, two Englishmen who were in company, declared that in all their travels they never had such brave divertisement; and if they should relate it in England, it would be concluded were rant and incredible!'

Just as incredible, perhaps, is that one Captain Whyte, a former owner of the Monar deer forest, once tried to open an iron mine by the banks of one of the burns that feed the loch; but the samples showed the ore to be of poor quality, and the thing was taken no farther. Nowadays, of course, there are no traces of industry, very little in the way of 'princely camps', and very few people willing to tramp over the lonely tracks from Glen Elchaig; but it's as well to remember that these lonely mountains haven't always been strangers to human bustle and activity.

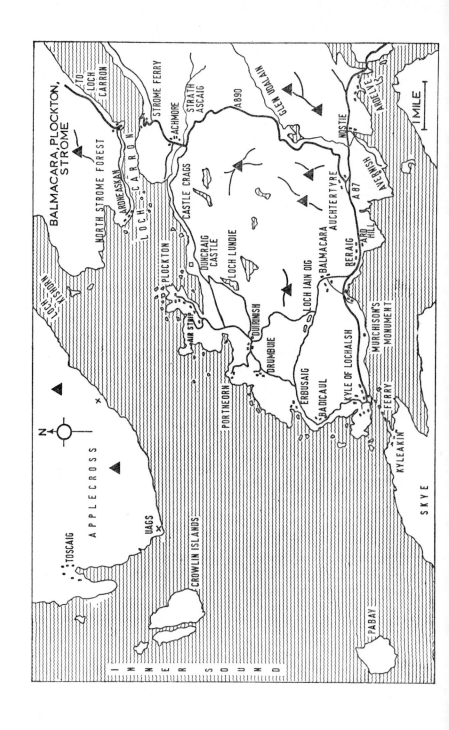

BALMACARA, PLOCKTON, STROME

CHAPTER 7

BALMACARA AND KYLE

THE MAIN ROAD FROM Ardelve to Kyle of Lochalsh has been in the throes of a massive rebuilding for several years past, and the work of bringing it up to modern standards is almost finished. There isn't much of a view from the first part of it beyond Ardelve, since it occupies the narrow stretch of flat ground between the rumpled, knobbly slopes west of Conchra and the separated hill of Fireach Ard that runs on the seaward side from Ardelve to Nostie Bay.

There's a turning to the left of the main road towards the little hamlet of Nostie, which is an old-fashioned collection of half a dozen cottages beside a post office. In days gone by there was a well-supported inn at Nostie, because it was here that the cattle being driven from Ardelve market turned uphill over a pass towards Strome; and with all of two miles covered, the drovers found that a wee dram was long overdue.

In the days of the Lochalsh clearances, at the beginning of the last century, several of the evicted families from townships inland had to settle in a most unprepossessing place near Nostie called Ceann-na-Moine, the Head of the Peat Moss; even the peat had been worked out, and the crofters had to buy fuel from Ardelve. The Ceann-na-Moine grazing land was regularly invaded by Conchra sheep, but the crofters' constant appeals for a fence round it were answered, so they told the Royal Commission when it met at Balmacara, only a few days before the enquiry began.

Duncan Sinclair, a local schoolmaster, said that Ceann-na-Moine 'used to be not very long ago a peat moss and quagmire; but at the commencement of the sheep farming mania, when the people were regarded as a nuisance to be got rid of by driving them out of the country like noxious vermin, or by crowding them into barren promontories or boggy hollows which were useless for sheep, this township was formed by locating families there who had been deprived of good land in other parts.' He was making a statement on behalf of the Ceann-na-Moine tenants, who had composed the original draft in Gaelic; when one of the commissioners quizzed him about the phrase 'noxious vermin', he admitted that his translation of the original had been perhaps a little too severe, and that the words intended were more like 'wild animals'. Throughout the five-volume report of the Royal Commission there is evidence that the crofters' representatives, although undeniably men with genuine grievances, were often inclined to overstate their case.

A recently built bridge that replaced an old ford leads the public road across the river at Nostie, and then through crofting land above the west side of the rocky Nostie Bay into the little district of Avernish. There's a good view out over Loch Alsh to the grazing land on the oddly-shaped Glas Eilean, the island where the Macdonald of Sleat who besieged Eilean Donan Castle was taken after being hit by a defender's arrow. There are some crofting cottages and one modern timber bungalow—which looks slightly odd, since it's really two built into one—on the water side of the little road, as it twists and turns across the side of the hill, often blocked by a minor congregation of cattle or sheep, before running down the other side to the end of the public way beside Avernish House.

Until fairly recently, the house had a thatched roof, although it is now more conventionally slated. It stands in a splendid position looking out over a rocky bay to the Ardintoul shore, with the entrance to the narrow strait of Kyle Rhea to the south-west, disguised by a wooded headland west of Ardintoul and the great north-eastern hills of Skye that fill the background. The houses at Ardintoul, and the farming land among the shelter belts of trees, are seen just to the right of Glas Eilean, with the steep and wooded hillside making a pleasant backdrop. Until the mid-1960s this outlook was outraged by the sight of some never-used wartime oil tanks at Ardintoul, but they have now been cleared away. In places it's just possible to make out the line of the footpath that is the only land approach to Ardintoul from Totaig, going high above the sea at the top of the steep-sloping birch woods. Directly over Ardintoul is the sharp-pointed summit of the hill above Glen Bernera where the Mathesons had their midnight fight with the MacCrimmons. Back to the east is an unfamiliar sight of Eilean Donan at the mountainous entrance to Loch Duich.

Duncan Sinclair reported to the Royal Commission that Avernish 'used to contain a large, prosperous, happy and contented population, but thirty-four years ago the bulk of the people were expatriated, as usual through the agency of the factor who wished to form a sheep farm for his son. Those who were allowed by the proprietor to remain after the factor had expressed his determination to have them evicted in these words, "Go you must, even though you should go to the bottom of the sea", were allowed a mere fringe of the township bordering on the rocky seashore.' This was during the ownership of Isaac Lillingston, who financed the building of the Free Church at Ardelve; it's only fair to say that it happened while Lillingston was in the early stages of a final mental breakdown, and was quite uncharacteristic of the man. It also appears that many of the Avernish tenants refused to comply with the sensible rules laid down for working the land. John McLennan the factor was reported rather grimly to have died at ninety-eight, 'quite a poor man after having been a great man'.

Back on the main road, there's a patch of rather boggy ground off to the left, with a small and surprisingly modern church standing towards the back of it. It was built in the early 1960s for the small Episcopal congregation hereabouts, and is reached by a kind of causeway across the poorly drained ground.

Not long after this, there's a bridge across the little river that flows down from the hills into Nostie Bay. Off to the left is a square building of local stone that looks from a distance to be a rather unobtrusive dwelling house, but is actually a North of Scotland Hydro Electric Board power station. It was built just after the second world war, when Nostie and the hills above it were chosen as a kind of small-scale pilot scheme for the great hydro workings that were soon to be put under way in many of the mountain valleys of the West Highlands; work on the scheme started in 1947. The power station is fed by a pipeline that comes sharply down the hillside from the reservoir in Glen Udalain; but it doesn't make much of an impression in this large-scale country. Local people were rather disgruntled when the scheme went into operation, because the charges turned out to be half as much again as they had been promised when they started converting their houses to electricity.

Glen Udalain is on the pass through the hills to Strome, but the lower reaches of the pass on this southern side are far too steep for any road, and the one from Strome comes down to join the Kyle road at the village of Auchtertyre a little way farther on. Once exactly on the meeting point of the two main roads, Auchtertyre has now been bypassed by a loop of the new road to Kyle. A hundred years ago the school here was the primary school for the whole of the wide district of Lochalsh, which was rather hard luck on the children who had to walk several miles every day to reach it.

It's flat farming land again that the road has to cross after Auchtertyre, with some forestry planting on both sides. The north shore of Loch Alsh is a series of wide bays, and looking out over the next one, the most notable feature of the view beyond the water is the hump of Beinn na Caillich, looming over the entrance to Kyle Rhea. The next little settlement is Kirkton, once Kirkton of Lochalsh, which was in the old days, before Kyle of Lochalsh was more than three or four houses, the centre of the whole district. Now it marks the start of the National Trust for Scotland's Balmacara estate, which takes up most of the ground in the western peninsula of Lochalsh.

The old church to the left of the road here is the parish church of Lochalsh, and there are gravestones or memorial plaques to many of the landowners and other notables of the district. It's a well-kept church, its surroundings dotted with snowdrops in the springtime, and it has a fine sunny site looking out over the fields towards the sea. There are window blinds to keep the sunlight out of the shallow interior during weekdays.

In 1849 the crofting township of Kirkton was broken up, when much of the arable land was taken over for sheep, and the mountain grazings up by Loch Monar became part of another sheep farm which the owner of the Attadale estate formed by rifling the summer shielings of crofters from many parts of the district. After that, since they had no summer grazings, the remaining Kirkton tenants had to drive their cattle over to Skye for the summer season.

Just beyond the church a private road runs down the west side of Ard Hill, to what was once the manse but is now a private house. The hill is often known as Tulloch Ard, and it was a place of great significance in the days of the Earls of Seaforth. Tulloch Ard is the 'burning mount' of the Seaforths' badge; when there was trouble or the prospect of a fight, a burning tar barrel would be set up on the summit, and by the next morning all of Seaforth's tenants in Kintail and Lochalsh who could bear arms would be gathered at Eilean Donan, ready to fight for their chief.

James Hogg, the Ettrick Shepherd, came to stay at the manse after he was rowed across the loch from Ardintoul. The Rev. Alexander Downie's house was full of a cheery company of ministers and elders of the Kirk, since communion was to be celebrated on the Sunday and they'd been gathering at Kirkton for a couple of days beforehand. Hogg noted that 'an extra-ordinary multitude assembled to hear sermon. I thought I never saw as many on the same occasion by one half, which convinced me that the lower classes of Kintail are devout. The men are generally tall and well made, and have good features. The women of the lower class are very middling.'

A great tent was set up in the churchyard; one minister preached in Gaelic at the tent, and another in English inside the church. Hogg was persuaded 'much against my inclination' to act as precentor and lead the singing at the English service.

Beyond Kirkton there are forestry plantations on both sides of the road. The older ones on the hill to the right are arranged in a kind of tartan pattern, while the more recent efforts on the north side of Ard Hill were originally made by the National Trust for Scotland, which got out of the unfamiliar timber business in 1970 by passing its forestry interests over to the Forestry Commission. There's a rather scattered collection of old and new houses at the entrance to Balmacara. Over to the left the most substantial feature of the view across the water is still the mass of Beinn na Caillich over in Skye, and as the road moves farther into the village, it becomes gradually possible to see right down the narrows of Kyle Rhea into the Sound of Sleat. Beyond Beinn na Caillich to the right, a sturdy sight in the background, are the high peaks of the Cuillin.

Balmacara is actually a rather vague name for a three-part settlement to which this first collection of houses is only an introduction. Calling this first part Balmacara is a good way to get into an argument in one of the other divisions. Until recently this string of houses, set in a fine situation looking down Kyle Rhea in one direction and through the narrow strait between Kyle of Lochalsh and Skye in another, was announced by a name board that said Reraig. Somehow or other, perhaps because the Balmacara Hotel and the NTS information centre are situated here, this single division began to take on the name more properly given to another part of the village, and in 1969 the county council road signs department capitulated; however, there are Balmacara nationalists lurking not far away, and an incautious word may lead to trouble.

One of the houses at the far end of Balmacara/Reraig used to be well known as a haunt of Sir Harry Lauder's. He was a friend of the family who lived there, came several times on holiday, and went to worship at the local kirk. Perhaps this association brought too many tourists to peer at the house, because since Sir Harry's day it has changed its name, not once but twice from the original Mo Dhachaidh, which meant My Home.

There are rocky cliffs above the road going out of Reraig, with the local war memorial occupying a now less obvious place in a bypassed section of the old road. Up on the hillside is a cave that is sometimes claimed to have sheltered Bonnie Prince Charlie in those dangerous, romantic days after Culloden; but there is not the slightest evidence in the well documented accounts of the Prince's travels to suggest that he ever came near Balmacara, and even local people admit that the cave is little more than an excellent vantage point.

Round the next corner from the war memorial there's a fairly new road junction. Until a short time ago, the main road to Kyle continued uphill to the right, and there was a private driveway off to the left into the grounds of Balmacara House. Now, the new coast road to Kyle goes more or less in the middle of the two older routes. Slightly to the left of it is the tree-lined driveway to the big house, an imposing long white building set behind some fields at the head of a curving bay, with a wooded hillside rising behind and a sweeping stony beach in front.

When Sir Hugh Innes bought the whole of Lochalsh from the last Earl of Seaforth in 1801, it was the start of a thirty-year ownership that was marked more than any other way by the clearing of large areas of inland grazings so that they could be rented out more lucratively as sheep farms. Innes died in 1831,

14 The holiday village of Plockton, at the meeting of Loch Carron and Loch Kishorn

15 Lochcarron village, with the 'Wellington's head' effect of Fuaral on the skyline

16 The single-track railway wandering down Glen Carron

17 Looking over fields of Kishorn to the Applecross mountains

leaving no children, and Lochalsh passed to his grand-niece Katherine Innes Lindsay. Some time before, she had married a rather singular Englishman called Isaac Lillingston, a nephew of William Wilberforce, who used to spend many of his vacations from Cambridge wandering about the Highlands. On one of these trips he stayed with Sir Hugh Innes, met his grand-niece Katherine and fell in love. They were married not long afterwards, and when Sir Hugh died, leaving Lochalsh to Katherine, Isaac Lillingston became its effective landlord.

According to the Rev. Alexander Beith, one-time minister of Glenelg, who came to know Lillingston rather well, he was a magnificent marksman but preferred not to shoot or fish on his estate. The great passions of his life were biblical studies, good works, and sailing; Lochalsh gave him plenty of opportunity for all three. His father had been born Abraham Spooner, but added the surname Lillingston after marrying an heiress from that wealthy Yorkshire family; when the old man was killed by a falling tree in 1834, Isaac sold off the family estates in Warwickshire, and came to live permanently at Balmacara. In the same year, his brother Charles bought over Ratagan and part of Glenshiel.

Although much of Isaac Lillingston's time was spent in research into the Second Coming that he was convinced was shortly to burst upon the world, he wasn't by any means just a library Christian. He was a very daring helmsman, who always took over personal command of his cruising yacht the *Elizabeth* when the weather grew really rough. Balmacara House looked straight down the narrows of Kyle Rhea, which was often used in bad weather by coasting and fishing boat skippers who didn't want to risk the dangerous passage through the Minch between Skye and the Outer Isles; at other times there were merchant ships going to and from the Baltic ports, and even occasional men-of-war to be seen in Loch Alsh. Lillingston devised a plan that brought two of his consuming passions together. He built up a great collection of religious tracts in most of the languages of mercantile Europe. They were packed in specially weighted parcels that a skilful seaman could throw a fair distance. The *Elizabeth* would sail up and down Loch Alsh and Loch Carron, hailing passing craft to ask their country of origin; when the answer came, the crew would hurl a parcel of religious books on board, and then move immediately away to find another customer. There were people who thought that Lillingston was daft to bother his head with such things, but there was no questioning his sincerity, and criticism was rarely voiced openly among his own tenants. The *Elizabeth* was well known in many creeks and harbours and sea lochs up and down the west coast; if the owner heard of a minister who needed transport to some island parish or remote coastal village, the *Elizabeth* was instantly put at his disposal.

Even more to the point was the sudden enthusiasm that caused the Lillingstons to turn Balmacara House into a free hospital, for the benefit of the people of Lochalsh and surrounding districts who had no chance to visit the established hospitals of Inverness and elsewhere. Isaac and Katherine moved into two rooms in the big house, turning all the rest into wards, kitchens and rest rooms; all the household staff became hospital staff, and on sunny days the patients would rest comfortably on chairs set out on the lawns.

Mr Beith recalled that the presiding genius was Lillingston himself, 'who had a passion for administering medicine, his two great remedies being mercury and Epsom salts, these being aided by a vast variety of pills, either original or adapted. The thing lasted for a while. At length it began to be believed (at least suspicions became strong) that the hospital was not a safe one. Nobody, it was remarked, got better. Persons who had not much to complain of when they entered there got worse. Customers fell off. In the end there were to be found about Balmacara, as patients, only the knowing ones, who managed to persuade the good man (not a difficult task) that they were in poor health, and so succeeded in getting food, clothing, and money—accepted his medicines, at the same time, but took care not to swallow them—so sorning on him till even they became ashamed of doing so any longer.' The situation was soon saved, however: 'The eccentricities of Balmacara life disappeared when a young family began to bless the house.'

Now and again, Lillingston discussed his theories about the Second Coming with Mr Beith. His often repeated calculations showed, as had those of many other enthusiasts, that 1837 would be the year in which the great event would come to pass. In September of that year there was a particularly superb aurora borealis, which can be seen from time to time in these latitudes;

the display persisted for nearly a week, with great columns of purple, orange, red, green and yellow light. It seemed to be a magnificent heavenly prelude to the great event. When nothing happened, Lillingston was puzzled but not downhearted. Convinced that he had missed something during his exhaustive studies, he continued with them and remained certain that the prophecy would soon be fulfilled.

Mr Beith's judgement of him seemed very fair: 'My affection for him was strong. With eccentricity, to a certain extent, the existence of which his warmest admirers would not gainsay, he was a holy man, devoted to doing good, never off his Master's work. In all the region in which his property lay he exerted a mighty influence of a most beneficial character. His liberality and generosity to the poor became proverbial. In one department it was eminently so: I mean in that of assisting promising young men with pecuniary aid for pursuing their studies with a view to the ministry. There were friends who thought that in this, as well as in his charities generally, greater discrimination of the cases which claimed his patronage would have been an advantage. He cared not to have such views presented to him. It could be no excuse, he would say, to withhold one's bounty, that the objects to whom it was extended were unworthy and ungrateful.'

Isaac Lillingston built churches, helped many of the coastal villagers with money for fishing boats, provided food in times of famine, and generally acted the paternalistic landlord. Unlike his predecessor Sir Hugh Innes, he kept most of the land in his own hands, and there was no suggestion in his time of existing tenants being cleared away to make room for incoming absentee sheep farmers. Towards the end, however, his eccentricity gradually became overpowering, and he lost his grip on affairs. That his factor could so casually evict the people of Avernish, even though Lillingston allowed some of them to stay on, was almost certainly a sign of this. The Avernish evictions were in 1849, and before another year was over, Isaac Lillingston had been laid to rest in the old churchyard at Kirkton of Lochalsh. To the left of the gateway there is a memorial raised by his tenants and servants. The text from Hebrews is particularly apt, beginning 'Remember them which have the rule over you, who have spoken unto you the word of God.'

Throughout the Highlands there are similar memorials to

landed gentry, often the result of sickening hypocrisy on the part of estate managers who assisted them in the task of clearing their tenants off the land like animals, to their own financial advantage; but the monument at Lochalsh is a fair and honest tribute to a man whose like these parts of Wester Ross were not to see again.

After Isaac Lillingston's death Lochalsh was bought by another individual character called Alexander Matheson. In the eighteenth century, the Mathesons had a wide circle of influence around Loch Alsh and Loch Carron, but the fortunes of the family went into a sad decline, and in the early years of the nineteenth century they were forced to sell off all their property; last of the estates to go was Attadale, which was sold in 1825. At that time, Alexander Matheson was twenty-nine years old, and employed in the Far East trading firm of Jardine, Matheson and Company, founded by his uncle Sir James Matheson and Dr William Jardine from Dumfriesshire. The company built up an immense trading connexion based on Hong Kong, had a large fleet of sailing ships, and made most of its money out of tea and opium. Alexander's brother James, who became a partner in the firm, later resigned because of the involvement with the opium trade, which clashed with his own position as Honorary Secretary of the Presbyterian Mission in India.

In a very short time the firm of Jardine, Matheson and Company made immense profits for its owners. Of the founders, Sir James Matheson was able to retire and buy over the Island of Lewis from the Earl of Seaforth; the Jardine side of the firm made so much money, and went back to their home county to establish such splendid estates, that part of Dumfriesshire came to be known as Chinatown. Alexander Matheson was only thirty-four when he retired with a very large personal fortune, and set about buying back the old Matheson lands in Wester Ross.

In 1840 he bought Letterfearn and Ardintoul, in 1844 Inverinate, in 1851 Lochalsh and Eilean Donan, in 1856 Contin over in Easter Ross, in the 1860s Attadale and other lands round Loch Carron; he ended up with such a vast amount of Ross-shire that he could have walked on his own ground from the Moray Firth to the Atlantic. To begin with, everything went well. He became Sir Alexander Matheson, Baronet of Lochalsh; already a Member of Parliament, he was made a director of the Bank of England; and his immense fortune was devoted largely to improving conditions on his Highland estates. Sometimes he reduced rents, and he regularly offered generous loans or grants for house improvements. On the other hand, he was no enthusiast for the peasant way of life provided by subsistence crofting, which he realized was one of the poorest ways of making use of the land. At the time of the Royal Commission in 1883, many of the properties around Loch Duich, Loch Alsh, Loch Long and Loch Carron were in his possession; so that many of the complaints offered were from tenants of Sir Alexander's. The usual reason put forward for the estate's reluctance to give the crofters more land was that it would have interfered with leases given to larger farmers round about.

He reminded the commissioners, in a statement explaining his position, that one of the great troubles of the West Highlands had been that in many places the land had been expected to support more people than was physically possible. When he bought over Lochalsh, 'it was not for the value of profit or making money by it, it was entirely from the love I had for the country of my birth, and to the country which formerly belonged to my ancestors. I was anxious to get it back when I had the means, and the moment I got the property I laid down a plan, which I have carried out ever since, that is to have tenants of all descriptions upon the estate. I don't wish to have any over £400 or £500 a year, and I wish to have the land occupied by resident tenants. I am very much in favour of small tenants paying £50 or £100 a year and I encourage them as much as I can, but I don't think it is desirable to have a number of small crofts where people can only subsist and where there is not sufficient labour for them to make a living by. At this moment I consider we have rather too many of that class on Lochalsh, and I would be glad if some of them would leave and better themselves elsewhere.'

He didn't force them out, though, even if he gave them little encouragement. His factor, who lived over at Ardross in Easter Ross, told the commissioners that Sir Alexander had three hundred and twenty-nine crofting tenants paying rents of £4 to £30 per year, and twenty-eight larger tenants paying up to £900. By 1883 the rentals had amounted to £205,000, and the £23,000 that came every year from his Ross-shire estates had all been ploughed back into them. More than £86,000 had been spent on improvements for the tenants, £11,000 on roads, and so on right down to £806 on a Commercial Bank office. At the same time, more than £80,000 had been spent on a new mansion house and shooting lodges.

There came a time, however, when even the Matheson finances were overstrained, partly because of the considerable drain on them of all Sir Alexander's improvement schemes. When he died in 1886, the property passed to Sir Kenneth Matheson, the second baronet, who lived elsewhere and finally sold off most of the Ross-shire estates. During Sir Kenneth's ownership, Lochalsh was leased to the second Lord Blythswood, who spent much of his time at Balmacara House and provided work for many of the local people. The Blythswoods owned important estates in Renfrewshire, Argyll and elsewhere, but the Rev. Sholto Douglas Campbell, second holder of the title, had been minister of various churches in Scotland and England, latterly of St Silas's in the west end of Glasgow. Like Isaac Lillingston, he was a student of the events leading up to the Second Coming.

After the first world war, the Mathesons sold the western part of Lochalsh—what is now the NTS Balmacara estate—to Sir Daniel Hamilton, another Scot who had made his money in Asiatic trade. During the 1920s, in a reversal of the historic trend, he broke up the home farm at Balmacara into smallholdings that were then rented out to returned servicemen, mainly from Skye. As in Glenmore on the far side of Mam Ratagan, the Department of Agriculture gave financial assistance to the new tenants, and is still involved today. Sir Daniel died in 1939, last of the private landlords who had done so much for Lochalsh in the century and more since Isaac Lillingston first appeared on the scene. After the war, on the death of Lady Hamilton, almost all of the estate was gifted to the National Trust for Scotland. The old mansion house of Balmacara was left to be used by the county council as an agricultural school, which is still its function today.

Balmacara House School offers a course 'designed for those seeking a career in practical agricultural and associated industries', although various non-agricultural studies are involved too. It takes boys of fifteen or sixteen, and prepares them for the City and Guilds examinations in three basic subjects: Crops, Livestock and Farm Machinery. It has a farm of about four hundred and fifty acres, whose dairy herd produces milk for various customers round about. Lessons are also given in forestry, farm accounting, bee-keeping and so on. There are no fees for Ross-shire students, and boys from other counties usually have their fees paid by their own county council education committees. Oddly enough, the current problem seems to be that there aren't enough boys applying for the available places.

A little way along the new coast road hill, which sweeps up through the old Balmacara House woodlands, is a staggered crossroads of two minor roads. Turning left here leads down a narrow wooded lane behind the mansion house grounds, to a most splendidly situated line of houses looking directly out over the loch at a little place called Glaick. Before there was much road transport in Lochalsh this was a very important spot, because from a now ruined pier a boat used to go out to meet the Glasgow steamers, and bring ashore supplies for the various parts of Balmacara. The steamer would then continue through the sea lochs to lie off at other villages like Dornie, Ardelve and Letter-fearn.

The public road to Glaick ends at the entrance to Lochalsh House, the headquarters of the National Trust for Scotland's estate, and the home of its representative here. This was the longest surviving link with the Lillingstons, because when Isaac's widow sold off almost all the rest of Lochalsh to Alexander Matheson, she retained this little corner of the district. The Lillingstons, who came to call themselves Innes-Lillingston, stayed here for a few generations more, and were still in possession after the second world war. After another merger, the surname of the main line of the family is now Inge-Innes-Lillingston, and their coat of arms still includes the arms of Sir Hugh Innes of Lochalsh.

The other minor road, to the right of the new junction, is another very pleasant wooded lane that looks more like something out of the Home Counties, with the arable fields of the agricultural school through the trees towards the loch. At the end of it is the little settlement of Balmacara Square, which is, according to the people who live there, the *real* Balmacara and a much more senior establishment than the upstart collection of houses at Reraig.

Balmacara Square is set round a junction where the lane that leads to Glaick turns off the old road to Kyle, which takes a line much farther inland than the new one above the coast. Some of

the houses used to be estate stables and so on, but when Sir
Daniel Hamilton provided smallholdings for returned soldiers
after the first world war, he spent a lot of money converting them
into private dwellings. There's a curious mixture of tenures in
the houses at Balmacara Square. Some are privately owned, some
belong to the NTS, others to the Department of Agriculture,
while the most recent ones are to the usual pleasant design of
Ross-shire County Council.

Ignoring for a moment the old road from Balmacara Square,
the modern way to Kyle of Lochalsh keeps high on the hillside as
it heads along the north shore of Loch Alsh, by this time looking
over, not to Kyle Rhea or the Ardintoul shore, but to the lonely
hills in the north-east corner of Skye, and the narrow strait of
Kyle Akin that separates Kyle of Lochalsh from the corresponding settlement of Kyleakin in Skye. This stretch of water got its
name from the Norse King Haco, whose fighting galleys came
this way in 1263 on their way to the rather indecisive Battle of
Largs, which nevertheless effectively ended Norse control of the
Western Isles and the north-west seaboard.

The new road is a most invigorating one, swooping and
dipping its way along the hillside with magnificent views always
off to the left over sea lochs and the mountains of Skye. It's
certainly well worth stopping in one of the many parking places to
soak in the view and the fine fresh seaborne air. One of the
stopping points is beside an imposing monument, previously
approachable only by a coast path from Balmacara or Kyle, to
Donald Murchison, one of the great heroes of Kintail and
Lochalsh.

He was the factor of the lands of Kintail at the time of William,
the fifth Earl of Seaforth, and lived at Tulloch Ard, at the foot of
the hill near the parish church at Kirkton of Lochalsh. The Earl
was 'out' in the Jacobite rebellions of 1715 and 1719, and his
estates were forfeited because of his actions in the first of these.
His people were instructed to pay rents to the government instead
of to their chief. It was one thing, however, to sit in a comfortable
city office and write an order that the rents previously paid to
Seaforth were now owed to the government; but an entirely
different matter to go out and collect them. Kintail was a far-off
mountainous area that couldn't be subdued by Parliamentary
resolutions. The Disarming Acts passed after the first rebellion

didn't really upset the Jacobite clansmen. All they did was hand over any old junk in the way of swords and muskets they could lay their hands on; their serviceable weapons were kept carefully concealed but always ready to hand. Even Wightman's sacking of the district after the abortive rebellion of 1719 didn't make things any easier for the government-appointed Commissioners of Forfeited Estates; in fact, for years after it the local people took advantage of the store of Spanish muskets that came into their hands after the foreign troops surrendered.

It took nearly five years for the government to find anybody prepared to make an expedition into Seaforth's country to gather the rents, which all that time Donald Murchison had been collecting and faithfully delivering to the exiled Seaforth. Finally, the year after the Battle of Glenshiel, one William Ross, who came from Tain on the other side of the county, was appointed to gather the rents of Kintail and Lochalsh, which by that time amounted to a substantial sum. First of all he sent notices of the impending collection into the rebel district. The locals sent back a deceptively mild reply that theirs was a poor country: it had no silver and no gold, only a plentiful supply of lead, which they would be delighted to pay over in small doses through the barrels of their muskets.

William Ross and his brother, who was also involved in the affair, decided to come west anyway, with a party of troops as escort. Murchison was not only very well informed, with a network of friends and informants practically lining the Rosses' route, but he was a canny military tactician as well. He knew all about their plans long before the armed expedition left for the mountains. An ambush was arranged in the upper reaches of Glen Affric, on the east side of the pass that ran from there to Dorusduain. As the government party crossed a ford, shots rang out from the hillside above. A musket ball grazed William Ross's neck, but even that unnerving experience didn't stop him, although he took a coward's way out. According to the story, he changed places with his son Walter, who then rode at the head of the group. Four miles farther on, Murchison's second party opened fire, aiming particularly at the leader; Walter Ross was fatally wounded. After relieving the Rosses of their parliamentary warrant to gather the rents, Murchison sent them all packing back to Inverness.

Next year the Rosses made another attempt, when a larger party approached the Seaforth country by another route, down through the northern glens by Loch Carron and Attadale; but this one too was driven back, and Donald Murchison was able to make his annual journey across to the Continent to hand over the rents to his exiled laird. The Commissioners of Forfeited Estates could make nothing of it; but the government had a stroke of luck a year or two later when the ship that was bringing Murchison back to Scotland fell into their hands. He was taken to London and imprisoned in the Tower.

By the middle of the 1720s the political situation was beginning to ease; General Wade, who years before had scuppered one of the earlier attempts to put James Stuart on the British throne by arresting the Swedish ambassador at his London home, was among those who were trying to have a pardon granted to Seaforth and his supporters. George I, whom the Jacobites were trying to depose, came to interview Murchison in the Tower, and seemed to be impressed by the independence and loyalty to Seaforth he displayed even then. The King offered Murchison a pardon if he would guarantee from that time to be as faithful to his King as he had been to his chief. Knowing that it was only a matter of time before the general pardon was approved, Murchison agreed and went home to Tulloch Ard. When he left London, he had in his pocket a token of the royal favour, a grant of some lands on the north side of Loch Alsh.

Seaforth's pardon followed soon afterwards, and the chief returned, although without his title, which was to remain forfeited for many years more. He had apparently promised Murchison a hearty reward for all his services, as was only reasonable. The story, however, does not have the traditional happy ending, although the details of it are by no means clear; it has been suggested that the popular version was invented as a political attempt to blacken Seaforth's character. Nobody seems to know for sure.

It is said that Seaforth, when he returned from exile, was not entirely happy with Donald Murchison's position; Murchison's great influence and popularity in Kintail and Lochalsh, earned during the long years when the chief was absent and he had been the supreme authority in the district, and the substantial grant of land that had been made to him by the King, did not suit Seaforth's book. All that he offered Murchison was a smallish farm at Bundalloch. With some reason, Murchison was bitterly hurt. He left the district altogether, and went to live away over the mountains on the eastern part of Seaforth's estates in Strathconon, not far from the chief's home at Brahan Castle. He never recovered from the disillusionment of his beloved chief's return, and died not long afterwards, still in middle age. Seaforth visited him during his last illness, but was given a very frosty reception.

Donald Murchison's brother Murdoch tried to get legal help to win back the royal grant of land which Seaforth had refused to hand over; but Murdoch was killed in the rebellion of 1745, and the story gradually faded from memory. Even the location of Donald's last resting-place was forgotten. It wasn't until 1861 that the famous geologist Sir Roderick Murchison, Donald's great-grand-nephew, searched for his grave so that he could put up a memorial beside it. By that time there was nobody alive with even a faint family memory of the place, and it could not be traced in any church records.

Sir Roderick compromised by setting up the memorial on the hillside above Loch Alsh, in a place that Donald Murchison must have known well. The inscription makes no mention of Seaforth's ingratitude:

Tulloch-Ard
To the Memory of
Donald Murchison,

Colonel in the Highland Army of 1715.
He successfully defended, and faithfully
preserved the Lands of Kintail and
Lochalsh, from 1715 to 1722, for his Chief
William, the exiled Earl of Seaforth.

The new road continues high above the lochside, often on a line blasted out of the cliffs, before sweeping down towards its destination at Kyle of Lochalsh, the railhead and ferry port for Skye. Kyle is on a rather unlikely and inhospitable rocky site, cramped on the north side of Kyle Akin looking directly across to the nearest settlement in Skye. From the approach road, there's a good impression of its situation at the junction of a tangle of sea lochs and narrow straits, with smaller islets dotted about, and the great mountains of Skye and the northern districts of Wester

Ross making a splendid backdrop. However, as with Dornie, it's worth remembering that the new coastal route isn't the only approach, and there's still the enterprising old road snaking its way along the line of least resistance farther inland.

From the junction at the entrance to the grounds of Balmacara House, the old road swings right to begin its climb up past Balmacara Square. Off to the right is a minor road that doubles back up the steep hillside to an old wartime anti-aircraft gunsite; after the war one of the buildings there was converted into a youth hostel, but today it is another of the NTS adventure camps.

Off to the right beyond Balmacara Square is a pleasant valley running towards the top of Auchtertyre Hill, with woods and plantations around the sides. Part of the wooded area is the remnant of the Coille Mhor or Great Wood of Lochalsh, which was cleared almost completely after the first world war. Here too there are traces of old arable ground, a reminder of the time before Sir Hugh Innes's clearances when Coillemore of Lochalsh was one of the biggest villages in the district; sixty-seven families made a modest living from crofting there. The house by the roadside at Coillemore was the home of Dr MacRae, whose practice extended from Kyle of Lochalsh all the way up Glen Elchaig to the lonely stalker's house at Millbuie.

The road begins to turn westwards through a landscape of wild rocky heather and occasional peaty lochans; it looks less like Ross-shire and more like the northern country of Assynt, far away over the county boundary in Sutherland. A minor road off to the right leads to Duirinish and Plockton in the north part of Lochalsh, and soon after this junction the main road passes above the little pools of Loch Iain Oig and Loch Palascaig. From a point between the lochs there is a most dramatic view over the mountains of Applecross on the far side of Loch Carron, the Crowlin Islands in the Inner Sound between Applecross and Raasay, and some of the peaks far away in the Trotternish peninsula in the north-east corner of Skye.

Beyond the lochs, the road begins to wind downhill again, having passed the highest point on its way from Balmacara to Kyle. As it comes down the valley, the upper part of which is a good example of how hopeless much of the North-west Highlands are for agriculture on any scale, the road passes another turning sharp back to the right, the second of the roads that lead

over to Duirinish and Plockton. At the foot of the valley is the
little settlement of Erbusaig, once a crofting and fishing centre,
but more or less deserted by the sea after the railway was pushed
through from Strome Ferry to Kyle, over a curving embankment
that leaves only a small gap for the burn to run through, and
blocks the village off from the waters of Erbusaig Bay.

Erbusaig is noted for being one of the select group of places on
the Scottish mainland that has a coral beach. At least, there's a
bank of coral sand, exposed only at very low tide; it isn't made
by little marine animals, as in the tropical atolls, but by a certain
kind of plant. The old crofters often made use of coral and shell
sand to fertilize their fields, and the custom has been revived in
the Hebrides today, allowing many acres of moorland to be
reclaimed for cattle grazing. The local minister noted in 1794
that all the tenants on Seaforth's estates had free access to any
banks of coral sand round the coast; from Erbusaig, small boats
would take loads of twelve to eighteen barrels and transport it to
the villages on the edge of Loch Duich, and it would be hauled in
carts to farms and crofts farther inland. The charge was sixpence
per barrel landed on the shore at Letterfearn.

Swinging round to the south again, the road winds past
another little settlement at Badicaul, dips and rises along the coast
beside the succession of embankments and cuttings made for the
railway, and soon arrives at the fringes of Kyle of Lochalsh. It
seems a most peculiar place to have built a village, a rough
peninsula of rocky hummocks and stiff-sided inlets of the sea,
with some of its houses haphazardly stuck down among gorse
and heather, bare rock and scattered trees. It was only the coming
of the railway that turned it from a tiny and lonely outpost into
the lifeline of the Isle of Skye.

CHAPTER 8

PLOCKTON AND STROME

EIGHTY YEARS AGO, Kyle of Lochalsh was composed of a shooting lodge of sorts, an inn and no more than four or five houses. There was an old-established ferry crossing to Skye, but it was a very half-hearted affair compared with Glenelg and Strome, which saw most of the traffic. The *Ordnance Gazetteer* of 1884 didn't think it worth mentioning Kyle at all. It was only in 1897, when the Dingwall and Skye railway was extended round the coast from Strome Ferry to a new pier at Kyle, that the village began to grow up. To build the single-track line those last ten miles from Strome cost something like £100,000, which was very reasonable, considering the number of cuttings and embankments, and the incredible way in which the line is stuck delicately to the foot of the enormous cliffs on the shores of Loch Carron. The final stretch to Kyle had to be excavated out of solid rock, and the pierhead facilities included such wonders as hydraulically operated cranes to lift cargoes on and off the boats.

It's the Skye crossing, of course, that brought prosperity and inhabitants to Kyle, which in its early days had something of the atmosphere of a frontier settlement; it wasn't for nothing that one of the businesses came to be known as the Pioneer Stores. Nowadays, Kyle is also the shopping centre for all the mainland villages and hamlets in five parishes.

During the summer season, most of the visitors to Skye go through Kyle at some point on their journey. It seems, however, as if some high authority feels that Kyle has had a long enough run, because its railway link may well be removed if the line from Achnasheen closes in 1971—a closure that was proposed during the great economies of the Beeching era, but postponed after vigorous local action—and there is a strong possibility that it will also lose its place as one of the main steamer ports on the Hebridean run. The railway line, of course, loses a lot of money, partly because most local households have to have a car to move around and partly because the efforts to promote it as a tourist attraction could hardly be called enthusiastic. It must seem from a cosy city office that finance is the only consideration; but in the often wild north-west winters, even the new roads that are being pushed through to Kyle will sometimes be blocked or dangerous. Removing the rail link will isolate the place even more. It has been said with some feeling that the service has been allowed to become so scruffy of late that it won't be much of a loss. The big disaster, however, may be not so much the removal of a communications link as the disappearance of the railway jobs.

Instead of the coastal and island steamer trade making up for this loss of work, it looks as if it too will be taken away from Kyle, which may shortly lose its position as the Ross-shire base to the more northerly village of Ullapool. All that may be left in a few years' time is the car ferry over to Kyleakin in Skye. Every year there are more and more council houses going up in Kyle; if the railway and steamer jobs disappear—and there isn't much hope of anything else to take their place—it's difficult to see who's going to occupy them. The ferry terminal is being improved and extended, and new ferries are being built—although, typically, the first one arrived too late for the 1970 summer season—as if to divert attention from the fact that Kyle seems to be destined in the planners' minds for a descent into the Celtic twilight. There are Skye people who would like to see the ferry replaced by a £3,000,000 bridge.

Nevertheless, Kyle is a busy enough little place in the summer season. It has a good selection of shops, restaurants, hotels, boarding houses and the like, crammed into the restricted space available. The western tip of the peninsula on which it's built is known as the Plock, or Lump of Kyle; on the hill leading over to it is a collection of rather pleasant council houses, arranged in a little settlement with the distressingly Lowland name of Heathmount. There's a great view out to Skye, the Inner Sound and the Applecross Hills from an old wartime observation post right at the top of the hill. A few years ago the golfing enthusiasts of Kyle began to hack out a course from the rocky and ill-drained land of the Plock, which had been left to the people by Lady Hamilton, and the result of their exertions lies between Heathmount and the edge of the peninsula.

All round Kyle there are pleasant little islands and rocky inlets, often used as sheltered anchorages for fishing boats. As you would expect from its situation, Kyle is a coastguard and lifeboat station; only half a dozen herring boats and some smaller creel boats operate locally. At the moment, the place is unhealthily dependent on the Skye tourist trade, even if the occasional six to eight hour queues for the car ferry mean that there's plenty of potential custom.

Continuing northwards along the Ross-shire coast means back-tracking for a short way beyond Erbusaig, where a minor road turns left across a bridge to head over the low hills towards Duirinish and Plockton. It goes up through rather barren heather moorlands with many lumps of exposed rock. From the summit level there's another of those fine prospects over the Applecross Hills, this time with Loch Carron shining in the middle distance. Over a brow, and the view is suddenly to a much more productive landscape, the little crofting township of Drumbuie, with the fields it shares with the neighbouring village of Duirinish spread out over a sweep of lower ground. Much of this is split into the strips of arable land that are the trademark of most of the crofting Highlands. Beyond the crofting ground is knobbly, rocky moorland, with a great panoramic backdrop made up of the soaring mountains of Applecross, the meeting of Loch Carron and Loch Kishorn, the steep hills of North Strome Forest over to the north-east, and the tops of the outstanding Castle Crags beyond Plockton on the south shore of Loch Carron. Farther down the road towards Drumbuie, in a dip of the foreground hills, is a sight of a large white building that turns out from closer up to be the very modern senior secondary school at Plockton.

Some of the Drumbuie and Duirinish crofts have been worked part-time by people whose main job was on the railway. This is really at the heart of what will be crofting's greatest problem in the next twenty years or so; most Highland crofters' sons feel that one job is quite enough, and that if they've done a full day's work there isn't much point in continuing to work through the gloaming on a smallholding that has little more than sentimental value. When the present generation of crofters is gone—and many of them are retired from other jobs anyway—many of their cottages will become summer holiday homes for their families who have had to go to the towns and cities to find work.

18 Crofting land at Loch a 'Mhuillin in Applecross, looking across to Skye

19 Looking down the Pass of the Cattle to Loch Kishorn and Achintraid

20 Winter in the mountains of Applecross: looking over Glen Shieldaig from Beinn Bhan

Most of the Drumbuie crofting land is still in good heart, and the place itself is a pleasant collection of whitewashed cottages looking over it and away from the sea. Although the one-inch map suggests that the croft lands round all these villages like Drumbuie and Erbusaig are outside the NTS property, the whole area does in fact form part of the Trust's Balmacara estate. There are, it has to be said, very mixed feelings throughout Wester Ross about the Trust as proprietor; a common complaint is that while it's supposed to be holding its lands in trust for the nation, it is sometimes out of touch with the needs of its tenants and inclined to act too much like an old-fashioned landlord.

These Drumbuie and Duirinish crofters have a hard time of it getting their stock to market, although in this way they are much more favoured than many others in Wester Ross. The rail and road freight charges are felt to be far too high, especially coming from government-controlled concerns. For example, if one of the crofters has a cow to take to Dingwall, which is the nearest market, the current rate for sending it by rail is no less than £15; it's hardly worth while sending an older beast to the sale at all.

The road winds on for a spell between Drumbuie and Duirinish, which is announced by a crop of corrugated iron roofs on top of some old stone barns and byres. This is a completely different kind of place from Drumbuie, being more or less one straight street with a line of houses on one side and a handful of scattered cottages opposite them on the other side of the Duirinish Burn that tumbles right through the village. The roughcast houses are mostly whitewashed, while the ones with stone outer walls are treated with a preservative that takes on a blackish tinge and then has the mortaring picked out in white. To a stranger, since the houses are split fairly evenly between black and white, it looks as if they imply some kind of political or religious rivalry, but there is no symbolism intended. From the road junction at the top of the village, beside a bridge over the deep and rocky gully of the burn, there's a fair view out towards the open sea; but it seems a pity that none of the houses in the main part of the village has its windows aimed in that direction.

Back at the entrance to Duirinish there's a little turning between the old stone byres that seems to come to an end at a gate between the buildings; but the public road continues beyond the gate to a little place called Portneorn, one of the most attractive corners in the whole of Lochalsh. It meanders over the crofters' arable land towards a couple of houses beside the Duirinish halt on the single-track railway line from Kyle; nowadays these little platforms are unstaffed request halts. It was near here that the wartime mines were stored, which provoked the fears of sympathetic detonation when the *Port Napier* went on fire out in Loch Alsh.

At the houses, the public road jinks back to the right and then turns left over a level crossing; drivers have to get out and open the gates for themselves. The recently tarred but narrow road, quite well supplied with passing places, winds up and down past banks of rowans, oaks and birches, alongside rocky bays until it comes down to sea level at Port Ban, a little opening off to the right where the Duirinish Burn comes down to the sea, and two of the Portneorn men keep a fishing boat. On a little farther, through a gate, and there is the unpublicized hamlet of Portneorn, the Barley Port.

Portneorn is no more than four houses and a handful of ruins, set round a bridge where a burn comes seeping down from Drumbuie. A little sheltered rocky bay faces north over a group of islands to the great hills of Applecross and Loch Kishorn; but there's no sight at all of any of the other villages nearby, and so a great feeling of peace and detachment comes over a stranger visiting the place, made more obvious by a chattering of birds, sudden indignant cries from the gulls, and a gentle breeze from the open sea. There are miniature cliffs on the east side of the bay, sometimes a dinghy or two lashed to the rocks at a cleared stretch of the stony shore, and, looking back up the overgrown course of the little burn, a sight of two mountain summits away in the background, in the north-east corner of Skye.

The Drumbuie and Duirinish crofters had the Portneorn ground taken away from them in the days when land was being rented out to incoming sheep farmers, and they also lost the right to take their cattle in summer to the shielings of Loch Monar. The memory of this seems to stay with the place even yet, in the form of ruined cottages and tangled ground that once was under the plough. There are only three families at the Barley Port now, and it's out of the way of most summer visitors. It's one of the most splendid little corners of Lochalsh, with a background of great distant cliffs and rock faces, from the west right round through the north to the eastern edge of the view. Like many of these places, Portneorn is seen at its best in the pale golden light of a summer dusk.

Back at the top of the village of Duirinish, there's a road junction beside the bridge. Dominating the whole village and its little valley is a very striking white mansion house on the wooded hillside. This is Duirinish Lodge, which was built between the wars by General Sir Torquhil Matheson, who retired here after a successful military career that extended from 1890 to 1935. He was the fifth of the Matheson baronets of Lochalsh; his son, the present baronet, lives in Somerset, and none of the old property around Loch Carron and Loch Alsh, which first came into Matheson hands in 1730 when John Matheson bought Attadale, remains in the family's possession. For a while Duirinish Lodge took in paying guests, but within the last two or three years it has become a private house once again.

The road that comes down past the lodge to Duirinish bridge is a winding minor affair that runs from the old inland route between Balmacara and Kyle, turning off it just before Loch Iain Oig. In its early stages from the loch, it's a pretty wild looking road over rocky, heathery ground. From the top there are the expected excellent views out over Loch Carron and Applecross; but as it dips down the valley to Duirinish, the whole landscape makes a dramatic change. The upper valley of the Duirinish Burn which lies to the east is heavily wooded, its structure a mixture of low rolling nearby hills with fine upstanding peaks and towers on the skyline. There are wooded ridges and deep hollows, and odd patches of rough grazing land among the plantations. Like Portneorn, this valley is seen at its best in the warm golden light of a summer evening. Away to the west from the hill down to Duirinish bridge is a fine view of the oddly-shaped Crowlin Islands off the Applecross coast. From this angle, the main island looks exactly like a picture that was once published of a great shapeless hump reputed to be a close-up of the Loch Ness Monster.

Past the entrance to Duirinish and over the old high-arched stone bridge, the road continues on its way to Plockton, getting alongside the railway and passing through another pleasantly wooded area. For a while, it runs exactly parallel with the railway line, until it suddenly curls over it and comes to the entrance to the fine modern Plockton secondary school that serves Glenshiel, Kintail, Lochalsh, Lochcarron and Applecross. Many of the

children from far-out districts who attend the school live in a
hostel in the grounds. When the hostel was built, the specially
subsidized bus services that used to bring pupils every morning
from places not too far away, like Inverinate and Ratagan, was
stopped; children who could quite easily have been taken home
every afternoon as before had no choice but to move into the
hostel.

Just to the left of the bridge is the Plockton railway halt, and
here the county council have built what must be the most
ridiculously sited houses in the whole district. With views of
almost unimaginable grandeur in nearly every direction, the houses
here look into nothing but the railway line itself.

While the road into Plockton drops downhill from the school,
there's another road that turns back behind the station, and
wanders through patches of gorse across the low-lying plateau
due west of the modern village which is the 'plock' from which
it took its name. Until the time of Sir Hugh Innes, the village
was a ramshackle collection of cottages on this low-lying ridge-
land; almost the first thing he did after buying over Lochalsh
was to clear it away and build the present village down on the
shores of a sheltered inlet of Loch Carron. It became a burgh of
regality, but that arrangement has long since lapsed.

The back road from the station leads over towards an orange
windsock that marks the tarmac airstrip that was built in 1966
by a party of Royal Engineers. It was originally intended as a
kind of emergency landing strip for hospital planes and the like;
but, although there's a little hut that contains a helicopter
emergency fuel store, most of the light planes that land here
belong to wealthy people who come to Plockton on holiday.
During the Festival of the Countryside that was run in Wester
Ross in the spring of 1970, flights were made from here up and
down the coast, and over to landing strips on some of the
Western Isles; it would be pleasant to think that something in
this line might become a regular service.

There can be few airfields in Britain with such a superb view
as this one above Plockton. It's a splendid place from which to
appreciate the fjord-like structure of the landscape round about.
To the north-east are what appear to be a pair of triangular peaks
occupying the ground between Loch Kishorn and the narrows
of Loch Carron as it heads for Strome; but one of these is simply

an end-on view of the steep ridge of the North Strome Forest hills, edged along the waterside by Forestry Commission plantations and sweeps of pleasant older woodland. In the other direction, of course, is the usual view out towards Skye, over the mouth of Loch Carron between the Applecross Hills and the mainland of Lochalsh; but to mention the 'usual view' hereabouts is not to suggest that anybody could ever become blasé about such a magnificent sight. The great mountains of Applecross look particularly grand and lonely.

The public road ends at the north end of the airstrip, at a turning place from which there's a fine outlook over the islands in Loch Carron, many with warning lights on them to advise sailors of the low-lying obstructions in the channel. Due west, along the south shore of Loch Carron, are the soaring cliffs of the Castle Crags, which have much the same appearance, from closer up, as the buttresses on Mount Rushmore that are carved with likenesses of American presidents. Just to the north of them across the loch is the superbly situated line of white cottages at Ardaneaskan, almost on the shore below the plantations of North Strome Forest, and with the wooded inlet of Loch Reraig a little way to the north again. Between the airstrip and the station junction there's another little tarmac road turning off to the southwest; but this one is a bit of a snare and delusion, because it remains passable just about as far as a sensibly-sited rubbish dump that's well out of sight of local people and visitors alike.

Going back down from the school into Plockton itself, there's a war memorial on a little rise of ground to the right of the road, commanding a fine view of the steep-sided rocky bay that provides the village with a famous anchorage. On the south side of the bay, and stretching along the south shore of the loch, are the wooded precipices and headlands around Duncraig Castle, with the even grander Castle Crags fading away into the distance much higher up the hill. The bay and the outer loch are still seen to be dotted with little islands, some of them with occasional clumps of trees. Plockton is seen in its magnificent situation, perhaps the most beautiful on the whole of Scotland's western coast; it's a village of fine, well-tended whitewashed houses, all with an outlook to sea loch and mountain. The whole place, however, faces to the east, which is not the best outlook for a west coast settlement, but gives it an air of seclusion and privacy.

On the hillside to the left after the war memorial there's a gateway to an old open-air preaching ground that is still sometimes used. The present Church of Scotland is a small but very neat building to the right of the road not far into the village. In its churchyard there are gravestones to Mackenzies and Livingstones and Mathesons; but the bright and well-kept interior, with its gallery on three sides, is devoid of decoration or memorial plaques or stained glass, and no prominent local men are remembered there. Local notabilities were buried at the parish church of Lochalsh, away over at Kirkton near Balmacara.

As the road bends left to go along Harbour Street, which is the main street, promenade and just about everything else in Plockton, there's a little car park overlooking the bay. Duncraig Castle is seen in its tremendously grand situation on the pine-wooded cliffs across the bay. There are mountains all around, and, almost exactly to the south-east, a break in the inland hills at a place called Gleannan Dorch, the Little Dark Glen. The summit just to the right of it is called Carn an t-Saighdeir, the Soldier's Cairn. The story goes that in 1719, after the Battle of Glenshiel, one of the wounded Jacobites tried to make his weary way home after the fight was over, and got as far as here before dying of his wounds.

At both ends of Harbour Street the houses have gardens on the far side of the road overlooking the loch, and there are some palm trees to demonstrate the mildness of the climate. The houses in the middle part of the street, however, have only a sea wall on the far side of the road, dipping down to a rather stony beach where dinghies are usually tied up and the seagulls wheel and soar above the rocks. Towards the north end of the village there are more houses off on a little peninsula to the right, and a camping site hidden away on the left.

In Sir Hugh Innes's day, and later on when Isaac Lillingston owned Lochalsh, Plockton was the biggest village in the district; in 1841 there were five hundred and thirty-seven people here at census time, which is about twice as many as live here all the year round now. For some reason, the story of Plockton has been rather confused by some of the people who have written about it. From time to time it has been said that Plockton in the early part of the last century was a place where sizeable ships were built, and local skippers were engaged in the Baltic trade.

All of this is rather an exaggeration; even if there are many gravestones in the churchyard to men described as 'shipowners of Plockton', the reality is not quite so grand. The safe natural harbour made Plockton a good base for inshore fishing, and there were some local men who fitted out small sloops to take the fishing catches to the Clyde ports, bringing back foodstuffs and other supplies as return cargo. Many of these fishing and trading boats were financed by Isaac Lillingston; but the trade was never fully developed, and there was the usual collection of landless crofters as well.

The potato blight of the 1840s was a desperate time in Plockton, and the people were once again lucky in having a proprietor like Isaac Lillingston. He sent fresh vegetables from the Balmacara home farm to Plockton and other townships along the coast, to supplement the dreary and inefficient rations of oatmeal that the relief authorities doled out, and gave the Plockton people bags of seed to plant in their gardens so that they could grow a more varied diet themselves.

Donald Macrae's recently published booklet *Lochalsh* reprints a circular letter from the inspector in charge of relief work in the district, to show what an offhand and sometimes grim attitude the relief workers often had towards those in their care. Writing from Kyle House on 10 February 1848, H. B. Rose instructed his officers how to deal with the supplies apportioned to the district.

There was no suggestion that this was any kind of simple charitable handout, because the half-starved people had to work very hard for their rations of meal. The relief officers under Rose's control had to employ local overseers to make sure that the work, mostly in road building, was carried out satisfactorily. Every man given work had to put in eight hours every day except Sunday, for which the pay was a munificent one and a half pounds of meal per day, or three ounces for every hour. 'But this full allowance is only to be granted to the man who works honestly and hard, not to him who merely gives his attendance and idles over his task. In this case the quantity is reduced to 1 lb.; and this is a rule which I trust to your strictly enforcing.' Officers had to keep a firm eye on the overseers, who were liable to lose their two shillings daily pay for any sign of neglect, and would lose their job altogether for two bad reports.

The women didn't escape the rules of this charitable relief

work, but were offered extra rations for real sweatshop labour. They could earn fourteen pounds of meal in a fortnight if they produced four pounds of spun wool, four pounds of spun hemp, four pairs of knitted socks, and four yards of twenty-five foot wide net. It wouldn't be fair to say that the whole arrangement was without its touch of humanity: 'one-half of the above requirement will be accepted from women who are partially infirm, or pregnant, or nursing, or who have large families.'

It sounded more like the treatment of a nation defeated in war than government assistance to people visited by a natural disaster. Like Rose, many of the men running the relief organization were not West Highlanders themselves; it has been one of the tragedies of this part of the country that many incomers who arrived to take control of some part of the people's lives despised and hated the whole west coast way of life, and the people who enjoyed it. Only a fool would suggest that this attitude has completely died out.

Small wonder that there were emigrations from here as well as from all the other villages in Wester Ross; and then Sir Alexander Matheson came on the scene. It was opposite Plockton that he decided to build his splendid new mansion house of Duncraig Castle; perhaps the most important result from the Plockton tenants' point of view was that they lost some of their land for the gardens and woodlands of the big house. Duncraig woods were said to have been planted with at least one example of every known species of tree that would grow in this climate.

When the Balmacara estate, of which this is the northern limit, was passed over to the National Trust for Scotland, Plockton became their property too. Duncraig Castle was given to the county council to be transformed into a school of homecraft and domestic studies, a girls' equivalent of the school at Balmacara House.

Although present-day Plockton looks a prosperous place, appearances are a little deceptive. Most of the houses here are summer holiday homes, rented out or occupied only during the summer by their owners, or belong to people who have retired here from the south, often having family connexions with the area. Plockton has attracted many well-to-do people over the years, and it isn't anything remotely like a Blackpool-on-Loch-Carron. In 1970 the BBC Radio 'Brain of Britain' quiz series was won by a retired surgeon who lives here.

There's a popular modern Scottish song called *At the Dancing in Kyle*, but the real social whirl in Lochalsh appears to revolve around Plockton. At least, any time a ferry crew decide to knock off a wee bit early, or some lonely hill road is deluged with traffic up to five o'clock in the morning, the reason seems to be that 'there's a dance at Plockton tonight'. During the summer months, the place is full of sailing enthusiasts; there's plenty of scope for social sailing off the shore, and for more intrepid work among the great sea lochs and islands of the Ross-shire coast. Plockton regatta is a well established summer attraction, when the bay is full of yachts and dinghies, and the squelch of gumboots and yellow mackintoshes is heard in the land.

In 1970 work began on a much grander vessel that will soon be a regular part of the Plockton scene. The Dulverton Trust announced that the keel had been laid in a Buckie shipyard of a three hundred and twenty ton three-masted schooner, costing £200,000, which would be based at Plockton and provide four-week training cruises for schoolboys and young men. It was decided to call the ship *Sir Francis Drake*, and this perfectly reasonable idea was greeted with the predictable barrage of criticism from the touchy fringe of Scottish nationalists, who get hot under the collar about references to anything or anybody specifically English and dated before the Union of Parliaments in 1707; they felt affronted that an Englishman's name should be involved. Now the ship is to be called the *Captain Scott*.

The most memorable sight from Plockton is probably the great wooded cliffs around Duncraig Castle plunging down to the sea. That enterprising railway line to Kyle manages to sneak along by the water's edge just below the castle, where it was swamped a few years ago by a very high storm tide that also invaded the lower-lying houses at Bundalloch on Loch Longside. Although it seems barely credible from the village, there is a public road that takes a very intrepid line behind Duncraig Castle, and on by the lochside cliffs of Castle Crags to follow the south side of Loch Carron on the way to Strome.

There are two ways to get from Plockton to Duncraig. Heading back along the Duirinish road, just where the railway line curves away, there's an unsignposted turning to the left, running along the edge of an old pinewood. To begin with, it has a tarred surface; in the summer of 1970, the tarred surface didn't

last for very long, because the whole road was being rebuilt on
an embankment that raised it above the generally boggy ground.
The road runs up through a little glen, with a rocky pine-clad
hill on the right and a rise of ground with birches dotted about
among miniature crags on the left. This is a pleasant enough
place when the trees are in leaf, but it loses some of its attraction
earlier in the year. Towards the low summit of the road, there's
a view at another angle to Castle Crags, with pinewoods sloping
down towards the castle itself, and from there into the loch.
From this point, where the road is higher up the hillside than the
castle, the dominating effect of the big house is much reduced.
Downhill again there's a good view out over the islands off
Plockton, and into the gash in the hillside below the castle where
the railway squeezes through a cutting. When the railway came
through, in the time of Sir Kenneth Matheson, Duncraig Castle
had a private station down by the shore. Downhill once again,
and the road comes to a junction with a splendid tree-lined
avenue to Duncraig, with plantations of all kinds round about.

It's the road that approaches this junction from the right that's
the more attractive way to Duncraig. Getting onto the start of
it means going back along the Duirinish road almost as far as the
bridge, and taking a left turn signposted to Duncraig. It goes
along through woodlands again, out of the National Trust for
Scotland property, and above the glen of the Duirinish Burn for
a short way before veering off into another valley. Some of the
lower hillsides round about here are being planted as part of the
timber operations of the investment group called Economic
Forestry Limited, but the Forestry Commission controls many of
the higher slopes. There are local people who feel that almost all
of Lochalsh may yet be turned into one enormous forest.

The road goes past the entrance to the farm of Achnandarach,
a place that seems to suffer from various attempts at spelling it;
the name means the Field by the Oak Trees. Authoress Margaret
Leigh was the tenant of the farm for a few years from 1933. In
1936 she published a very good book about the place called
Highland Homespun; in it Achnandarach is disguised as 'Achnabo'.
The book is realistic yet full of colour, and mercifully free from
the sentimental junk often offered in similar situations by other
writers. That her account of a farming year in Lochalsh, with
stories about all the different kinds of people involved, was very

popular is shown by the fact that *Highland Homespun* went through three printings in its first year. Other books by Margaret Leigh deal with life in Moidart and on Barra.

Up on the hillside beyond Achnandarach is Loch Achnahinch, which suffers from much the same spelling trouble; it's one of the hill lochs in Lochalsh where some trout fishing is offered jointly by the NTS and Balmacara Hotel. There are some others south of the Gleannan Dorch, but they are best approached from the road between Auchtertyre and Strome. On Loch Achnahinch, it is said, there used to be a fortified lake-dwelling that was one of the strongholds of the Macdonalds of Lochalsh before they were driven out of the territory by the Mackenzies.

From the Achnandarach road-end, the view ahead is to a very rough and craggy hillside, with birches on the lower slopes and newer plantations of spruce higher up, some of the tiny conifers peeping over the skyline like a few thousand Red Indians massing for a film-set ambush. To the right of the road there appears an apologetic puddle of water that is the first notice of the presence of Loch Lundie. This is a most pleasantly situated little loch, in a depression among the woodlands, and with a spit of ground out towards the middle where some old pine trees grow. There are birches on the far side, gorse bushes along the road, craggy slopes going up from the water's edge, and some really splendid reflections in the loch. This is part of the public water supply, and is also stocked with brown trout, which are said to provide good sport for the angler from April to July; permission to fish it, as with the hill lochans, is available from the Trust and Balmacara Hotel, which offers free fishing in these lochs to its guests. Going along past Loch Lundie, the road enters an avenue of stately hardwoods planted at the time of Sir Alexander Matheson's building of Duncraig, and this continues down a winding hill, with views down over Plockton Bay, that meets up with the other approach road from nearer the village.

The two roads merge to continue along a very fine, dignified avenue towards the entrance to the castle grounds, where the through road to Strome bears right uphill again, above the old walled garden, and makes for the most enterprising stretch below the cliffs of Castle Crags. It's difficult to explain just how splendid this narrow and winding little road really is, with a most magnificent outlook down over the island-dotted loch and over to the mountains of Applecross and Kishorn. Beyond the Duncraig Castle woods it comes nearer to the sea, although still a few hundred vertiginous feet above it. Away down at the bottom, worming its way along the edge of the rocky coastline, is the little toytown railway line; it's no surprise to learn that landslides have sometimes closed both railway and road. At one time during the 1960s the railway authorities were so worried about the falling rock that the road was closed to all but essential local traffic. Between the wars there was a long dispute about which of two private landowners controlled the road, and later some argument about whether it was public or private. About ten years ago the whole thing was settled when the county council took it over and gave it a tarred surface.

There are one or two cottages tacked onto the very steep hillside above and below the road, which is by this point no longer on NTS ground but running through the estate of Fernaig, owned for several generations by the Forbes family. It has wooded edges, banks of rhododendrons and other shrubs, and a fair number of passing places into which it would be inadvisable to dash too suddenly, because there's a very long drop to the water's edge below. Actually, the road has been sensibly rebuilt and widened a little in recent years, and there are crash barriers at the most likely spots. From this road, running at the foot of the great 'Mount Rushmore' buttresses of the Castle Crags, but with a lot more steep hillside plunging down to the water off the nearside edge, there is one of the grandest coastal views available from anywhere in the north-west; Plockton is seen as from an aeroplane, and the strung-out little hamlet of Ardaneaskan on the far shore of Loch Carron looks particularly fine. There are 'falling rock' signs here and there along the road, and it's as well to remember that they are not purely ornamental.

At the far end of the Castle Crags the lochside begins to curve round at the entrance to Fernaig Bay; the railway line follows it, and cuts across the head of the bay on the usual embankment, but the road keeps swinging inland along the little narrow valley of Strath Ascaig. The road is on the southern flank of the valley, and over on the far side is a very fine example of a raised beach, with a wide curving plateau above it and the substantial craggy tower of Creag Mhaol rising grandly over all. Due east, and farther up the valley, the green arable lands are guarded by steep-rising hills carpeted with the plantations of South Strome Forest.

Fernaig has a long-standing association with Gaelic literature. It was here that a seventeenth-century Duncan Macrae of Inverinate, a famous poet and anthologist, collected a series of songs and poems that have come to be known as the Fernaig MS.

It's a pleasant view over the productive arable lands of the little valley towards the sheltering hills of the South Strome Forest, and then the Duncraig road comes to an end, at a junction with the main road from Auchtertyre to Strome. Getting onto the main road at its southern end means leaving the new Dornie–Kyle road, going into the now bypassed hamlet of Auchtertyre, and turning up the steep, narrow and winding hill over the shoulder towards the Glen Udalain reservoir that was created to turn the turbines down at Nostie. From the hill there's a final superb view over the mountains of Loch Duich, Kintail and Glenshiel. This is wild, lonely sheep country nowadays, but there was a time in the eighteenth century when the Mathesons were said to have been able to summon up seven hundred fighting men from this one valley alone. That may have been something of an exaggeration, but the activities of Sir Hugh Innes left the place in the condition it is in today—deserted by humankind. Over the summit of the road, though, the outlook cheers up considerably with a sight of the green splash of the cultivated fields of Strath Ascaig. Even this ground was cleared for sheep in Innes's time, and it's worth remembering that many of the nowadays lonely and almost barren valleys of inland Wester Ross were well-farmed cattle grounds before the people were turned out to make way for sheep.

Sir Alexander Matheson turned none of his tenants out to make way for sheep or deer, but there were people in the district who thought he could have helped to bring back some of the population that had been evicted from these upland grazings. Farquhar Macrae, a shepherd at Bundalloch, pointed out that Sir Alexander's deer forests of Dorusduain and Killilan in Kintail, and this great sweep of Lochalsh Moor, had previously been the home of several families who made the estate good money from the sheep flocks. These three deer forests alone, he calculated, could support enough sheep to produce every year about two hundred thousand pounds of mutton and eighty-four thousand pounds of wool; but now they were reserved for sport. Lochalsh Moor itself was worked by only one gamekeeper; but Macrae could remember when it supported the families of four shepherds, three wintering shepherds, several other helpers, and also provided plenty of seasonal work at smearing and clipping. In the cattle days, of course, there had been countless more.

For a main road, this one from Auchtertyre to Strome is almost hilariously inadequate: narrow, none too well surfaced in parts, and provided with passing places. Over the bridge in Strath Ascaig, just beyond the Duncraig turn-off, it widens for a little, but only to go through the little forestry village of Achmore. This is the service village for South Strome Forest, but some of the houses in it, as elsewhere in the Highlands, have become surplus to the Commission's requirements. When the Achmore estate was bought over to be transformed into a state forest, most of the hill land was planted, but the arable farms were kept more or less intact. In the village, another road turns off to the left to run down the north side of the valley at Fernaig, a pleasant little lane with several fairly substantial houses along it, that finishes up before a bridge under the railway embankment at Fernaig Bay.

Walking on under the bridge towards the very stony shoreline reveals yet another splendid outlook over Loch Carron, this time from an unfamiliarly low level looking over to Plockton. A footpath to the right leads round the coast past a couple of shoreline farms, towards a place called Portachullin and on to Strome Ferry itself.

Portachullin was a particularly badly-hit place during the last century, after the people had been cleared to it from better ground inland, and then had their summer pastures barred to them. Their houses were pitiful, and always in some danger of being swept away in a storm. One of them complained bitterly to the Royal Commission of 1883 that for forty years they hadn't even been allowed to take the normal seaware from the shoreline as fertilizer for what bits of arable land they had, but were forced to go out in boats and grapple for the coarser weed four or five fathoms down. As manure it was almost useless. And this pathetic settlement had to support not only its normal crofting and fishing tenants, but seven families of landless squatters who had to scrape along as best they could.

Going back to Achmore, and continuing over the last hill to Strome, leads through more of the state forest to the summit overlooking the Strome narrows. Hereabouts there are great roadworks. To the right is the start of the new Strome Ferry bypass road that comes down through the Attadale estate on the shore of Loch Carron, and was finally opened, after various postponements, in October of 1970, four years after government approval of the long-overdue scheme was finally given. The new road, which was closed to traffic until after this book was written, swoops and dips up and down some very stiff gradients on the way to close the long-standing gap at Strathcarron. Part of the way, it uses the line of a forestry road. Some very suspicious local people feel that the soon to be abandoned railway line, which runs at the foot of the hills on the same side of the loch, is destined to become an extra carriageway of the new road; it is certainly rather odd that the bypass has been built with such a restricted width.

The main trouble in building it has been that the work along the steep hillsides of the South Strome Forest has tended to start landslides, and the roadmakers have been forced at one place to build a concrete apron out over the very exposed road and railway, which run almost together there, so that any rocks that come crashing down from above will simply bounce off the concrete roof and career into the loch without flattening any of the passing cars or railway coaches. Local opinion is that the new road will be very tricky in winter, when its one-in-seven gradients will sometimes be coated with ice. At the opening ceremony, a county official said that the road might not be very good, but it was the best they could do with the money available. Less than a month later a landslide blocked both railway and road.

As this book was being written, then, the way to the north still zoomed downhill from the new road works, through the sharp corners that take the road into Strome Ferry over a great railway cutting, the first obstacle that had to be reached when the line was extended to Kyle. Even in its busiest years, Strome wasn't a very big place: just a hotel, a post office and half a dozen houses hanging onto the steep slope to Loch Carron. From the hill, there's a fine view up the loch along the wooded Attadale shore, and over to the other side in the direction of the very long and strung-out village of Lochcarron itself. Generations of motorists have had plenty of time to sit and admire it, because the summertime queues for the ferry have often had to be seen to be believed, when two hours and more of a wait wasn't unknown; and there was really no way of avoiding the ferry, because to get to the north shore by road involved a journey of something like a hundred and forty miles, away back to Loch Ness-side and round by Beauly, Garve and Achnasheen.

James Hogg came to Strome during his tour in 1803, and discovered even then that the official ferry arrangements couldn't be short-circuited: 'There was a boat just coming to land, freighted from a house several miles up on the other side of the loch, by some people bound to the place from whence I came. I waited their arrival, thinking it a good chance, but in this I was mistaken. No arguments would persuade them to take me along with them. They alleged that it was depriving the ferryman of his right. But effectually to remove this impediment, I offered them triple freight, but they dared not to trust themselves with such a sum, for they actually rowed off, and left me standing on the rocks, where I was obliged to bellow and wave my hat for no small space of time. The ferryman charged sixpence and a dram of whisky.'

Over the years, the car ferries here, which never ran on Sundays, made a very handsome profit; and there's a cynical body of local opinion that thinks they could well still be needed in wintertime even after the new road is open.

Down at the ferry landing stage, which is close to the railway station that used to be the end of the Dingwall and Skye line, are some remains of an older pier. A story about a 'Sabbatarian riot' was given some prominence in Lowland newspapers in June 1883. It was a dispute about Sunday loading that grew to such an extent that police had to be drafted in from places as far away as Elgin, Perth and even Lanark, more than a hundred and fifty of them arriving by rail to deal with two thousand men of Wester Ross gathered at Strome for the second Sunday of the trouble; the whole thing petered out very peacefully when the Free Church ministers of the surrounding parishes came back from their Assembly in Edinburgh.

The best story about the place happened only a couple of years earlier, has a much more international ring about it, but is rarely mentioned nowadays in any detail. At the time, though, the mystery of the s.s. *Ferret* made very good reading. The *Ferret* was usually based at Strome, where she handled cargoes brought this far by rail on their journey to Skye and the Outer Isles. She was a coaster of three hundred and forty-six tons, fitted out for journeys in the heavy waters of the Minch and the Inner Sound. One day in 1880 the *Ferret* disappeared, and vanished more or less from human ken, despite cabled messages from her owners and worried consultations with her insurers' agents in ports all over the country.

Nothing at all seems to have been heard of the ship until June 1881, when readers of the London *Times* and the *Glasgow Herald* were informed by a Reuters telegram, sent almost four weeks before, that the steamer had been discovered as far away from her home port as was physically possible—at Melbourne in Australia: 'The reputed owner, the captain, and the purser of the steamer India, *alias* Ferret, have been arrested on a charge of forging the ship's register, and have been remanded. The discovery of a telegraphic code on board the vessel leads to the belief that there were accomplices in England concerned in the fraud.' And there, because of the rather clumsy method of getting news from the Australian colonies, the story was left for a full tantalizing week until it was the turn of the *Herald*'s own correspondent to have his ration of print and cable time again. The whole thing was fairly leisurely: the story broke in Australia at the end of April, and the correspondent's cable of 10 May reached Glasgow in time for the issue of 23 June.

Melbourne had its fair share of emigrant Scots, and one of them was a police constable who still kept in touch with the Glasgow papers. He saw the good ship *India* steaming quietly into Melbourne roads, and was struck by her resemblance to the *Ferret*, whose description had been widely reported back in Scotland. Along he went to the head of the port customs, and together they searched through Lloyd's register; there was no entry for a ship of that size under the given name, but it was described perfectly under the entry for the long-lost *Ferret*. A party of armed marines and police boarded the ship, arrested her crew, and moored her safely alongside a warship called the *Cerberus* so that there could be no sudden escape.

The three ringleaders were obviously Captain Wright, alias Carlyon; William Wallace, alias Walker, the purser; and a most ingenious character called at various times Henderson and Smith, who was supposed to be the owner. Obviously, the hijacking of the *Ferret* hadn't been intended as a short-term adventure; on board her were all kinds of forged documents and official stamps, even a small printing press for producing bogus bills of lading, and a fair supply of arms and ammunition. Most damaging of all, perhaps, was the discovery of a special telegraph code book, obviously designed for sending secret messages back to agents in Britain. The codes could hardly have been more incriminating. Among them were coded messages for: 'Everything wrong. No one contented. Dangerous.' 'Vessel seized. Everything U.P. Could destroy nothing.' 'Destroy everything, and be on guard. Failure.' 'Lloyd's agents will call to make inquiries. Be prepared as previously agreed upon.' 'Game is up; all discovered; destroy or hide everything, and make yourself scarce. Communicate with me through the arranged channel.' It was clear that the ordinary crew members didn't know what was going on, because the code book contained sinister entries implying that members of the crew might have had to be summarily disposed of.

It took a long time for the story of how the *Ferret* got halfway round the world to be pieced together; even then, only half of it was ever told. She had been stolen in the Clyde, and sailed from Greenock to Cardiff for coal and a new crew. On to Milford Haven, and then she sailed through the Bay of Biscay towards Gibraltar. There was a touch of the Keystone Cops about her approach to the Rock, because she didn't actually steam into the harbour, but passed within a couple of cable's lengths, with a board prominently displaying her original name pointed towards the dock. On she went into the Mediterranean, but as soon as darkness fell she whipped round, back the way she had come, and sailed out into the Atlantic again with all lights doused. This manoeuvre, of course, was intended to trap her expected pursuers into thinking she was heading for Suez; but after all that melodrama, nobody seemed to notice.

Henderson and Wright took her across the Atlantic in easy stages to Santos in Brazil, having changed her name to the *Benton* after slipping out past Gibraltar into the open sea. At Santos they picked up coal and a cargo of coffee for Cape Town. Unfortunately, they ran out of coal a few days from the Cape, but Henderson, never at a loss, ordered several hundred bags of coffee to be burned instead. Even with that reduced cargo, he sold the coffee for more than £10,000. Henderson got £2,000 in cash, and £8,000 in bills of exchange were sent to his mysterious principal in London.

The *Benton* sailed on into the Indian Ocean, tried unsuccessfully for a cargo of sugar at Mauritius, and came empty into Melbourne, now under the name of *India*. Perhaps because of the failure to pick up a cargo at Mauritius, Henderson tried to sell her. He was offered £8,500, but decided to hold out for £10,000, and the crew were busy freshening up her paintwork when the gendarmerie arrived. If he had accepted the first offer, he might well have got away scot free. Instead of that, he, the purser and the captain were tried, found guilty and sentenced to seven years' penal servitude each. The *Ferret* stayed in Australia, and was wrecked in a storm in 1920.

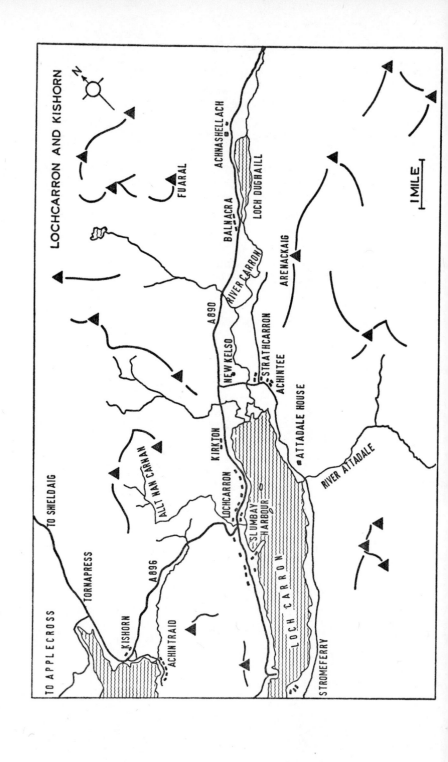

CHAPTER 9

LOCHCARRON AND KISHORN

EVEN AFTER THE CUSTOMARY WAIT on the south shore, it used to be a very pleasant trip across the narrows of Loch Carron on the Strome ferry. The cliffs on the seaward side look very grand from here, and there's a fine view towards the head of the loch, which stays much the same width all the way and is simply squared off as it gets near Strathcarron. The hills on the south-east or Attadale shore rise sharply and directly from the sea, the nearer slopes being part of the South Strome Forest, through which the railway and the bypass road are taken. The other shore, towards the village of Lochcarron, also has little in the way of level waterside ground, but the gradient is not so steep. Away in the background in every direction are great ridges and mountain peaks, often in the lonely reaches of the deer forests. As an example of that union of sea loch and mountainside that makes the West Highlands such a striking landscape, Loch Carron would be hard to beat.

On the north side of the narrows, just above the ferry slipway on the rocky shore, stand the shattered remains of Strome Castle, which is now in the care of the National Trust for Scotland. For a long time it was one of the strongholds of the Macdonells of Glengarry, whose territory was mainly farther south around Knoydart and the glen from which they took their name. In the 1600s the castle was besieged by one of the Mackenzie chiefs, who was pursuing the clan policy of adding more and more lands to their empire on the west coast. The little garrison held out, and Mackenzie was about to abandon the siege when one of his men, who had been a prisoner inside, suddenly leaped from the walls —laming himself for life in the process—and told him that the Macdonells' defence was finished. Some women held in the castle against their will had dumped water from the well into the barrels of gunpowder, which were now useless; there are, it need hardly be said, several more ribald versions of how they managed to soak the powder. The Macdonells asked for quarter, which Mackenzie granted, and then the castle was blown up.

James Hogg wasn't the only literary man to visit the narrows at Strome: sixteen years after his wearying attempts to get a ferry from the south side, Robert Southey arrived at the northern shore during his tour of the Highlands with Thomas Telford. He had been agreeably surprised by the state of the newly-built roads in Lochcarron parish, and mulled over how they had come to be built; throughout his diary of the tour, in fact, he was much more concerned with civil engineering than with poetical impressions of the passing scene: 'To hear of such roads in such a country, and to find them in the wild western Highlands is so surprising, everything else being in so rude a state, that their utility, or at least their necessity, might be doubted, if half the expenses were not raised by voluntary taxation. The Lairds indeed have one inducement for entering largely into the scheme, which explains what might otherwise seem, on their part, a lavish expenditure on such improvements. Large arrears of rent were due to them, which there was no chance of their ever receiving in money; but the tenants were willing to work for them, and so discharge the debt. When therefore the estimated expense of a road was 5000£, they received from Government 2500£, and the tenants did for them 5000£'s worth of labour; thus they were clear gainers by all which they received, and by the improved value of their estates.'

Telford and Southey's was the first carriage which had ever reached the ferry, such gentlemanly conveyances not having been seen in the district before; but if they thought they were about to have a quiet journey across to Lochalsh, they were sadly mistaken. Nobody could raise a ferryman, and the party just had to go back the way they had come. This delay allowed Southey to jot down some more observations about landowners in the Highlands and Islands. Not long before his visit, a character called Brown had held the job of factor for the vast Clanranald estates in the Western Isles. From 1796 to 1811 he controlled the finances of the estates for the Clanranald chief, who was up to his ears in debt, incurred mostly when he began to spend money like water to keep upsides with the aristocratic London society which he favoured; later on, Clanranald began selling off his patrimony island by island in an unavailing attempt to keep himself solvent. Brown's ideas about managing an estate, as recounted by Southey, must have seemed very attractive to the extravagant chief:

'Some years ago a villainous adventurer, by name Brown, made his appearance . . . professing that he had a "capability" of improving estates—not in their appearance, but in their rents. His simple secret consisted in looking at the rent-roll, and doubling, trebling, or even quadrupling the rent, according to the supposed capability of the tenant, without regard to any local circumstances, or any principal of common justice. Some Lairds allowed this fellow to make the experiment upon their estates, and it succeeded at first, owing to accidental causes. The war occasioned a great demand for black cattle; and the importation of barilla being prevented by the state of affairs in Spain, kelp rose to such a price that it enabled the tenants to pay the increased rent without difficulty. This brought Brown into fashion, and whole districts were brought under the ruinous system of rack-rent, in some instances even to a sixfold augmentation. The war at length was brought to an end; cattle and kelp fell to their former prices; the tenants were unable to pay; and some of the Lairds were at once unthinking and unfeeling enough to go thro' with their extortionate system, and seize their goods by distress. They suffered doubly by this: by the entire ruin which was brought upon their poor tenants; secondly by the direct consequence of the process. For, according to the forms of their law, they took the cattle at a valuation, in part payment of arrears; the valuation was made at the then market price, and before the cattle could be driven to market, there was a very considerable fall; so that, both causes operating, these grasping and griping landlords have gone far towards ruining themselves.'

Up from the slipway, and a little way after the roadside ruin of Strome Castle, is a minor road off to the left towards Ardaneaskan. In many parts of Wester Ross, some of the most attractive corners are the ones just off the main roads, and this is certainly the case here. The Ardaneaskan road was rebuilt and widened in the 1960s, but the character of it wasn't altered, and it remains one of the most beautiful byways in the whole county. It's a splendid up-and-down little road through the fringes of North Strome Forest, rising and falling above the rocky shore, which is seen in glimpses through the woodland to the left. There's a good view over to the wooded cliffs above Portachullin, and a sudden sight of the great crags above Duncraig, seen at an angle which is perhaps unsurpassed from any other viewpoint.

In places, the road to Ardaneaskan is not unlike the wooded sections of the one to Arnisdale, although without the same sense of exposure. There are dozens of little rocky bays down to the left, sometimes with boats moored nearby. Through the trees there are continual glimpses out past the tangle of islets around Plockton. Although it's a single-track affair with passing places, the surface is very good throughout. At one point the road suddenly widens out, but this seems to have been just a momentary burst of enthusiasm on the part of the contractors, because by the time a driver has shifted up a gear, it narrows back down again. There are traces here and there of the rather less prepossessing road that was used until about ten years ago. Although it goes through part of the plantations of the state forest, there are still many acres of the old hardwoods left. At a place called Port a' Mhairlich or Smugglers' Bay, there's a very pleasant picnic spot.

Ardaneaskan itself is the little strip of houses above the shore that is seen to such advantage from the Duncraig road. Following the habit of even the smallest West Highland settlements, it is divided into several different parts. The first has some very neat newer houses built along the shore, with some rented caravans down by the beach, and is set among some old crofting land. They were crofter-fishermen at Ardaneaskan in the old days, but now there is only one boat seriously engaged in the fishing trade. The second part is older, originally a purely fishing settlement, and there are still net-drying frames on the rocks by the water's edge. A little way farther on, the public road comes to an end at a parking and turning place looking out over the open loch to Plockton. The western skyline is still made up of the towering mountains of Applecross, the rocky islands show up very well, and there's a good view over to Skye except on the dullest days. An untarred road continues for a while up to the top of a hill, where three caravans are lucky enough to have an unsurpassed sea view, and there's a wee white cottage down by the shore that seems to sum up all the physical attraction of life on this wonderful West Highland coast.

Going straight on along the main road, and ignoring the

turning to Ardaneaskan, leads through a fine stretch of country, well wooded and with excellent views out to the mountains of the Attadale deer forest across Loch Carron. Over on the far side, among the plantations of South Strome Forest that sweep down to the water, there can be seen the difficult line of the new bypass road, although much of the traffic on it will be hidden by the trees. There's a very pleasantly situated old croft cottage on a green patch of ground at Ardnarff, now reached by a public road for the first time. Through a high, deep-cut gully above it, a single long waterfall dips gracefully to the sea.

Lochcarron Weavers, an enterprise financed by an earlier owner of the local estate, have a mill and shop to the right of the main road, and it isn't long afterwards that the first fringes of Lochcarron village appear, although there have been odd cottages and bungalows on the way from North Strome. It is still marked on some obsolete maps as Janetown or Jeantown, having been named after a girl friend of one of the Mackenzies of Applecross whose property used to extend for many miles to the east and west of here. The Applecross family were fairly well known for the number of unofficial liaisons in which they became involved.

This is just about the most pleasant village in the whole of Wester Ross. Scattered along three or four miles of road, it's a succession of very bright and well-kept houses, usually with flowery gardens proving that the local claim to a mild climate isn't just imagination. Although there are many older people in the village, because, as usual, there isn't much in the way of work for young folks, even in the forestry, Lochcarron has a livelier look about it than Plockton, which has all the marks of being mostly a summer holiday village. In Lochcarron too, there are many patches of crofting land still being worked, even if some of them are little more than vegetable gardens, or have been rented out to neighbours. There's plenty of very pleasant cottage accommodation available for visitors. The bright houses, and the splendid outlook over the loch to bank upon bank of mountain ridges beyond, give the whole place a very settled and comfortable air.

This first part of the village is actually called Slumbay, although nobody is very keen to use that name nowadays. Slumbay Harbour is little more than a name on the map now, a sheltered bay formed by a curving spit of land that protects it from the harsh movements of the distant sea; the little building at the top of the peninsula is a relic of the wartime Observer Corps network. On the south side of the old harbour is a line of houses in one of the most attractive situations in Wester Ross.

Slumbay means the Safe Bay, but the great days of the Loch Carron fishing, when hundreds of boats would take advantage of its protection, are long since gone. The Rev. Lachlan Mackenzie, writing about his parish in the late eighteenth century, had seen the place in its busiest days, but recalled in a rather detached and bloodthirsty way that even a glut in the fishing wasn't always an advantage: 'In 1791, there was a remarkable herring-fishing in this loch. During low water, the children . . . went often to the strand, and carried lapfuls of herring with them. The people fed entirely on fish. They were visited by a fever. Their blood was vitiated. When they were let blood in the fever, it had the appearance, when it congealed, of the blood of a boiled pudding, or of an ugly kind of jelly. Their breath smelled strong of fish. In proportion as they fed, soberly or voraciously on the herring, the fever was more or less severe. Such as lived mostly on fish, and other strong food, suffered dreadful agony. The poor people, that lived mostly upon water-gruel, suffered very little.'

In Mr. Mackenzie's day the centre of the village, if such a strung-out place can have such a feature, was a little way to the north, nearer the head of the loch. He didn't think much of the Lochcarron weather, and reported gloomily: 'The seasons are always wet in this place, but within these four years seem to be turning worse. Every thing is reckoned a sign of rain. If there be a warm or a hot day, we shall soon have rain; if the clouds be heavy, or if there be a mist upon the top of the hills, we shall see rain. In a word, a Highlander may make any thing a sign of rain, there is no danger he shall fail in his prognostication.' Nowadays, a fairly sure winter forecast is that if there's much snow on the ridge behind the village, the mountain road to Applecross, farther up the coast, will certainly be blocked.

Although the weather in Mr. Mackenzie's time may have been damp almost beyond endurance, it can't have been too severe; this mildness may have led to a feature of Lochcarron life about which he allowed himself the nearest thing to a good giggle that appears in his public writings: 'There are many instances of longevity in this parish. There have been likewise instances of some old couples in this parish, who have felt the sweet passions of love, after passing the grand climacterick. Their union has given rise to some curious anecdotes and verses, which would move the risible muscles, even of a cynick philosopher.' But he didn't dare give any examples.

By 1836 Jeantown, which is the main part of the present village, had begun to be built up; towards the end of the previous century there had been only three families living on that section of the lochside. The herring fishing had been declining steadily since about 1825, but the loch was by no means deserted by fishermen: 'In a calm summer evening, when hundreds of boats are seen shooting their nets, and scores of vessels lying at anchor, Lochcarron exhibits a scene of rural felicity and of rural beauty that is seldom to be witnessed.'

Although the village continued to grow, the fishing, at least on a commercial scale, faded out more and more. By the beginning of this century there were still half a dozen Lochcarron boats engaged in the inshore fishing, but now there are none at all. There's plenty of casual fishing, though, and visitors can hire boats for this and for picnic trips to some of the deserted islands in the lower part of the loch, beyond the narrows at Strome.

Getting towards the main part of the village, the road heads towards an irregular mountain summit a few miles to the north. This is Fuar Tholl or Fuaral, and it's often pointed out to visitors as Wellington's Face; but there's no point in looking for a normal profile view, because the Duke is lying on his back with his Roman nose pointing to the west. Fuaral is very nearly a Munro, missing that distinction by a regrettably small margin; since it's so high, the Duke's features are sometimes obscured by cloud.

The main part of the village—the old Jeantown—comes after a road junction where the left turn leads over a pass towards the district of Kishorn. Shortly, there's a sharp bend over a bridge, with another new settlement of those pleasant Ross-shire council houses over to the right. Beyond the bridge is the start of a long main street, the houses mostly to the left of the road with, later on, a wall down to the pebbly lochside shore on the other side; as in several other west coast villages, there's so little room behind the houses before the hillside begins, that washing is hung up from poles along the shore. There are several well stocked shops, some of them like miniature supermarkets, plenty of parking space and a useful information centre which, like the ones in Kintail and Kyle, keeps track of rooms available as well as providing the usual tourist information.   For the locals, though, the great attraction is the fine unrestricted view out over the loch to the mountains beyond; directly across the loch is the great valley that runs through the middle of the Attadale deer forest.   For much of the day, the sun pours down on the Lochcarron houses, which face in a handy direction only a few points east of south.   Out in the middle of the loch are a few rocky islets, on one of which, Sgeir Fhada, the Long Rock, a wedding was once celebrated. Nowadays there are more and more seals to be seen out there, which has not, of course, done anything to help the fishing.

Going northwards out of the village, the road passes the local garage, the biggest of the hotels and the modern primary school, and then heads towards the wide valley of Strathcarron, with majestic mountain peaks rising up all round the skyline.   Just about level with the start of the tidal area at the head of the loch, and before a little bridge, are the remains of the old parish church of Lochcarron, and a rather overgrown graveyard.   From here there is a splendid view over to the mountains of Attadale and, farther back, to the lonelier summits of the West Monar deer forest, especially to the spire of a shapely Munro exactly to the east and standing imperiously on the edge of the visible world.

The original church on this site was built in 1731 and given the name of the Great Church of Lochcarron, because it was so much bigger than the modest scale of Highland kirks in those days. The Presbyterian church of Lochcarron had a pretty wild history, as a result of the political and religious inclinations of the people of the parish.   In the early years of the Church of Scotland the reformed religion had many traces of Episcopalianism about it, and there were some places where the later modifications of the new regime were not regarded very highly.   Many of the Jacobite north-western parishes were strongholds of Episcopalianism, especially as the established church was no friend of the Stuarts, and when the Rev. Aeneas Sage was ordained as first Presbyterian minister of Lochcarron parish in 1726 he had a very rough time of it.   Only one family in the whole district came to his church; the rest of the people, staunch Jacobites in that time when the rebellions were not yet over, almost spat on the 'Whig minister'; his life was often in real danger; and things got so bad that, five years after his arrival, he petitioned the church authorities to remove him from his uncomfortable charge, thinking he would never be of any service in the place.

Writing in 1836, a local man wasted no time in laying about him concerning the previous generations who had treated the early ministers so roughly: 'No farther back than the middle of last century, the inhabitants of this district were involved in the most dissolute barbarity. The records of presbytery, which commence in 1724, are stained with an account of black and bloody crimes, exhibiting a picture of wildness, ferocity, and gross indulgence, consistent only with a state of savagism. The people, under the influence of no religion, but, from political considerations, attached to Episcopacy, conceived a rooted dislike of the Presbyterian system, which all the prudence of the clergy was for some time unable to eradicate.'

As with the similar quotation about Glen Elchaig noted in an earlier chapter, all this has to be approached with some caution. Jacobite feelings ran high in this part of the country, which in those days was included in the territory of the Earls of Seaforth; and the Church of Scotland was an open opponent of the Stuart cause. The Presbyterian ministers directed to these Jacobite parishes were hardly coming to convert the heathen, since the local people were quite happy with their own form of worship, but were seen as the advance guard of a political and sectarian attack.

For all its faults, the Church of Scotland of that time had one great advantage in these affairs: an unerring ability to direct to the dissident parishes its most devoted servants, men of unrelenting patience and strength of character, who could, when necessary, fight muscle with muscle and guile with guile. In Aeneas Sage, the Kirk hit upon one of its doughtiest heroes.

Lachlan Mackenzie, writing in the more peaceful days fifty years later, reminisced about his sturdy predecessor: 'The people were so barbarous, that they attempted to set fire to the house he was boarded in, at a time when there was a meeting of the clergy there. Such usage made it necessary for him, not only to make use of the sword of the Spirit, but likewise to have recourse to the arm of flesh. . . . Mr Campbell, Seaforth's factor, sent him once a challenge upon the morning of a Lord's day. Mr Sage knew his own situation, and accordingly, accepted the challenge. He went out with his claymore, and no sooner did he begin to draw it out of the scabbard, than Mr Campbell made a pair of heels, and did not look behind him for some time. . . . Mr Sage was subject to sudden starts of passion, and this was his great weakness.' In the circumstances, sudden starts of passion were just what the Lochcarron minister required.

In the end, despite his earlier plea to be taken away from this apparently hopeless charge, Aeneas Sage won his parishioners round, and served them well for forty-seven years before being laid to rest in the churchyard. His successor Lachlan Mackenzie was another individual character. There are many stories about his apparent gift of prophecy, and he seemed to have the second sight. There came a time when he took very ill, and a party of local men carried him through the mountains, across the pass on the near side of Fuaral, to the nearest doctor over in Torridon. On the way, the weakened minister asked them to look out for a spring that was often used by travellers over the hills. If the spring was burbling, he said, everything would be well; but if the water had dried up, they might as well stop, because he would never come back to his parish alive. The spring water had stopped flowing, and Mr Mackenzie, as he had foretold, never recovered.

By the 1830s the Great Church of Lochcarron had become so dilapidated that it was described as 'a miserable edifice, almost unfit for the exercise of public worship', and it was soon condemned. Now there are only parts of three walls of the roofless ruin still standing, and the present church is down at Jeantown, which, whatever else it may lack, certainly isn't short of churches for various denominations of Presbyterians. The old graveyard is partly overgrown, but the stones marking the graves of Mr Sage and Mr Mackenzie are still to be seen. Aeneas Sage lies under a flat slab on the south-west side of the church, and the mason who carved the stone was so affected that he cut an accidental extra letter into one of the words. Lachlan Mackenzie's grave is inside a railing, where he was laid on the return from his last journey over the hills in April 1819. The railing is kept freshly painted, and the memory of the man is kept fresh in the district too. He foretold that after his death a strange tree would grow over his grave, and there did indeed appear a curious little tree rather like an aspen, which nobody was able to identify for sure. In the last few years, though, it seems to have died off.

Beyond the old Kirkton of Lochcarron, the tidal area at the head of the loch is a mixture of tawny seaweed, rough grass and a variety of channels through the delta of the River Carron. Angling is good on the river, and both banks are controlled by the nearby Strathcarron Hotel. There's a little golf course that spreads over both sides of the road, with moderate fairways and nicely kept greens. Golf isn't the only sport in the district, because the Lochcarron shinty team is making a good name for itself in the junior league. There are farmlands to the left of the road, rising gently towards the foothills of the mountains to the north-west, and then a patch of peat moss. Sheep graze around both sides of the road.

It's important to realize here that there's a sharp difference between a Highland strath and a Highland glen. The wide lower valley of the River Carron, extending some way north-east from the head of the loch, is called Strathcarron, and the name implies a fertile valley floor between bordering mountain flanks. Farther up the course of the river, the landscape changes to a narrow groove between the mountains, with room for little more than the river and an occasional patch of farmland; and this is Glen Carron.

The main road hugs the north-west side of the strath, and soon comes to a junction where a B-class road turns right towards Strathcarron station, over the flat ground through which the river makes its final meanders to the loch. To the left, just before the station road crosses over the main channel of the river, is a place known as New Kelso. It got its name from a weaving operation that was started here in the late eighteenth century, an attempt to create a centre of the tweed industry just like Kelso in the Scottish Borders; but the project failed. It seems to have been from here, several years earlier, that General Wightman wrote his famous despatch about laying waste the rebel country after the Battle of Glenshiel, when this was part of the Seaforth territory.

During the early part of the next century, New Kelso market, held on the first Monday of June, was the only organised stock sale in the wide parish of Lochcarron; but by 1836 it had lost much of its previous importance: 'At one time, it was a considerable fair for cattle, but now it has dwindled into an annual term for settling accounts and drinking whisky'.

Later on, New Kelso was the scene of one of Sir Alexander

Matheson's attempts to ease his smaller tenants away from the unproductive business of subsistence-level crofting. Although some of his factors and managers didn't give the smallholders much opportunity to make a decent living, and although he would have been quite happy to see more of the crofters emigrating to give themselves a better chance abroad, he did devise a number of schemes to turn them from peasants into genuine farmers. In several places, he started club farms, which were created by merging a number of uneconomically fragmented crofts into a larger single farm in which all the original tenants had a £20 share, and which was run as a single unit. The tenants were given sound advice on farm management, which they did not always put into operation.

On his Easter Ross estates the club farm scheme worked very well; there was a prosperous example at Ardross, north of Dingwall. In Wester Ross two of these club farms were created, one at New Kelso and one at Sallachy on Loch Longside; but they were never anything like as successful as the one at Ardross. In evidence before the Royal Commission, Sir Alexander reckoned the trouble might well have been that the Wester Ross men just weren't as good farmers as those in the east, an opinion which through the years has raised some violent emotions on either side.

A little way beyond the New Kelso road-end comes the little settlement of Strathcarron, mostly a hotel, a railway halt and a terrace of houses that look as if they were built by the railway company but were actually put up by Attadale estate. A minor road off to the left beside the hotel wanders along the eastern edge of Strathcarron, bends over the railway at a rather casual crossing, and continues for a while towards the crofting lands of Arenackaig. To the right, banks of birches climb the steep slopes of the deer forest; to the left are narrow strips of arable land leading over to the windings of the Carron. The tarred public road comes to an end about two and a half miles from Strathcarron, by which time the narrowings of the glen at Achnashellach are clearly seen.

There's a modern automatic level crossing at Strathcarron, one of the few immediately obvious concessions to the 1970s to be seen on this line, which was built from Dingwall to Strome largely at the instigation of Sir Alexander Matheson, who was chairman of the railway company. Its fifty-three miles were built on an easy route which cost only £330,000. The road then goes over

21 The whitewashed houses of Shieldaig, with the North Applecross hills behind

22 A pine marten exploring in Glen Torridon

23 Winter on Mullach an Rathain, with the houses of Torridon village crouched at the water's edg

another river and past the little farming settlement of Achintee, and this is the northern end of the Strome Ferry bypass that was finally opened in the autumn of 1970. There always was a road of sorts from Strathcarron to Attadale House, but the new one is a much more satisfactory affair which, in its early stages, goes alongside the railway line that hugs the shore at the tidal area near the head of the loch. Looking along the eastern edge of Loch Carron from here, there's a rather fine view down towards the folds of the low but striking ridges that hide the narrows at Strome. Looking directly across the loch, the view is to the rather shapeless lump of Glas Bheinn, the mountain behind the old Kirkton of Lochcarron, and, farther to the right, a selection of spikier peaks in the Ben Damh deer forest; there are Munros galore here, and a surprising number of summits that fail to meet that mark by only a tiny amount.

Beyond Achintee the railway keeps right down alongside the loch, but the new road has to soar steeply over the top of an unbreachable cliff to reach the valley of the River Attadale. It's a very stiff climb indeed round the shoulder of a hill, from the top of which there's a pleasant outlook over the white cottages of Lochcarron village, the cultivated land behind it, and across the little pass that takes a main road from there to Kishorn. Downhill again towards Attadale House, with a patch of young forest to the left, and it still looks as if the loch must be landlocked down at Strome. If anything, the new road is steeper downhill than it was coming up, and it will be no easy drive in a wild winter.

Beside the Attadale railway halt there are woodlands to the left that shelter Attadale House from searching winds or prying eyes. There are splashes of colour from banks of rhododendrons and then, in the valley of the River Attadale that comes down a steeply-guarded course from the wilds of the deer forest, a wide spread of well tended arable land, protected from marauding deer by the usual unjumpable fence. There are craggy rock faces on the north side of the glen, and a tremendous view of mountain ridge succeeding mountain ridge, away to the east by Killilan, Monar and Kintail.

Mathesons were at Attadale for several generations before the family fortunes waned in the early part of the last century, but this was one of the properties bought back by Sir Alexander. It was sold off in the time of Sir Kenneth Matheson to Baron Schröder, member of a famous London banking family. The title was Prussian, and the Schröders wisely gave it up during the first world war. In their time the Attadale fishing and deer stalking were sternly preserved against intrusions by local poachers; but it is recalled with a quiet smile that the various river watchers and gamekeepers couldn't be in a thousand places at once. The Schröders were very enthusiastic tree planters, and the pleasant surroundings of the mansion house owe a great deal to their activities. After their time the estate changed hands a couple of times, and is now owned by a Macpherson family. An estate track leads away up the glen and through the mountains towards Bendronaig Lodge, which is in a very remote area more than halfway to Loch Monar; it has been said that the deer forest should really be called Bendronaig instead of Attadale, but that's rather an academic argument. One story about Bendronaig concerns Bonnie Prince Charlie, who is supposed to have spent some time hiding in the wilds of the mountains there; but, although it has plenty of circumstantial detail, other accounts make no mention of his ever having been near the place.

The bypass road continues beyond the bridge across the Attadale River, but as this book was being written traffic was not allowed any farther. There's another stiff climb away above the lochside from here, over to the little croft of Ardnarff by another brae that local opinion suggests will need careful driving in winter, and then a final stretch to the top of the hill above Strome. It's proof of how long this road has been in the planning and building that there's a man still living in Lochcarron village who worked at the original survey—more than seventy years ago.

Back down on the main Lochcarron road, ignoring the Attadale turning, leads along the west side of the strath towards the splendidly Highland place names of Achnashellach and Achnasheen. For a while the road has maintained the adequate double width with which it leaves Lochcarron, but it soon comes back down to single-track. In front of the scree slopes on the southern edge of an outlier of Fuaral, it crosses a bridge over one of the Carron's tributaries, which comes down from the mountains through the pass over which Lachlan Mackenzie made his last strange journey. To the right of the road is a rather ugly quarry.

The strath gets perceptibly narrower as the road proceeds farther up the windings of the Carron. The next settlement at Balnacra is just a little hamlet beside a level crossing over the single-track railway, at the foot of Loch Dughaill. Hereabouts the strath turns very firmly into a glen, and on the far side of the loch there are steep hillsides rising up through old natural woodlands. The rest of the mountainsides are mostly covered by the plantations of the state forest of Achnashellach.

In the old days, one of the clan chiefs had a house on an island in the middle of the loch, but it's a long time since this part of Wester Ross had a Scottish proprietor. Achnashellach was once part of the vast estates of the Mackenzies of Applecross, whose property extended far to the east of the district that's called Applecross today. In the middle of the last century, the whole of this Mackenzie territory was sold off to the Duke of Leeds, who later split it into various minor divisions. At that time the whole estate covered 144,000 acres, and the Duke of Leeds paid rather less than a pound an acre. In the 1860s and 1870s the whole area was sold off in smaller lots; Achnashellach was stalked for a while by a man called Tennant, who entertained the Prince of Wales at a deer drive on 5 October 1870. There was said to have been good sport, with nineteen fine beasts accounted for; also almost accounted for was the future King Edward VII, because he narrowly escaped injury in a rockfall at one of the corries on the north side of Fuaral. Soon after that, Achnashellach was sold to Sir Ivor Guest, later Lord Wimborne, who was the owner of considerable estates in Dorset. It was during his ownership that the railway came through to Strome, and the present Achnashellach halt was originally provided for his private use. Later on, the property was sold again to Emerson Bainbridge, who had begun his career as a mining engineer, then became a colliery owner and railway company director in Yorkshire. He was Member of Parliament for a Lincolnshire division, and was well known south of the border as a philanthropist.

After the first world war, the Achnashellach estate passed from the ownership of the succession of sportsmen who had owned it for the previous seventy years, and had been interested in little more than the deer stalking, and loch and river fishing. It was bought over by the Forestry Commission, and the planting of the lower mountain sides began. Recently, the high ground

where conifers won't survive was taken over by a member
of one of the Wills families, and is used for deer stalking once
again.

There's a very pleasant wooded approach through shaded banks
of rhododendrons to the gates of Achnashellach Lodge. Guarding
the entrance are two of those curious Wellingtonia trees from
whose rubbery bark a blow will simply bounce back. A little
wooden bridge over the main road was built by the owner of the
house so that his dogs wouldn't have to negotiate the light traffic
to get down towards the river. Beyond the lodge is the rough
road up to Achnashellach station. From the road-end there's a
splendid view of the bare rocky crags and buttresses on the north
side of Fuaral, in one of which Edward VII almost came to a
sticky end. There are snow patches in the gullies well into late
June in most years. The whole effect is quite different from the
green slopes of the forestry ground, but it's as well to remember
that fifty years ago the whole district looked like that.

The road that's marked on the one-inch map going over the
Coulin Pass towards the estate of Coulin, which is another Wills
property, is a private one, although a right of way was established
after a long and often bitter dispute between the wars. The road
was built by an earlier proprietor to connect his shooting lodge
with the useful Strathcarron railway. Higher up Glen Carron is
more deer stalking ground beyond the Forestry Commission
property. There's a roadside loch there called Loch Sgamhain,
which got its rather curious name of the Loch of the Lungs
because of an old story that's almost identical with the one about
John MacInnes's Loch in the hills above Glenelg.

Following this main road leads to an important junction and
railhead at Achnasheen, but it can't be pretended that this inland
part of Wester Ross is as attractive or interesting as the coastal
districts. To continue along the direct coast road to the north
means going back into Lochcarron village, and turning uphill
along the road to Kishorn. It's a fairly steep, narrow road that
climbs up to the top of a bare windy moorland of rough grass
and heather. On the way it passes the entrance to a house with
the incongruous name of Patagonia; this may recall the exploits
of an old Scottish settler in South America, because several of
them became involved in the Argentinian government's 'civiliz-
ing' programme in the middle years of the last century, when the

going rate for shooting Patagonian Indians out of hand was £1 per head.

Away to the west a great towering peak appears on the skyline, but it's actually another end-on view of a distant ridge, this time guarding the entrance to the Pass of the Cattle and the spectacular mountain road over to Applecross. The Kishorn road begins to head westwards away from the course of the Allt nan Carnan, the little river of whose narrow final valley it took advantage to climb up from Lochcarron. In the higher reaches of the river, on the slopes of the rounded mountain to the north, the Nature Conservancy have established a small reserve. The Allt nan Carnan gorge houses a varied collection of pine, rowan, aspen, ash, elm, oak, birch and so on, and the Conservancy carries on studies of the trees and plants which it hopes will be of use in other larger reserves.

Going downhill on the west side of the little pass, the right-hand side of the road becomes rocky, with crags and scree and loose boulders. This kind of country looks much greener in summer than it does earlier in the year, thanks partly to the thin covering of grass and perhaps more to the sad rank growth of bracken. There's a fine long waterfall in a gully up to the right, and then a plunge down to a Z-bend over a bridge; in this part the glen becomes much steeper, narrower and, in suitable weather, rather more forbidding. With the mountains of Applecross still filling the skyline ahead, there comes a sight of some woodlands, and then the valley opens out, with cultivated fields down by the river on the left of the road. It's characteristic of the limestone outcrops which occur here and there on this coast that there should be pockets of good soil among the generally rough country of the mountain slopes.

There's some new forest planting to the left of the road as it comes into the casual little hamlet of Kishorn, right at the head of the loch of the same name. There are two roads off to the left, which merge and continue past the little 'suburb' of Ardarroch, round the edge of the tidal bay to Achintraid. Ardarroch is just a line of cottages above a rocky shore, with lobster pots and net-drying frames here and there, and a most magnificent outlook straight down the loch, with the lonely mountains of Applecross on the right and the gentler wooded slopes round to Loch Reraig and Ardaneaskan on the left. At the mouth of the loch, where it joins the grander waterway of Loch Carron, lie Kishorn Island and a batch of satellites. It was here one day in May 1719 that the *Assistance* and *Dartmouth* came to lie at anchor while the rest of Captain Boyle's squadron knocked lumps out of Eilean Donan Castle.

Through the opening of the loch there can sometimes be seen the mountain peaks of Skye. Looking slightly north of west, the view is to a great series of towers and ridges over at the edge of the Applecross country, and it still seems unlikely that there can possibly be a motorable road snaking its way through that tangle of dizzy peaks. On that whole imposing shore across the loch there is only one patch of arable land to be seen, at the little farm of Russel, with a white wandering stream coming scrambling down the mountainside towards the house.

There's a pleasant sweep of grazing land round the head of the bay to Achintraid, which is in a most pleasant lochside situation. To the left of the road in the village is a youth hostel, about whose position the Ordnance Survey map and Bartholomew's half-inch currently argue; Bartholomew's is more up to date. The public road ends soon afterwards, having curved up a short hill towards some cottages below the crofting land at the far end of this little settlement, at the start of the lochside woodlands that sweep round the indentations of the coast by Reraig and Ardaneaskan to the north side of the narrows at Strome.

Back at Kishorn village, the main road north continues through woodlands and cultivated fields past the ruined mansion of Courthill House, which stands in a sorry condition behind a wall to the left of the road. In the old days of the Mackenzies of Applecross, there was a substantial family of Macdonalds of Courthill, and the old mansion later became the centre of the Lochcarron estate that was carved out of the older and much more extensive Applecross property. The estate of Lochcarron runs from the village and the Strome narrows, in a northerly direction beyond Kishorn right up to Shieldaig on the shores of Loch Torridon. It was owned for a while in the last century by Sir John Stewart, who turned the crofters' hill grazings into deer forest, and then passed into the hands of Charles Murray, Member of Parliament for Hastings. The Murrays, very popular landlords, held the Lochcarron estate for many years, disposing of it only in 1945 to Alexander Greg, the present owner. Although the northern part of the estate is made up of the Glenshieldaig deer forest, the stalking is usually rented out, because Mr Greg's own interest is in angling. When he bought over the estate he sold Courthill House, which had been the Murrays' local residence, to a firm of demolishers, the rates on a mansion of this size being very high. The demolishers did rather well out of the job, and are said to have covered their costs by the price of the lead that was stripped from the roof.

Kishorn wasn't always a purely agricultural district. In his Statistical Account of 1836, the Rev. Roderick McRae mentioned that there had once been a copper mine here that produced high quality ore. He hoped that Mackenzie of Applecross would re-open it, 'as that might considerably benefit his own family, and afford employment and support to persons who now lose their time in sloth and wretchedness'. But Mackenzie had worries enough of his own, and it wasn't long before the whole district passed into the hands of sporting landlords who were not remotely interested in any mining potential.

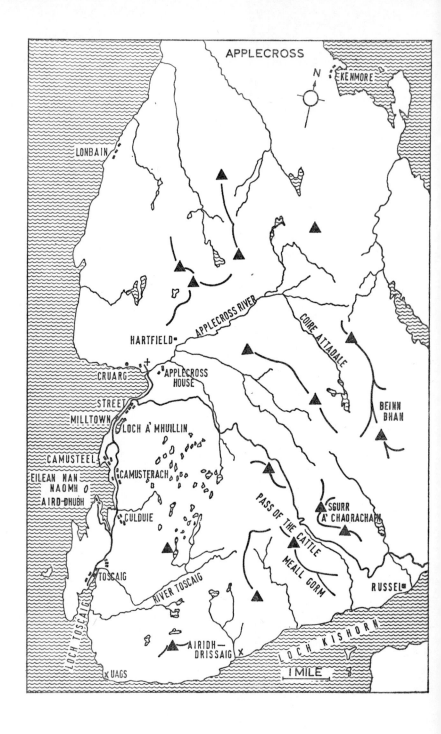

CHAPTER 10

APPLECROSS

BEYOND COURTHILL HOUSE the main road runs along a ledge just above the east side of Loch Kishorn. Soon the lochside bears away to the left, and the road runs beside a burn that comes down from the Lochcarron hills; after a double bend across the burn there comes the farmhouse of Tornapress, before which is a side road to the left, the only way for a motorist to reach the heart of the wild mountain country of the Applecross peninsula.

After crossing the low-lying farmland at the head of the loch, the Applecross road turns sharp left over the River Kishorn, and begins the gentle introductory assault on one of the most spectacular mountain roads in Britain, which rises to a summit at 2,053 feet only six miles or so after leaving the shore of the sea loch. Straight ahead from the approach to the river is the south-west side of Beinn Bhan, steep-rising slopes of bare rock, boulders and heather that sum up the appearance of much of the interior of this giant Applecross peninsula. There's a very fine view over the loch to the ruins of Courthill House and the fertile fields of the Kishorn limestone country. Beyond a turning down by the shore to the farm and stalker's house at Russel that's seen so clearly from Ardarroch way, the road climbs to the right over the shoulder of a hill, past some new tracks being built through the deer forest, and suddenly comes to a most impressive view of the towering summits that guard the entrance to the stiffest part of the Pass of the Cattle. To the right is the great chunky outline of Sgurr a' Chaorachain, the Shepherd's Peak, with another similar summit lying just behind; as happens so often with views of the Applecross peaks, this is really the end of a long winding ridge that reaches its highest point more than two thousand feet above the road. Over the lower slopes of the hill, across which the road makes its snaking way, is an entirely different view to Meall Gorm, a similarly scaled ridge that is seen in full face as a series of towers and gullies; as this ridge disappears to the right, there's a line of cliffs above the still invisible final valley that leads to the Pass of the Castle. It takes some time for the narrow road to round the shoulder of Sgurr a' Chaorachain, but when it finally does there is a most magnificent view up the precipitous valley that leads to the summit. The road hugs a ledge on the north side, and the gradient becomes much stiffer; for most of the way there's an adequate view ahead, but in one or two places there are half-hidden loops round which another car may suddenly appear. All the way from Tornapress to Applecross, it need hardly be said, the road is single-track, although there are enough passing places to make driving in traffic fairly simple; if there are ten cars in thirty minutes during the holiday season, the traffic is reckoned to be very heavy.

On the far side of the great ravine, the sides of Meall Gorm are seen to be formed of a succession of buttresses and deep-cut gullies, with sloping grassy ledges angled across the face. The near side is precipitous in the extreme, with scree runs and boulders above the road and, rather nerve-wrackingly, exactly the same effect below. There's a retaining wall at places on the right, and sturdy crash barriers most of the way along the outside. The series of hairpins by which the road reaches the steep sided saddle that leads towards the invisible summit of the pass can be seen for a mile or two along the approach.

The top of the road is marked on some maps as the Bealach nam Bo, and on others as the Bealach na Ba; both mean the Pass of the Cattle, and the second is said to be more accurate Gaelic. Applecross folk themselves talk about reaching the outside world by going 'over the Bealach'; the pronunciation is roughly *byaallach,* with the accent on the drawled first syllable and the *l* sounded farther forward than in English. Years ago, the Bealach was a hard test for any car, and there are still tales of passengers who become so nervous at going over the summit that they chicken out and take a ferry back to Kyle of Lochalsh rather than face the journey again. In fact, the final assault on the highest part of the pass, with the road twisting and turning through a series of hairpins, is one of the more exhilarating moments in Scottish motoring.

From the hairpins, the view back down towards Loch Kishorn is most impressive, with the narrow road climbing wearily up from sea level and completely dominated by the beetling cliffs that frown over it. This outlook may be one of the clichés of Scottish mountain photography, but it still manages to raise a thrill long after the novelty of it has worn off.

The actual summit of the road is some way beyond the hairpins, at a point 2,053 feet above the sea. It's well worth parking the car and having a wander around to look over this vast, wild, empty landscape. Near the top of the pass are some stone cairns; but they aren't a sign that there are Buddhists over at Applecross, or even relics of the old habit at Highland funerals of piling stones at the points along the coffin road where the cortège rested. The cairns were just built haphazardly by modern travellers, and have no special significance.

To the right of the road at the summit, there's a view into the empty hills, towards another saddle that separates two roadless glens. The valley that goes south-east from this saddle leads down to Russel on the shores of Loch Kishorn, while the other one drops north-west into a steeply guarded glen known as Coire Attadale. More than a hundred years ago, when an owner of the Applecross estate took off the roof of the mansion house, it was discovered that the original slates had been fixed on, not by metal nails, but by pegs of heather root; to make them, a man had worked all summer in Coire Attadale, ripping up the heather and carving the pegs with a knife. In those days it seems to have been the habit, since metal nails were so scarce in this district, for Applecross people who had occasion to travel across the country to Dingwall or Inverness to bring back a pocketful of them for their coffins.

The outlook from this high viewpoint is mostly of bare rock and boulders, with sparse vegetation of grass and heather scattered amongst them. Before the heather blooms, there isn't much colour about the great deserted wasteland; the camouflage is perfect for deer, which are often seen by the roadside out of the stalking season. Out to sea there's a splendid view over Raasay and the mountains of Skye, and the smaller islands in the Inner Sound. South of the road the wild moorland is full of tiny lochans, sixty of them in sight at one time, which are scattered over the landscape like silver coins shining in the sun. There are brown trout in almost all of them, and no restrictions on angling. Perhaps the Bealach is at its most exciting on a day of cloud and mountain mist, when none of these details can be seen at all and the visibility is down to a dozen car's lengths: occasional traffic looms up out of the murk, headlights showing practically nothing but the smir of rain sweeping over the road, and the sound of its passing soon smothered in the ghostly vapour. At a lower level, the cloud seeps down through the giant corries.

In the old days of the Mackenzies of Applecross, whose massive estate included not only the 80,000 acres of the modern Applecross property, but the whole district of Lochcarron and Achnashellach as well, most of the people of the Applecross peninsula had grazing rights in the great mountain valleys. According to the Rev. John McQueen, writing about his parish in 1792: 'Black cattle is the great article, from which the farmer principally derives his emolument, and the landlord his rent.' There were something like three thousand cattle in the district; Mackenzie of Applecross's tenants were never behind with their rents. Even at that time, of course, the hills abounded in red deer, but the proprietor hadn't turned the place into a hunting preserve, since it was big enough to allow him to have his sport and his tenants to graze their cattle on the hills in summer without the two interests clashing. Times changed, however, and Applecross followed the pattern of most other West Highland estates. In the middle of the last century the Mackenzies sold off the whole of their 144,000 acre property to the Duke of Leeds, from Hornby Castle in Yorkshire; the price was £135,000. The new owners didn't keep Applecross itself for long, although they held onto the other lands for a while. In the 1860s Applecross proper was bought over by another wealthy Yorkshire landowner, the eighth Lord Middleton, and this family controlled the estate for several generations.

It was after the Middletons arrived that Applecross became first and foremost a deer forest, strictly preserved against incursions by any other interest; this rule applied even when the Middletons did not themselves do much stalking, but rented the forest out. At that time, many of the people in Applecross were Roman Catholics, but Lord Middleton is said to have forced them to change or leave their houses.

That first Middleton landlord died in 1877, and it was noted of his successor Digby Wentworth Bayard Willoughby, the ninth Earl, that a few years later he had estates in Yorkshire, Nottinghamshire, Lincolnshire, Warwickshire, Derbyshire and Ross-shire, with a total rent-roll of no less than £54,014 per year; but the Applecross estate, which was by far the largest single property, was worth only £1,957.

The ninth Earl died in 1922, but his heir had been killed at the Battle of Jutland, and he was succeeded by his brother. A series of sudden deaths in the family led to hefty demands for death duties, and Applecross was sold off in 1929, to become yet another of the Wills estates; the present owner is Major John Wills.

The far side of the pass is not nearly so dramatic as the climb from Loch Kishorn, but a roadside shed that usually has a snow-plough outside is a good reminder that the Bealach—very nearly the highest public road in Scotland, and beaten only by the Cairnwell above the Devil's Elbow—is often blocked by snow in winter. In the winter of 1969/70, which was particularly severe on these high slopes, the road was blocked as many days as it was open from October all the way through to March. There's a blower snowplough, which often gets clogged by the wet snow it can't digest too well; and local people who have lent a hand with the clearing remember many days when a short 'tunnel' of road has been cleared, only to be engulfed soon afterwards by snow drifted across it by the driving wind. Even when there isn't much snow, the Bealach is often made very dangerous by long slivers of ice.

As the road goes down through the dun-coloured moorland, there is nothing but the metalled surface and the accompanying telephone wires to point to any trace of human occupation or activity; for nearly a dozen miles after Russel there are no houses or crofts or cultivated fields: nothing but the great empty heart of the deer forest. Suddenly, the eye is caught by a flash of emerald green away in the distance; just appearing in a fold of the hills are the rich arable fields around the Applecross River, in the floor of the valley which shelters the estate mansion house.

It takes a little longer to reach them, though, during which time people with memories of the early 1950s may find the surroundings somehow familiar. The classic film comedy *Laxdale Hall* was made at Applecross, some years before the Bealach was given its first-ever coating of tarmac; the great chase after the poachers was filmed around this part of the road, other scenes were shot in the village down at the west side of the pass, and Applecross House played its true part as the laird's mansion.

Down towards the lower reaches of the pass, the fields and woodlands around Applecross House are seen to the right of the road, which begins to run through normal farming country for which the wilderness of the Pass of the Cattle is an unlikely introduction. The home farm here used to be one of the most productive and best run in the West Highlands, but some of it, as well as ground a little higher up the road, has been turned over to forestry.

Most of the Applecross people used to live in the glen, where they had crofts and larger cattle farms; but they were cleared off to the coast, where they had to build new houses for themselves. The Rev. Roderick McRae wrote in 1836 that there were three thousand people in the whole of the parish, of whom only thirty or so were on the poor roll; but since there was very little money in the poor fund, there wasn't much advantage in being entered on the roll, and the statistic wasn't worth very much.

Towards the final stretch of the Bealach road there's a sharp bend to the right beside some farm buildings, straight on from which is a recently established camping site. The public road continues down through a wooded stretch—the Applecross House policies were long ago planted with a fine variety of ash, elm, larch, fir and so on—and comes very shortly to a junction at the side of Applecross Bay. Turning right leads past the entrance to the big house and round the head of the bay.

It's a very pleasant part of the district along this way, with the curving public road backed by all manner of trees in the policy ground of the big house. The main entrance to Applecross House is at the north-east corner of the bay, where the public road swings round to the left, and traces of an old fish trap can be seen off the shore. There's a most magnificent picnic area on the grass right at the head of the bay, among a scattering of birches, with a splendid view out to the south-west, towards the presumptuous little summit of Dun Caan on Raasay, and the much grander peaks of Lord Macdonald's Forest and the Black Cuillin on Skye. At low tide there's a fine sandy beach, with crescents of sea water left behind on the ebb. When the Rev. John McQueen was writing his account of the parish in 1792, he could say that everybody in the place went fishing: the farmers all had boats of their own, and the smaller crofting tenants would club together and operate them in groups. The herring fishing had gone back, and with low prices at the cattle sales, the people were having rather a bad time. In Mr McRae's time, forty years later, the people would come down to the strand with peat creels, which they managed to fill with a great number and variety of cockles, mussels and other shellfish.

Behind the picnic area are the woodlands and fields around the mansion house. During the time of the Middletons' ownership, and for several years afterwards, the home farm, deer forest and mansion house provided a fair amount of work for local people. In 1929 there were more than twenty men working for the estate, including nine gamekeepers; the amount of work available has gone down with the changing times, and there is now only one full-time keeper. Since there are fewer estate men about the hills, foxes have become less controlled, and are now a real menace to the crofting tenants: in many of the crofting townships, lambs have to be taken indoors to be hand-fed during the early weeks of their life, because they would otherwise soon be killed by marauding foxes. There's trouble too from pine martens, which were previously never seen on the low ground, but have begun to go after different prey, the local people think, since myxomatosis cut down the rabbit population; now they occasionally break into henhouses and make a meal of some of the inmates.

At the turn of the century, and right up to the second world war, the estate proprietors, who for the last hundred and fifty years have lived in the south and paid more or less occasional visits to the district, supplied all that the people needed in the way of essential equipment and materials for their crofts and houses. It used to be the habit during the stalking season for all the dozen or so crofting townships on the Applecross estate to be given a stag to be cut up for meat; then it became a haunch to each household; and for the last few years the old custom has lapsed, although the local people can buy venison in season at a very reasonable price from the estate store. In years gone by the owners of the estate used to go stalking for a spell every season at Coulin, the deer forest north of Achnashellach, and took portable huts with them; now the huts have been converted into the garages at Applecross House.

There's a bridge over the River Applecross just above the point where it flows over a rocky course into the bay. When Augustus Grimble was writing his book *The Salmon Rivers of Scotland* before

the first world war, he was able to note: 'Lord Middleton preserves it strictly, as it runs through the deer forest . . . it is fished
only for about a mile above the mouth. It is one of the very few
west coast rivers that has not altered very much for the worse
during the past forty years. This is because Lord Middleton
neither works nor lets any fixed nets on his foreshore, while he
has a sharp lookout kept for poachers. Convictions have been
obtained on several occasions.' Nowadays the position is much
easier, and visitors can rent the fishing for a small fee. Access to
the hills and to the multitude of tiny mountain lochs and pools
is unrestricted; but it would be unfair to wander about the
stalking grounds unannounced during the stag season.

A little farther on, the tarred public road comes to an end
beside the old parish church and manse. Most of the early
history of Applecross comes from ecclesiastical writings, because
it was here that St Maelrubha—the *bh* is silent—founded one of
the earliest Christian churches in the north. Like that more
famous seventh-century cleric St Columba, Maelrubha came from
Ireland; he is said to have been descended from one of the great
Irish kings, Niall of the Nine Hostages. In 673 he founded a
church at Applecross, and went about his missionary work in
many parts of Ross-shire until his death in 722. Loch Maree,
the most beautiful inland waterway in the north-west, took its
name from him. Maelrubha is supposed to have been buried in
the old churchyard, about a thousand years before the present
building was raised. In the old days, Applecross folk who were
about to begin a dangerous journey would take with them a
pinch of soil from near his grave. For hundreds of years
after his death, Applecross was a sanctuary where fugitives
were guaranteed safety; the Gaelic name of the place, in fact, is
A'Chomaraich, the Sanctuary.

In the later days of the Mackenzies of Applecross, the church
here was in a pitiable condition: the Rev. John McQueen, writing
in 1792, noted that it had been condemned in 1788 but was still
the only place for public worship in the parish. For a time the
parish of Applecross included the whole of the modern district
of Lochcarron, and the local minister was a man of wide influence.

As a remote district, Applecross was particularly susceptible to
the doctrinal arguments that raged rather fruitlessly in Scotland
during the nineteenth century. Mr McRae wrote rather huffily

4 The mountains of the Ben Damoh and Coulin deer forests seen from the hillside above Inveralligin

25 Dick Balharry, warden of the Beinn Eighe nature reserve, feeding a young golden eagle

26 Looking out over Loch Torridon from Wester Alligin

in 1836: 'Religious knowledge has no doubt been increased of late; but it is questionable if moral improvement had kept pace with that knowledge. Supposed knowledge puffeth up many, but it unfortunately appears, that they are very deficient in that charity which edifieth. There are also disputes and hurtful divisions which may, in many cases, be ascribed to the conduct of improper teachers employed by well-meaning Societies, both in the metropolis and other places, who are unacquainted with the state of the Highlands, and misled by the reports of interested persons and busy bodies. And it is a matter of much regret, that no small share of these remarks applies to the case of superintendants and catechists, under the ludicrous denomination of local missionaries, though ignorant and illiterate, employed by so respectable a body as the Highland Missionary Society.' In those days, with the very poor travelling facilities in the remoter districts, partially qualified preachers had to be employed; but Mr McRae's exasperatingly oblique remarks were signs of the great schism that was to come upon Scottish churchgoers. The established Church of Scotland and the breakaway Free Church both claimed a substantial number of adherents in these parts of Wester Ross which, as mentioned in the Lochcarron chapter, had been firmly Catholic or Episcopalian not eighty years before; and there is still a division at Applecross today, as throughout the north-west Highlands, complicated by twentieth-century fragmentations and reunions.

The old parish church here was abandoned many years ago, and it suffered during the second world war when thieves stripped the lead from its roof. Today, however, it is completely rebuilt inside; but the renovation has nothing to do with any of the courts of the Kirk. In April 1964 Major Wills, as chairman of the central executive committee of the Dockland Settlements, opened the one-time shooting lodge of Hartfield, which lies on the west side of the Applecross River some way above the mansion house, as the West Highland School of Adventure. It operates month-long courses in outdoor activities like sailing, canoeing, trekking and rock climbing, and is open to boys from Scotland or from the areas in which the Dockland Settlements work, who are sponsored by local authorities, schools, youth clubs, industrial firms and so on.

In 1970 the estate decided to renovate the interior of the old

parish church, which had long since been replaced by a new
building in another place. There are still plain stone walls inside,
with new roof beams from which hang electric lights in the form
of old oil lamps. A plain but beautifully kept building, it is used
for church services held by the Adventure School.

Beyond the church an unsurfaced track leads by the house of
Cruarg at the side of the bay before launching itself up a steep
hill and heading for the series of cut-off hamlets on the north-
west coast of the peninsula, looking out over the Inner Sound to
Raasay, South Rona and Skye. There are settlements at Lonbain,
Kalnakill and Cuaig on that coast, and beyond the north-western
tip of the peninsula five more. The three western townships have
never had a proper road, and it wouldn't do to be misled by the
apparent suitability for motor traffic of the first stretch of the
track above Cruarg. It was widened in 1968 by a party of army
engineers; the local people were under the impression that the
engineers would be back every year to make more improvements,
but they have never reappeared. Before the top of the hill, the
track deteriorates again to little more than a bridle track, the way
marked by unexpected telephone poles. The Free Church
minister, local shepherds and some other hardy souls are prepared
to travel along it on motor cycles, but it is really suitable only for
pedestrians. This, of course, is the way the doctor has to go too.

The three isolated townships have naturally become almost
completely deserted, but there are sturdy souls who still hang on
to their crofts on that lonely and neglected coast. At Lonbain,
where seven families lived at the start of the second world war,
only two houses are occupied; the old school there, which served
until recently as a youth hostel, has now been taken over by the
Adventure School. Only one house is lived in at Kalnakill, and
two or three at Cuaig, where the North Applecross postman lives,
doing his rounds along the path by pushbike; and yet, there's
some fine arable land out that way, and at least one of the tenants
is a sheep farmer in a fairly substantial way. Even the oldest
remaining residents, who are well into their eighties, have to trek
up to ten miles along the path to Applecross village to visit their
nearest shop, and go back the same way of an evening. As one
of them remarked: 'We were used to walking all our days.'
Supplies also come in once a month by boat from Shieldaig.
Round the coast, the people are sorry that the youth hostel has

gone: 'We miss the hikers—they were very helpful.' As described in the next chapter, a road has been started round the North Applecross coast; but it comes from the far end, and the people of Lonbain, Kalnakill and Cuaig will have to wait another few years before the twentieth century condescends to do anything about them. Until then, there will continue to be features of North Applecross life like lowering coffins over the edge of the path into boats waiting below.

The main part of Applecross village itself lies to the left of the road junction at the east side of the bay. It was built at the time when the people were cleared off the rich inland ground, in much the same way as happened elsewhere in Wester Ross. Even before then, times were hard. Mr McQueen's 1792 account pointed out: 'The local attachment of the Highlanders hath, for some time back, been gradually abating. The influx of money, and their communication with other countries, hath introduced a desire for better living; and the rapacity of the superiors, in applying all the advantages of the times to their own private interest, hath effectually relaxed these attachments. The increasing population of the country at large is favourable to the interested views of the proprietors. For every farm, a multitude of candidates is ready to appear; and the culture of the ground being the sole occupation of the inhabitants, the disappointed have no other option, but either to emigrate or beg.'

At that time the population of the parish was 1,734, having doubled in forty years. Mr McQueen was unable to work out a mean density of population because the area of the district was only roughly known: 'The extent of the parish is considerable, but cannot, with precision, be ascertained, as there is neither public road nor bridge from one extremity of it to the other. The foot-traveller is guided, according to the season of the year, what course to take, over rugged hills, rapid waters, and deep and marshy moors. Besides here, as in all the adjoining parishes and Western Isles, the computation of miles is merely arbitrary, always terminated by a burn, cairn, well, or some such accidental mark, which renders them so remarkably unequal, that it is impossible to reduce any given number of these imaginary miles to a regular computation.'

Applecross village is just a line of houses called the Street, to the left of the road that runs above the shore, all of them with uninterrupted views across the water. The local shop, post office and hotel are here. There's a small pier hereabouts, but the one that played the most significant part in Applecross's recent history is at Milltown, a separated settlement a little way farther on. In 1745 Coll Macdonell of Barrisdale moored a ship off the shore here, and proceeded to interview some local men with the help of the instrument of torture that bore his name; but it was a long time afterwards that a more normal shipping service came into operation. The Pass of the Cattle road is about a century and a half old, but it played an insignificant part in the transport of the district until it was tarred at the end of the 1950s. Before that there was a regular MacBraynes' service, when steamers on the Outer Isles run would call at three o'clock in the morning and three o'clock in the afternoon on their way to and from Stornoway. There was no pier at Applecross that could take them, and boats used to be rowed out from the jetty at Milltown to load and unload passengers, parcels and livestock. When the Wills family took over the estate, they had a boat, called the *Passing Cloud* after one of their cigarette brands, which used to bring all the estate supplies over from Kyle of Lochalsh, and carried goods for the handful of local shopkeepers as well. Its latest successor, the *Dancing Cloud*, can be hired by visitors. During the second world war it was impossible to take the steamer directly to Kyle: Applecross folk had to sail all the way to Stornoway first, but were mercifully charged only the previous fare to Kyle. There were arguments after the war, when talk was heard about allowing the Applecross district to have twentieth-century transport facilities, about whether the local people should press for a road round the coast that would be open all the year, or for a full-sized pier in Applecross Bay; in the event they got neither. The steamers stopped calling in 1953, when a ferry service to Kyle was established at Toscaig, a village a few miles to the south.

Going out of Milltown, the road passes along a kind of embankment between the bay and a stretch of water at Loch a' Mhuillin, the Mill Loch. There's well-tended crofting land on the far side, and some of the old 'lazy beds' that used to be turned over by foot ploughs and fertilised with seaweed. Soon there's a Y-junction where the unsignposted right fork heads over to the little fishing hamlet of Camusteel. At the brow of a hill down the

Camusteel road there is suddenly a magnificent west coast outlook of sheltered rocky bays and the wide inlet of Poll Creadha, beyond which can be seen Eilean nan Naomh, on which Maelrubha is traditionally believed to have landed when he came here for the first time. Over the often silvery sea can be seen the Crowlin Islands off the coast of south-west Applecross; the islands of Raasay, Scalpay and Longa off the east coast of Skye; and, over on the Misty Isle itself, the summits of Glamaig and Beinn Dearg in Lord Macdonald's Forest near Sligachan, then Marsco and Blaven farther south and, away on the skyline, the great ring of peaks in the Black Cuillin from Sgurr nan Gillean to Sgurr Alasdair almost on the southern coast.

Camusteel is just a handful of cottages round a rocky bay; but the situation and outlook are very fine and, like all of these Applecross townships, it has an atmosphere of peace and quiet that can hardly be equalled anywhere. Peace and quiet, of course, are not enough these days, and making a living in the Applecross district is not the relatively easy business it is in places less remote. There are crofts round about here, but not worked to any great extent; one of the great attractions about a croft and the house on it is that they can be passed from generation to generation of a family, unlikely to be enough from which to make a living, but offering independence and a guaranteed rent. Camusteel never did have any hill ground, which put its crofters at a disadvantage compared with their neighbours at Milltown and Camusterach, the next village down the coast, where the smallholders had enough land for thirty sheep and two cows; the Camusteel crofters came to an agreement with some of their neighbours to provide ground for wintering stock, but the present tenants are not all involved in crofting any longer.

Places like Camusteel, with their good anchorages, are plentiful on this coast, and would seem to be ready-made for fishing boats. Before the second world war there were twenty-five or thirty boats manned by Applecross crews, but now there are only three in the whole vast district. Most of the people who might man them have long since left the place, away to the towns and cities where work is available. The owners of the three boats that are left make a fair living all the year round, with a healthy prawn fishing season from April to October.

Back on the 'main' road there's a winding climb to the brow

of a hill towards Camusterach, with a rock-strewn hillside over to the left. The prevailing south-west wind often brings days of damp weather, with mist rolling over these low foothills of the greater mountains behind. Over the brow, there's another splendid view out over the wide inlet and its islands. Eilean nan Naomh shows up well from here, generally called Saint Island by the local people. There's a deeper inlet at the south end of Poll Creadha, and on the promontory that guards it from the open water lie the whitewashed cottages of Aird Dhubh, another one-time fishing hamlet.

At Camusterach there's a small Free Presbyterian church and then the primary school that now serves the whole district; it's one of the great disadvantages in living at Applecross that secondary school children have to go away to Plockton or Dingwall, where they can't even get home regularly at weekends and often lose their taste for their faraway home life. As the parents say: 'They go to school, and that's the last you see of them.'

In the main part of Camusterach there's a small Free Church place of worship, not to be confused with the Free Presbyterian, and then, after a road junction on the way to the little pier, the Church of Scotland place that was built after the church at the head of the loch collapsed; it's all rather confusing for a non-Scottish visitor who doesn't understand the denominational differences. Services are held in Gaelic and English. A shop and petrol station, this last the only one in the whole Applecross peninsula, make up, with a handful of other houses, all there is of Camusterach, which is in many ways the most important of the Applecross townships today.

Beyond it the road goes along a ledge below some cliffs, and not far above the edge of the sea; another small hill takes it back down towards the perfect anchorage at the head of Poll Creadha, where there are always some boats moored, and net drying frames beside the shore. The crofting township of Culduie lies angled off to the left of the road.

These crofting townships of Applecross, although much of the ground in them is well kept, demonstrate the great weakness of the whole crofting system, which may be picturesque but is a most unholy way to make a living from the soil. There are something like eighteen or nineteen thousand crofts in the seven

Crofter Counties: Orkney, Shetland, Caithness, Sutherland, Ross and Cromarty, Inverness and Argyll. Some of them are no bigger in size than a respectable suburban garden, while others, partly through amalgamations, may be as large as a hundred acres. The croft is actually the piece of land that a crofter occupies; not his house, which he or one of his forefathers may well have built by their own labour. Nowadays crofters can have substantial government grants and loans to build their houses. The land belongs to the estate and is leased out at a fair rent decided on by the Scottish Land Court. As well as some arable ground, a crofter usually has a share in the hill grazings that are held in common by all the tenants in a township; these are usually administered by a grazings committee.

Before 1886, when the deliberations of the Royal Commission and the activities of some M.P.s who were sympathizers gave them legal security, crofters had very few rights, were often evicted to make way for sheep or deer, and might well be charged extra rent by their landlords for improvements to their houses or land which they themselves had made. Nowadays the legal position is much more in their favour, and there is a Crofters Commission based in Inverness which takes to do with the multiplicity of regulations with which these holdings are surrounded. Legally, however, the crofters do not own either the land they work nor the houses that have been built on them, and therefore cannot actually sell them; but they are due compensation for the improvements they have made—usually in the form of buildings—when they give up their crofts, which is why advertisements appear in the Highland papers about 'improvements' for sale.

It's the houses that matter most, because they are handed down from one generation of a family to another, and guarantee that some of them at least will always have a house in their home village to come to when they retire. Many of the houses are very pleasantly modernized inside, completely rebuilt, or newly put up thanks to the official grants, loans and low interest charges. The croft itself, although a remnant of a truly West Highland way of life that is elsewhere passing away, is often in agricultural terms no more than an absurdity: suitable for a retired man, it would rarely be able to support a younger family that didn't have a source of income elsewhere. In the Applecross townships, the incredible fragmentation of the holdings that makes working them a laboured and uneconomic business is most noticeable. When a crofter died, it was always the custom to split up the holding among his sons, which meant that eventually each croft came to be in perhaps a dozen different patches of land, no two of which ran alongside each other. In Applecross, to make the share-out as fair as possible, each son was given a part of the good land and a part of the rougher land; the result was that, as can be seen today, some of the crofts hereabouts shattered themselves into tiny fragments, many of them not the size of a normal dining room carpet. Nobody could possibly support himself from such a scattered holding, and several of the crofters who are not retired men and therefore do not regard their crofts as more of a hobby than anything else, have work elsewhere and more or less ignore their holdings. Three or four of the older men still use the *cas chrom* or foot plough, but this is not typical in an age when tractors are available.

Some of the crofts are little more than vegetable plots; but this is not to say that there are not some very well run holdings at Applecross as everywhere else in the north-west. Many of the holdings are really farms in miniature. In townships where all the tenants agree, the Crofters Commission try to re-amalgamate the disintegrated holdings. In general, though, it's useful to remember the explanation given by Sir John McNeill in 1851, even if the retired man was not a feature of crofting life in his day: 'It is a misapprehension, and one that may lead to many others, to regard them as a class of small farmers who get, or are now expected to get, their living and pay their rent from the produce of the croft. They are truly labourers, living chiefly by the wages of labour and holding crofts or lots for which they pay rent, not from the produce of the land but from wages.' Having said that, and having admitted that crofting is sometimes not much more than a colourful anachronism bolstered up by grants and subsidies, nobody can fail to admire the spirit of the men who work the little holdings; and it should be remembered that almost two million acres of Scotland is occupied by crofters: ten per cent of the total land area of the country.

There's a pleasant little road round the lochside to the hamlet of Aird Dhubh on its point of land across the water, but the main road continues through some rather wild rocky country of heather and marshy land before going downhill towards the neatly kept fields of the last of the crofting townships at Toscaig. Drivers have to keep an eye out for flying post office vans on these narrow coastal roads throughout the West Highlands; fifty years ago at Toscaig the situation was much calmer, because the postman came from Applecross village on a tricycle. Toscaig is really in three separate parts: off to the left of the road is Upper Toscaig; the middle part of the village is on lower ground beside the final stretch of the little Toscaig River; and the third section is near the pier at the head of the loch of the same name.

In the days when he was establishing himself as the parish minister of Lochcarron, which was then included with Applecross, that sturdy man Aeneas Sage had occasion to come here to deal with an unruly parishioner: 'There was a wicked fellow in Tosgag, who kept a mistress in the same house with his lawful married wife. When Mr Sage went to see him, Malcolm Roy drew his dirk; Mr Sage drew his sword; and the consequence was, that Malcolm Roy turned his mistress off.'

Toscaig is a very pleasant place, looking down a little strath towards the narrow inlet of its long rocky bay, just cut off from a sight of the Crowlin Islands beyond the mouth of the loch; there were within living memory seven families living on the islands, but they had to come to the mainland many years ago. A footpath goes from Toscaig round the foot of the Applecross peninsula to Russel and Loch Kishorn, along which there are ruins of other townships that saw the start of the twentieth century but did not survive much longer. At Uags, down on the southern tip of the peninsula, there was not only a small hamlet but also a school, and there were several families at Airidh-drissaig halfway to Russel. That part of the coast is now the home of little more than otters and seals. In Toscaig itself, sixty years ago, there were more pupils at the primary school than are taught at Camusterach, where all the children of the district go to school today.

The most significant feature of Toscaig is the modern pier part of the way down the loch, often piled up with lobster pots. This is the terminus of the ferry service that has run from Kyle since 1953, and is the only lifeline of the Applecross people when the Pass of the Cattle is blocked by snow. Now that the steamer service has stopped and this generally inadequate replacement has taken over, the local people think they were better off thirty years ago, when they had the choice of paying full fare on the steamer, going to Kyle on the estate boat *Passing Cloud*, or just thumbing a lift from a friendly fishing boat skipper. Freight charges have a minimum limit, which often makes the cost of bringing something like fish from Kyle of Lochalsh as high as the cost of the fish in the first place. For the most part, it's only perishable goods and the mails that come across on the ferry; when the Bealach is open, everything else comes in by road. The ferry had to be depended on until early May in 1970 because of bad weather on the hill; in these conditions, getting sick people to hospital is an uncomfortable business.

The first ferry that was put on when the Kyle–Toscaig service started in 1953 was very suitable for the job; then a smaller boat was used, and there were various other replacements, one of which was so rotten that it had to be sunk. The present ferry, the *Vital Spark*, is not held in high regard by the local people, being considered more of a boat for inland waters than for the rough conditions that often occur in the Inner Sound, when it is sometimes unable to make the crossing.

It has to be admitted that not many people make use of the ferry service to Kyle. Chartered from a boatman there, the *Vital Spark* takes about fourteen hundred passengers a year on its Toscaig run, about one a day in winter and three in summer; the service makes a loss of about £5,000 in a full year. At the same time, it is unquestionably for a great part of the year the lifeline of the Applecross peninsula, and the only way out of the district in an emergency. In the Spring of 1970, therefore, a great furore arose when the Scottish Transport Group, the nationalised body responsible for the service, appeared to give the impression that they wanted to close it down. That year was a particularly bad time for many of the west coast ferries, with a shambles developing over the late delivery and interrupted service of the bigger car ferry from Kyle to Kyleakin, and accidents on one of the new Firth of Clyde boats which convinced some of its regular users that it was simply not seaworthy and likely to capsize. It did nothing for their image, therefore, when the Scottish Transport Group took several weeks to make an official comment on the Toscaig run. Their spokesman made one of the more bizarre of official pronouncements when he said that they did not want to stop the service, but had to say they wanted to stop it because of the statutory procedure. What they were after, in fact, was some other body, like the county council, to meet the deficit from local rather than national funds. Applecross people did not seem to appreciate either the long delay in making the assurance that the ferry would not be stopped, or the weird procedure that prompted the original statement.

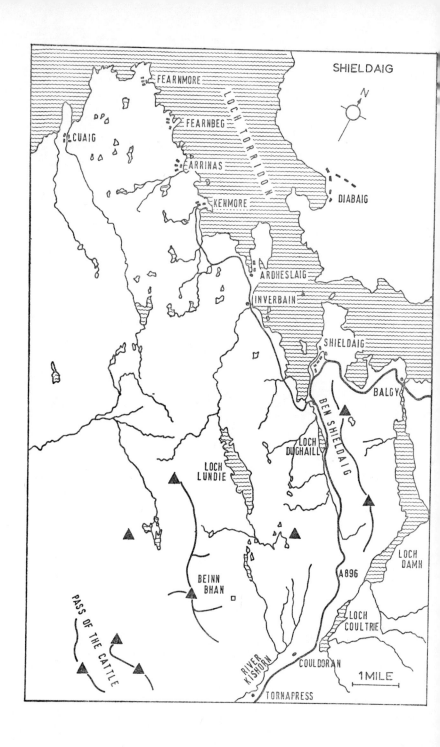

CHAPTER 11

SHIELDAIG AND GLEN TORRIDON

FROM THE APPLECROSS ROAD-END at Tornapress, the Shieldaig road continues northwards up the rather damp and winding course of the River Kishorn, with fine views of the mountains of the Glenshieldaig and Ben Damh deer forests always ahead. After a while, there's a small Nature Conservancy reserve over a rise of ground to the right. The Rassal ashwood was declared a reserve in June 1956 after an agreement between the Conservancy and Mr Greg of Lochcarron estate, like the one that produced the other nearby reserve at the Allt nan Carnan gorge. The old ashwood is a result of the limestone outcrops that occur throughout the Kishorn district, and the Conservancy has enclosed an area of it to preserve and regenerate the woods of ash and hazel.

Not far away on the other side of the road is a patch of woodland around the big house of Couldoran. Some of the Murrays used to live there, and it remained a separate small property when they sold off the rest of the Lochcarron estate at the end of the second world war. It was C. W. Murray of Couldoran who presented the ruins of Strome Castle to the National Trust for Scotland.

There are some old farmlands in the valley floor near Couldoran, where the River Kishorn is formed from a tangle of mountain burns that come down from the slopes of Beinn Bhan, and the little valley that runs north-west from Couldoran forms the boundary between the Applecross and Lochcarron estates; from here on, the Lochcarron property extends farther to the west of the road than it does along the course of the River Kishorn, and it's this northern part of the estate that forms the deer forest of Glenshieldaig. The western hills here might easily serve as prototypes of typical deer forest country. Nearer the road, there's rough heathery moorland; but the most striking sight is the great succession of towers and peaks and corries on the north-east side of Beinn Bhan.

The narrow road winds on, with the rather unremarkable and strung-out Loch Coultrie in a depression down to the right. Soon, however, there's a glimpse of a much more impressive stretch of water, as Loch Damh is seen in the great steep-sided valley between Ben Shieldaig and Ben Damh. There are woodlands around Ceann-loch-Damh at the head of the loch, a brief sight of imposing cliffs on the east side, and then the road swings away uphill and the loch is lost to view. It forms the boundary between Lochcarron and Ben Damh estates, and is fished by either side on prearranged days.

Having climbed over its summit, the road then goes down through the narrow and fairly steep-sided valley of Glen Shieldaig, often on a little ledge above the burn that runs through it. Road improvements are in progress here, but the higher part of the glen, from a scenic point of view, has little to recommend it.

Suddenly, however, there comes a view over Loch Dughaill and, farther into the distance, Loch Shieldaig, an arm of the sea. On the steep hillside to the east of Loch Dughaill there's a very fine old wood of pine and birch climbing up a remarkable rocky-terraced face. Back in the 1830s, the fir trees here were often used for building fishing boats and houses. Osgood Mackenzie's *A Hundred Years in the Highlands* recalled an election around that time, when the Glen Shieldaig woodlands were much larger. Mackenzie of Applecross was one of the candidates, having been M.P. for Ross-shire for several years. A rather cunning gentleman called Macdonald, who came from Lochinver, devised a scheme which was based on the fact that votes in those days didn't have to be registered direct: they could be given in the form of letters addressed to the candidate, who would then hand them over to the returning officer.

This Macdonald had had his eye on the Glen Shieldaig fir wood for some time, because he wanted to buy it over and ship the timber south for sale; but he didn't particularly want to have to pay hard cash for it. He reasoned that, as the election was coming off, Mackenzie of Applecross might be more interested in guaranteed votes than in money; so he suggested to Mackenzie that he should sell the woodland in return for letters of mandate from all the qualified voters in Stornoway. Mackenzie agreed, and Macdonald sailed over to Lewis in his yacht the *Rover's Bride*, did some fast talking, came back with letters giving Mackenzie all the Stornoway votes, and took over the timber for no more outlay than that.

The towering effect of the Ben Shieldaig terraces and the old birch woods that occupy every level almost to the very top, is seen to even greater advantage from the road beyond Loch Dughaill; this is, indeed, one of the great sights of Wester Ross. There are remains of an old pine wood lining the edge of the road at the waterside, and the whole effect must be very much as many of these West Highland districts appeared two or three hundred years ago. Between Loch Dughaill and the head of Loch Shieldaig there's a side-road off to the left, which may look unremarkable but was the centre of one of the biggest rows in Wester Ross this century.

Loch Shieldaig is really just an inlet of Loch Torridon, which stretches north-westwards out towards the open sea, with the Torridon Mountains on its north-east side, and the hills of North Applecross on the other. For generations there have been several little crofting townships along the North Applecross coast: Ardheslaig, Kenmore, Arrinas, Fearnbeg and Fearnmore, stretching away out to the northern tip of the Applecross peninsula, and in much the same isolated positions as Lonbain, Kalnakill and Cuaig, the similar settlements on the west coast above Applecross village itself.

In 1883 the Royal Commission heard that there were four hundred people in the North Applecross villages; one or two of them wandered along to the meeting at Shieldaig, but said they were only there to see what was going on. They had three good schools, enough ground and good fishing, and all they really wanted was more deer fencing and a road; their only land link was a stalkers' track that had been built by the estate owner, and it was too narrow and rough for any kind of cart. Six or seven years before, the tenants had asked Lord Middleton for a road, promising that they would do most of the work on it. He sent along his ground officer, who measured the route and took note of the various rivers and mountain burns that would have to be forded. Unfortunately Lord Middleton was then involved in a riding accident, and after being bed-ridden for ten months as a result, died at his home, Birdsall House in Yorkshire. Nothing more was heard about the road.

The decades wore on, and still nothing was done about the road, although the whole of North Applecross, cut off from most normal amenities, was steadily depopulated. For a while, the MacBraynes' steamers called at Loch Torridon, and local boats could go out to meet them as they lay off the shore; but that service did not survive the first world war. Then the Board of Agriculture and Fisheries began a government-sponsored service, which involved a regular freight run by fishing boat from Kyle of Lochalsh. That too petered out in the 1930s when the government grant was withdrawn; as far as government help was concerned, the thirties were one of the worst times in recent years for the remote settlements of the north-west. Later efforts were made to provide some kind of sea transport service, but they have all been fairly half-hearted, especially now that the long-awaited road has actually been started.

What really got things going was a report in the early 1960s by a Ross-shire county official who suggested that, since North Applecross was now practically deserted, the most sensible thing would be to evacuate the few people who were left, and forget about the place altogether. It may well have been meant seriously, but it would be pleasant to think that the proposal was simply an oblique Highland way of getting things done. Immediately there was an uproar, as newspaper and television reporters descended on the district, in which nobody had taken the slightest interest for years gone by, and played the story for all it was worth. A plan was devised to build a single-track road from Shieldaig to connect the five hamlets with the outside world; eventually, it was to be continued right round the coast by Cuaig and Kalnakill and Lonbain to meet up with the public road at Applecross village itself. Several of the surviving residents of North Applecross had been about to leave the district, but when they heard that somebody was at last prepared to haul the transport facilities screaming into the twentieth century, they decided to stay.

Alexander Greg of Lochcarron estate, through whose ground the first part of the road would have to run, was quoted as saying that the North Applecross crofters didn't really want a road, and that was worth a few more column inches of newspaper publicity. Work on the road began in 1965. It was practically hacked by hand out of the unhelpful hillsides, and there were never more than eight men working on it at any one time. In five years it had got as far as its present terminus at Kenmore, which was reached at a total cost of only £115,000, which must be the best bargain for seven and a half miles of road anywhere in Britain. As a plaque by the side of the new road announces, it was officially opened in May 1970 by Princess Margaret; Mrs Wills of Applecross is her cousin.

The new road starts with a downhill swing through a patch of pinewood, with a glimpse, from after a bridge across the little river that runs from Loch Dughaill to the sea, of a pine-wooded ravine. There's a splendid view back to the east of the great wooded cliffs, galleries and ledges of Ben Shieldaig, which is seen from this farther-away point to be much higher than can be imagined from the more restricted Loch Dughaill road. As it heads along the west side of Loch Shieldaig there's a very fine view out over the water, with rocky bays and inlets close by, and the tightly wooded Shieldaig Island, recently acquired by the NTS. An 1885 account was accurate enough in saying of the loch: 'In its bosom lies Shieldaig Island, 50 feet high. A stupendous cliff of shelving precipices, tier above tier, rises immediately behind the village to a height of 1,691 feet, and completely screens the inner part of the neighbouring marine waters.'

Beyond the island lies the outer part of Loch Torridon, with the sturdy headland at Ardheslaig to the north-west, the wild rocky north shore around Diabaig across the water, and the great peaks of Ben Alligin back to the north-east. There's a sight of the narrow mountain road to Diabaig winding and climbing its way over a difficult pass and, more gentle and nearer at hand, the trim whitewashed houses of Shieldaig village down by the water's edge.

The whole west side of Loch Shieldaig is a succession of most attractive bays and headlands, often with old birch woods between the road and the rocky shore. It isn't surprising that there are new houses going up here and there since the road was opened; even before that time, old croft cottages were being snapped up, mostly for nothing more than holiday houses.

As the undulating road continues, a group of abrupt grassy and heathery islands appear in the wider bay off Rhurain and Inverbain, and round about here there's plenty of opportunity to

see the old narrow motor cycle track that was the only land access
to Ardheslaig and Kenmore until a year or two ago, having been
built first of all away back in the middle of the last century. It's
as well to remember that a continuation of this miserable path
remains the only way apart from sailing to get to the hamlets
that still haven't been reached by the road. From Loch Dughaill
to Inverbain, the new road has opened up one of the most
beautiful parts of Wester Ross.

At Inverbain the old ford across the river that falls down from
Loch Lundie has been replaced by a bridge. It marks the boundary
between the estates of Lochcarron and Applecross, and the cottage
above the road is the home of one of the Applecross stalkers.
There's a very pleasant spread of hardwoods around the mouth
of the river, and some arable ground down by the edge of the
loch. Inverbain is the start of one of the old footpaths through
the deer forest, over to the head of the valley of the Applecross
River and down to Applecross village itself.

The road climbs over the shoulder of a hill to leave Loch
Shieldaig and come down towards the narrow rocky inlet of
Loch Beag, around which are dotted the houses of the little
hamlet of Ardheslaig. There's some crofting done here, and some
local men own one of the few remaining fishing boats on the
Applecross coast. There's even a side road, signposted to Aird,
which turns right over a cattle grid and heads along the far shore
of Loch Beag; but as this book was being written it was closed,
like the Strome Ferry bypass, by a minor landslide. It goes over
a wooded hillside to a little suburb of Ardheslaig, where the great
headland that's so obvious from farther back along the new road
is almost turned into an island by a pair of deep-cut inlets of the sea.

Beyond Ardheslaig the character of the new road changes, and
it begins to run through very much wilder, rougher country as
it makes a steep sweeping climb out of Ardheslaig, running
alongside the old track for a while, before taking a more inland
route behind the hill of A'Bhaintir. From near the top of the
climb, where the crash barriers are interrupted to provide some
parking places, there's a superb view of the mountains and
lochsides round about. To the north-east is the wild derelict
coastline that hides Loch Diabaig, an inlet on the far shore of
Loch Torridon; due east are the narrows that guard the entrance
to the more sheltered waters of Upper Loch Torridon, the south

side formed by a long peninsula going north from the village of Shieldaig; south of that is the end of the long high ridge of Ben Shieldaig; around the higher reaches of Upper Loch Torridon are those supremely elegant peaks of Ben Alligin and the majestic Liathach, and more and more independent summits marching away eastwards up Glen Torridon.

Inland is the steep mountain wilderness of the Applecross deer forest. The road begins to force its way through this wild country, and away from the lochside for a spell. It's rough tussocky moorland hereabouts, with great stretches of marshy ground, one of the wildest districts explored by any public road in the Highlands. Around little Loch na Creige the old footpath reappears, winding and plunging along through a desperately inhospitable landscape. Some way beyond this is the first sign for a long way of any human activity, at some peat beds that are still worked by the people of Kenmore. Soon afterwards the road comes winding down a valley towards the birchwoods above Loch a' Chracaich, an inlet of the sea. On the west side of the bay is the little hamlet of Kenmore, which is currently the very end of the road.

Any visitor who has been expecting that Kenmore will turn out to be a primitive and ill-kept collection of ramshackle croft houses is in for a pleasant surprise. In fact, this is one of the neatest little settlements on the west coast, half a dozen whitewashed houses looking brightly over the rounded bay. The houses are modernized inside, there's a local post office, and overnight accommodation is available. There's some crofting ground, and Loch Torridon still provides plenty of fish for local use. Altogether, this is no mean, inward-looking township, but a place which obviously deserves the road access that almost everywhere else in Britain is taken for granted. The north-west side of the bay, beside which the houses stand, is sheltered from the open waters by a little peninsula; on the other side of it is Camus an Eilein, where an estate gamekeeper lives.

Kenmore is rather more than halfway along the North Applecross coast from the main road at Shieldaig, and it has to be remembered that there are other similar townships farther along the coast that are still reached only by a continuation of the miserable goat track whose early stages can be seen alongside the new road. Plans have been made to extend the road from

Kenmore to Arrinas, Fearnbeg, Fearnmore and Cuaig, which is round the corner on the west coast of Applecross. If the road gets to Cuaig, the Army have announced that they will be prepared to link it, by a rougher track, with the other public road down at Applecross village. It's worth pointing out here that some references in print to the Kenmore road as having a gravel surface are not true; the whole splendidly engineered stretch from Shieldaig has a fine tarred surface.

Arrinas is a rather blunt version of a much more mellifluous Gaelic name; thanks to the steady depopulation it now has only one occupied house out of the eight that are still habitable. Before the second world war, there were more than thirty-two pupils at Arrinas school, about fifty fewer than at the turn of the century. Next of the coastal settlements is Fearnbeg, which now has much the same population as Arrinas. Almost at the tip of the peninsula is Fearnmore, which was, until the 1930s, the biggest of the North Applecross settlements, with twelve families and more houses available, but nobody to occupy them. Now there are only two houses in use. It has been suggested that once the complete all-weather road is built from Shieldaig to Applecross by Kenmore and Arrinas, the population will begin to grow again, as there are plenty of empty houses that need little work to be put into first class order; and there should be many people who have had to leave their native Applecross ready to come back and make a go of the crofting and fishing, with finance available from government loans. Another school of thought, however, feels that the damage has been done, and that all that can be hoped for is an influx of holidaymakers and retired people, with the whole of Applecross only an extension of the traditional tourist trade, which provides summer income but on its own is worth no more than that to a Highland community.

Back down on the main road at the south end of Loch Shieldaig, it's only a short way into Shieldaig village itself, a very bright and tidy place looking westwards over a bay to the lonely hills of North Applecross. Among the settlements of Wester Ross it has a unique history. Villages like Dornie were built to house crofters evicted from their good grazings inland; Ullapool was established by the British Fisheries Society; Kyle of Lochalsh grew up with the railway; but Shieldaig was officially created to provide cannon-fodder for the Royal Navy.

In 1800 Napoleon's ships were very active off the north-west coast of Scotland, causing a great deal of inconvenience, and some destruction of fishing boats and coasters. The Duke of Argyle, a member of the Board of Admiralty, made a speech in which the British government's answer to the marauding Frenchmen was given:

'We are able to build ships, but the great question is how to man them? Every person who has knowledge knows that a ship of war is a costly article: to trust such an article to the scum of cities and towns, such as tailors and shoemakers, country shepherds and ploughmen, would be foolishness. We want different sort of people. The greater portion of the people fit for manning our ships lies between Corsewall Point [in Galloway] and the Orkney Isles, and unless the Highland proprietors grant sites for building villages, we are not able to man our ships at a short notice. In this year, 1800, His Majesty George III and his Lords in Council marked the village of Shieldaig for bringing youths to the knowledge of the sea. The site is good for a village, having a fall of water from 15 to 18 feet. His Majesty's Lords in Council promised the best of terms to a society for building the said village on a lease renewable for ever.'

Before King George pointed his finger on a map to the site of Shieldaig, there had been some fairly well-off local cattle farmers, working on long leases from Mackenzie of Applecross. It stayed that way for some time more, because nobody could be found to build the village which the government had ordered. In fact, it wasn't until 1810, after some very straight talking from government officials, that a consortium was formed of contractors and businessmen, some from Glasgow and even from south of the border, and the building of Shieldaig began.

The government did indeed offer very generous terms, creating something like one of the development areas of the present day. There were official grants for boat-building, guaranteed prices for catches of fish, adequate supplies of duty-free salt, which was itself no small concession, plenty of land for all the tenants, and a new road to connect Shieldaig with Kishorn and Lochcarron, basically the same one as there is today. Every one of the government's promises was kept.

With a government bounty payable on all the boat-building and fishing catches, the people who came to live at Shieldaig did rather well. They were able to build fair-sized boats that could fish in the outer waters, and the duty-free salt allowed them to cure their catches at low cost and send them off at a fair profit to the markets of the south. The fishing has always been good here, judging by the name of the place, which comes from the Norse *sild-vik*, or Herring Bay.

All went well for several years. Then the Mackenzies of Applecross sold off their vast estates, which stretched all the way from Applecross to Achnashellach, to the Duke of Leeds. It was said that from 1810 until that time, Shieldaig was one of the finest villages in the west; but the Duchess of Leeds changed all that. She was one of the family who had been responsible for the brutal Sutherland clearances, and didn't much bother about the special rights of the people of the 'parliamentary village' of Shieldaig. In any case, although the people didn't seem to realise it, the bounty system and the permanent leases offered in these villages were passing away. The Duchess let her gamekeeper deal with local matters, and he soon made it clear that he preferred 'shepherds and sheep to mariners and sailors'.

He made new regulations about the land holdings, taking cattle grazing away from the smaller tenants and adding it on to sheep farms that were rented out to the innkeeper and a local merchant. The fishermen/crofters sank into poverty, protesting that their permanent leases from the government would be scrapped as soon as they stopped making their living from the sea. Worse was to come. When the Duke of Leeds broke up the vast Applecross property into smaller sections, the modern Lochcarron estate, including the village of Shieldaig, was sold to Sir John Stewart, whose sons went deer stalking in Glenshieldaig forest, and who dispossessed many of the Shieldaig tenants, taking over their houses for estate use. Most of the ground was rented out to incoming sheep farmers who were, as happened so often in the north-west, only absentee tenants.

By the 1860s, so the Royal Commission was told when it met at Shieldaig on 1 August 1883, there was only one offshore fishing boat left in the place, and the people were too poor by that time to do anything about it, although the fishing was still very good. The estate was also criticized for allowing cartloads of shingle from the shore to be taken away for road building and ballast, the village people being worried that their protection from storm tides was being removed. By that time the stone pier that had been built by the Destitution Board during the potato famine in the 1840s was still surviving, but lack of maintenance by the estate had allowed it to crumble away almost completely.

Shieldaig fared better once the Lochcarron estate came into the hands of the Murrays. Today it looks a very bright and well-tended village, but the effect is rather illusory; there are far too many houses occupied only during the summer months.

Until the early 1960s the road from Lochcarron stopped at Shieldaig, and there was no way round Loch Torridon except by a rough footpath just like the one that goes along the North Applecross coast. In the last ten years, however, a fine modern road has been built to the head of the loch, connecting with the Glen Torridon road that meets up with the main route from Achnasheen to Gairloch. It should be no surprise that the Applecross coast road is taking so long, if within the last ten years Shieldaig itself was on a dead-end.

The new main road to Torridon branches off uphill just before the entrance to the village, but there is a through route along the old coast road in front of the houses that look out over the bay to the wooded Shieldaig Island. At the far end of the village there's a short climb and then a sharp bend to the right in front of a modern primary school, onto a little plateau beside a couple of houses, a petrol station and a small caravan site, all with a fine outlook from this more elevated position over the long wooded inlet at the head of Loch Shieldaig. In the other direction the view is to the great bulk of Ben Shieldaig, and as the link road joins the new main road to Torridon, over the first brow there suddenly bursts upon the traveller one of the most spectacular mountain-surrounded lochsides in the whole of the Highlands. There's a parking place down to the left, behind an old pile of bulldozed rubble, where the view can be enjoyed in peace.

These great ranges of Torridonian sandstone are among the oldest rocks in the world, dating back something like 750,000,000 years. Looking north-east from the parking place, high above the sheltered sweeping inlet of Ob Mheallaidh, the first mountain on the far side of the loch is Ben Alligin, with the scattered village of the same name powdered along its lower slopes before the final plunge into the waters of the upper loch. It's a characteristic of Torridonian rock that it forms splendid upstanding

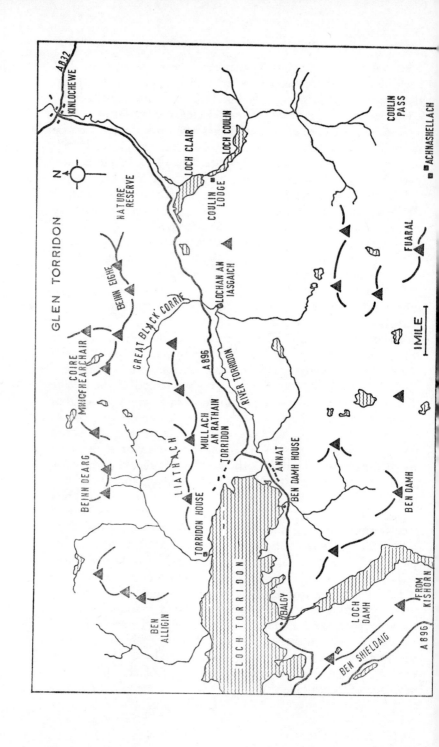

individual summits, and there are several of these in the background ranges beyond the eastern shoulder of Ben Alligin, form-
ing the minor massif of Beinn Dearg, the Red Peak.   Most
substantial of the mountains of Torridon, starting immediately
to the east of the valley through which Beinn Dearg is clearly
seen, is Liathach, a series of peaks soaring up almost directly from
the water's edge, dominating the head of the loch and the lower
reaches of Glen Torridon.   From this angle, the summit ridge is
a jumble of towers and buttresses, with scree slopes on the very
steep and spidery gullies that plunge down three thousand feet
and more almost to sea level.   The highest summit, Spidean a'
Choire Leith, the Pinnacle of the Grey Corrie, is 3,456 feet above
the sea; some idea of the colossal steepness of the whole mountain
can be given by the bare measurement that its western neighbour,
Mullach an Rathain, called the Ridge of the Pulley after a fancied
resemblance to part of a spinning wheel, is 3,358 feet high and
only 2,100 yards from the high water mark on the shore of Loch
Torridon, a gradient for the whole distance steeper than one-in-
two.

   Liathach used to be spelled Leagach, which is a better guide to
its pronunciation.   The name means something like the Hoary
Place, partly because of the scree slopes that suck the summit
debris down to the valley below, and partly because of the whitish
quartzite cap that crowns the highest points, and sometimes gives
the impression that the summit is lightly dusted with snow.   On
the near side of the loch from the parking place, the northern
face of Ben Shieldaig is seen to be formed from the same spectacular series of rocky terraces, towers and even more dramatic
gullies as the one above Loch Dughaill; the lower slopes are
covered in birches.   Beyond it are the less exciting mountains of
the Ben Damh deer forest, which stretch from Ben Shieldaig to
the head of the loch.

   Here and there alongside the road can be seen the remains of
the old track that was the only defined way along the lochside
until the 1960s.   The track went as far as a place called Balgy, at
the mouth of the river that drains Loch Damh into the sea, and
since there was a ford suitable only for foot traffic, this Balgy Gap
made direct road transport between Shieldaig and Annat, the
village at the head of the loch, quite impossible.   Until ten years
ago, the only way a car could get between the two places, which

are six or seven miles apart, was to go away round by Kishorn, Lochcarron, Achnashellach, Achnasheen and Kinlochewe, which is a distance of something like sixty miles.

The now-bridged Balgy Gap marks the boundary between the Lochcarron and Ben Damh estates. South-east of it is the finely shaped summit of Sgurr na Bana Mhoraire, northern outlier of Ben Damh itself. Beyond Balgy, but often hidden by woodlands to the left of the road, is a motorable track that used to lead from Annat to Balgy before the new road was built. Soon there's a view out over the beautiful narrow inlet of Ob Gorm Beag, towards the old church of Torridon directly across the loch. Just to the right of it are the sheltering woodlands around Torridon House, with the great valley of Coire Mhic Nobuil, MacNoble's Corrie, stretching up behind it, separating Ben Alligin from Liathach, with the Beinn Dearg range occupying the middle background. On the rocky peninsula of Ardmore that stretches out between Ob Gorm Beag and its larger eastern neighbour Ob Gorm Mor is a fishery research centre, still occupying a building that was set up for the purpose something like a hundred years ago.

Ob Gorm Mor is itself a fine anchorage, seen to its best effect from a parking place just at the summit of the road, where the dominant feature of the view, however, is the majestic bulk of Liathach. It is seen from here in much more detail, beginning with a long steep western ridge that rises just behind the Torridon House woodlands towards the first summit at Sgorr a' Chadail, the Peak of Sleep. There are several gullies sweeping down towards the lochside here, one of them with a fast-plunging waterfall, and the quartzite tops show up very well. Mullach an Rathain is the most substantial peak from this viewpoint, with a barrage of scree coming down from various high tributary gullies to join in a great southern corrie into a single line of rubble. Beyond it, on the north side of Glen Torridon, a curious flake of rock marks the next part of the great summit ridge as it moves slightly out of sight to the highest peak of Spidean a' Choire Leith. In summer the slopes of Liathach are lightly swept with patches of grass on the solid rock between the scree runs; but in winter the whole mountain is often a tremendous mass of ice and snow. W. H. Murray has written of a winter climb on Liathach when his party, well armed with ropes and ice axes, came upon a tramp who couldn't visualize that people might be climbing about the mountain for fun; he managed to convince himself that their axes were for hacking off great lumps of ice which would then be sold to ice stores in the fishing ports.

More recently, when asked about the activities of some helicopters that were flying about the district, a Torridon woman made the puzzling reply that they were carrying monuments to the tops of the mountains. In fact, the helicopters were being used by a party of surveyors, who were ferrying triangulation pillars to some of the previously unmarked summits.

The main road continues a little farther inland for some way, until it runs down again to cross a bridge in the woodlands around Ben Damh House, usually spelt in the anglicized form of Damph which leads native Gaelic speakers to think dark thoughts about the impossibility of getting a Lowlander or Englishman to pronounce the nasal 'vee' sound, which simply cannot be reproduced in English script. The real pronunciation is something like *Damv*, but with the *m* sounded through the nose and not the mouth.

Unravelling the ownership of Torridon through the years, which has to be attempted to explain the background to Ben Damh House, is not something that can be done very briefly; part of the trouble is that the modern Torridon estate, which is really the north side of the loch, and the Ben Damh estate which runs along the south side from Balgy to Glen Torridon, have been separate and combined at different times. For a time in the fourteenth and fifteenth centuries the whole district belonged to the Macdonald Lords of the Isles. After the break-up of the Lordship of the Isles, Torridon came into the hands of the Macdonells of Glengarry, but the affair at Strome Castle, when it was successfully besieged by a party of Mackenzies, ended Macdonell influence and put Torridon, like the rest of Wester Ross, under Mackenzie control.

The south side of the loch, including what is now the Ben Damh estate, came to be controlled by the Mackenzies of Applecross, and passed out of their hands in the way mentioned several times before. In 1873 both parts of Torridon were bought by a rich Lowland laird, Duncan Darroch of Gourock in Renfrewshire, whose story will be more conveniently told in the next chapter. Darroch held onto the north side of the loch, which is the modern Torridon estate, but sold off Ben Damh in 1885 to the Earl of Lovelace. The earldom of Lovelace was a coronation peerage of Queen Victoria, granted to the King family, later known as King-Noel. The same Lord Lovelace also owned for a while the stalking ground of New Kelso, which he bought from Sir Kenneth Matheson.

Lord Lovelace built Ben Damh House, a rather imposing turreted mansion to the left of the modern road, very much in the sporting estate style of those days. Woodlands were planted round the mansion, for shelter and ornamentation, extending up the steep and curving course of the Coire Roill burn; some distance up the valley there's a splendid waterfall seldom seen by casual visitors.

The Lovelaces held onto Ben Damh, although Darroch's old estate of Torridon on the far side of the loch had several different owners during the fifty years after his death in 1910. At the start of the 1960s the Lovelace family bought over Torridon too, and having converted Ben Damh House into Loch Torridon Hotel when the new main road came through, they moved to Torridon House on the north side of the loch. The fourth Earl died suddenly in 1964, and the Ben Damh estate was sold to a Major Braithwaite. Torridon had to go too, in part payment of death duties, and was handed over by the Crown Commissioners to the National Trust for Scotland. The present Earl was left with Torridon House and the policy woods round about, and a few houses on the south shore between Balgy and the hotel.

The Braithwaites continued to run Ben Damh House as a hotel, and there are now a modern bar and cafeteria near the roadside. Naturally, the sporting rights are available to guests, with deer stalking in the mountains, loch fishing in Loch Damh and angling in various small rivers. Going up the far side of the Coire Roill burn is a stalkers' track into the mountains, but the main effect of that side of the burn is horror at the state of the devastated hillside. The old ornamental woodland there was sold off in the early 1960s, the contractors didn't seem to make a very tidy job of it, and the shattered remains of hacked-about timber that are still lying about make this the only ugly patch of ground in the whole district.

Beyond the hotel, the road comes right down to the lochside as it makes for the little hamlet of Annat. Across the tidal area at the head of the loch is the village of Torridon, a string of houses tucked right under some of the precipitous scree runs of Liathach. Between Annat and Torridon there's a triangle of good arable land at the foot of Glen Torridon, with fields and some croft houses, at the west end of which stands the much more substantial building of Torridon Mains, which used to be the home farm of the estate.

Above the water here, the main road runs along a little embankment below a spread of rhododendrons and pine trees, with the old Balgy track just to the right of it, into the scattered settlement of Annat. There are mostly older houses here, with sheep pens beside the rocky shore, and strips of crofting land inside a deer fence to the left of the road. It seems that the crofters once had ideas about putting holiday caravans on their land, but the whole idea was squashed by the landowners.

The local graveyard is just beyond Annat, the older part being mostly invaded by sheep and the more modern enclosure safely fenced off next door. In the first part there are some very old slabs whose inscriptions have long since been worn away by the weather. A more recent one remembers a local blacksmith who died rather unusually for a Torridon man, of sunstroke at Cincinnati in 1887.

From round about the graveyard there's a fine view down the loch; since it's a view along rather than towards the hillsides, the mountains seem to have retreated a little from the water's edge. The great scree gully on Mullach an Rathain that seems ready to engulf Torridon village is seen very clearly from here. Going beyond the graveyard, there's a framed view through pines and birches to the neat terraced hill of Seana Mheallan, guarding the southern edge of Glen Torridon and somehow looking much higher than its 1,431 feet. Away beyond it are the greater peaks of the Coulin deer forest. The white farmhouse of Torridon Mains is seen among some trees at the head of the loch, and then, as the road swings left over a bridge across the River Torridon, there comes a much clearer view into the heart of the Coulin forest.

Three peaks in particular stand out prominently. Just over the shoulder of Seana Mheallan is Sgorr nan Lochan Uaine; then, going farther south, comes the usual fall away to a saddle and a climb to the summit of Beinn Liath Mhor, which is really an end-on view of a long ridge above the River Lair that flows into the

Carron near Achnashellach station; finally, steepest of them all,
is the apparently double summit of Sgorr Ruadh, which is 3,142
feet high and the neighbour of Fuaral, the 'Wellington's face'
mountain that's seen so clearly from Lochcarron.

The main road sweeps away round to the right to head for the
entrance to Glen Torridon, passing on its way the start of the
splendid road along the north side of the loch, which will be
described in the next chapter. Unlike the modern affair from
Shieldaig to Annat, the Glen Torridon road is narrow with
passing places. It begins under the great towers of Liathach,
which is all part of the National Trust for Scotland's property.
For the first part it runs through rather boggy low-lying ground,
with the windings of the River Torridon to the right. There are
one or two patches of old pinewood between the road and the
river, often used as base camps by climbers in the Torridon hills.
There's a warning notice nearby: 'Cattle graze in this glen. If
you camp here you do so at your own risk.' It doesn't seem to
put many people off.

The first building is a fair way up, at Glen Cottage, a house
sheltered by the usual patch of woodland. It has replaced the
youth hostel at Alligin, on the north shore of Loch Torridon,
which was given up a few years ago. The floor of Glen Torridon
is not very interesting to the casual visitor, although more
observant types will notice evidence of old glacial action. From
this low-down and close-up position, even the soaring hillsides
of Liathach look fairly dreary.

Liathach comes to an end at a monstrous curving gully called
the Great Black Corrie. The mountain burn that sweeps down it
is the main source of the River Torridon, and flows under a
bridge to gather its forces in the little Lochan an Iasgaich on the
other side of the road before ploughing down the glen to the
sea. The Great Black Corrie separates Liathach from Beinn Eighe,
the File Peak, called after its serrated summit ridge, another great
mountain complex that is dwarfed only by Liathach itself; the
south-west part of Beinn Eighe, above the Great Black Corrie,
is part of the National Trust for Scotland's Torridon estate, and
the south-east side is now a nature reserve.

In the old days, the Great Black Corrie of Liathach was one of
the traditional routes of the cattle reivers, and there are tales of
several minor battles between the robbers and the robbed. Much

farther back in time, one of the great Highland glaciers drained down that steep valley, and the collection of mounds and hummocks known in Gaelic as the Corrie of a Hundred Hillocks, hides the old glacial debris that poured down the valley. For all its small size, Lochan an Iasgaich must have been held in high regard at one time, because its name means the Little Loch of Good Fishing.

Among the many travellers who have come this way over the years, one of the most notable was the Rev. Aeneas Sage, that stout-hearted minister of Lochcarron whose Jacobite parishioners went to considerable trouble to try to get rid of him. The story of how he went from Torridon to Gairloch, accompanied only by a young lad who carried a 'bonnet' containing their provisions, was told in John Dixon's classic book *Gairloch*, published in 1886 and perhaps the most comprehensive account ever written of a Highland district:

'Two of Mr Sage's parishioners had conspired to put an end to his life. They followed him, and after a time joined company, beguiling the way with conversation, until a fit place should be reached for the carrying out of the projected murder. When they came to the burn of the Black Corrie the minister announced that the luncheon hour now had arrived, and asked his parishioners to join him. He took the "bonnet" from the boy, and began to dispense the viands. The would-be assassins seated themselves quite close to the minister, one on either side, and the leader now at last mustered pluck enough to inform Mr Sage that he had been condemned to die, and that his hour had come. The powerful minister instantly threw an arm round the neck of each of the villains, and squeezed their heads downwards against each other and upon his own thighs with paralysing force, holding them thus until they were on the verge of suffocation, when, in response to their abject screams for mercy and promises of safety for himself, he released them from his strong pressure, and they went away both better and wiser, let us hope, for this display of the good minister's muscular Christianity.'

From the Lochan an Iasgaich bridge, the north side of the glen is made up of the even steeper slopes of Beinn Eighe—pronounced *Eay*, as it is sometimes written—to the highest point on this side at 3,188 feet. From the summit ridge an incredible succession of scree runs is aimed at the depths of the glen. At the north-western corner of the Beinn Eighe massif, but out of sight from Glen Torridon, is the famous horseshoe-shaped Coire Mhic Fhearchair, with thousand-foot cliffs plunging down into a little loch. Although Liathach and Beinn Eighe look splendid enough from the road, it's a feature of these Torridonian mountains that their northern slopes are perhaps the most magnificent; although there are many others farther north along the edge of Wester Ross, these two keep their grandest sights for climbers and walkers who shun the easy routes of the public roads.

On the south side of the glen, the view is to an irregular lumpy hillside, like the spiky back of some prehistoric beast, that rises more and more steeply until it meets the towered summit of Sgurr Dubh. Continuing along that way, the National Trust for Scotland property soon gives way on the north side of the road to the Nature Conservancy's Beinn Eighe national nature reserve, marked by some patches of fenced-in woodland. This was the first national nature reserve in Britain, established in 1951. It spreads round the corner of Beinn Eighe above the village of Kinlochewe at the far end of the Glen Torridon road, and above the west side of Loch Maree. Most significant part of the reserve is Coille na Glas Leitire, the Wood on the Grey Slopes, which rises above the shores of Loch Maree beside the Kinlochewe to Gairloch road. A remnant of the great Caledonian Forest that once covered most of the Highlands, it is being used for a study of regeneration of the old natural woodlands. Plants and animals are also studied: notably the pine marten—one of Britain's rarest and most rarely seen creatures, which is now prepared to forage for food at the picnic sites—wild cat, otter, fox and deer. Occasionally, there's a glimpse of birds of prey like the golden eagle, buzzard, peregrine falcon and so on. There are various mild regulations for visitors to the reserve, which should be heeded to avoid disturbance. The far side of the ridge is still privately owned deer forest, and visitors should not wander that way during the stalking season without having a word with the estate owners' representatives. Since the whole reserve is more than ten thousand acres in extent, there isn't much need to wander beyond its boundaries.

At the north end of Sgurr Dubh there's a little stretch of water called Loch Bharranch, which is an introduction to the much grander Loch Clair; it marks the watershed of Glen Torridon, because from here all the rivers and burns flow east and north into Loch Maree. Loch Clair is a fine curling waterway, splendidly situated with a substantial area of old pinewood stretching up the hillsides to west and south, and there's a pleasantly imposing summit, Meall an Leathaid Mhor, directly south of the loch. This is the northern end of the deer forest of Coulin, which is pronounced as if the first syllable were *cow*. Coulin Lodge is at the south end of Loch Clair, and through a narrow valley beyond it is Loch Coulin itself; the private road through the estate extends all the way from Glen Torridon to Achnashellach station.

Coulin was at one time the north-eastern limit of the massive estates of the Mackenzies of Applecross. For a time in the last century it was owned, like all the rest of the old Applecross property, by the Duke of Leeds; he sold the modern Applecross estate to Lord Middleton about 1861, but held onto Coulin for some years more. Lord Elphinstone bought the place over, and it was in his time that the present mansion was built; of all the members of the peerage who have owned sporting estates in this part of Wester Ross, he was about the only one who was actually Scottish. After ten years or so he sold Coulin to Lord Wimborne, who also owned Achnashellach and Glencarron for a time. Lord Wimborne then sold Coulin to Sir William Ogilvy-Dalgleish, a wealthy and philanthropic Dundonian, who had an estate at Errol Park in the Carse of Gowrie between Perth and Dundee. He was a patron of the Dundee Royal Infirmary, but left his mark at Coulin mainly in the form of eight hundred acres of woodland that he planted about 1890 around the sides of the valley, partly as ornamentation and partly to improve the wintering for the deer. Later, Coulin became one of the Wills properties, and Mrs Gibbs, the present owner, is a daughter of the last Wills laird.

Around the Coulin road-end, there is some newly-planted forest ground that will soon obscure the fine view down Loch Clair and into the massive peaks of the deer forest which stretch to the horizon. On the other side of the main road, there are new plantations of the Forestry Commission, on ground leased from the nature reserve. From here the valley becomes rather gentler, with wide meanders of the river that drains Loch Clair past Kinlochewe into Loch Maree. The long regular hillside on the far side of the river has recently been forested too.

Kinlochewe itself is a small scattered village around the junction of the Glen Torridon and Achnasheen-Gairloch roads.

The local Nature Conservancy headquarters are in various places round about here, and there's an information centre just before the road junction. Among the details contained in a display in the centre is a note that a pair of eagles need fifteen thousand acres of country to feed a family; so it isn't surprising that they aren't seen very often.

Kinlochewe used to be the centre of a substantial deer forest of the same name, part of the considerable territory of the Mackenzies of Gairloch; it was one of the earliest forests in Wester Ross to be rented out to a shooting tenant. The first of the tenants was a Colonel Inge, who had the reputation of running the place like an army camp, but was so little interested in the stalking that he allowed Osgood Mackenzie, the creator of Inverewe Gardens, to rent the shooting rights of a whole valley while Mackenzie was just a boy—for a rent of £5 per year.

The Mackenzies of Gairloch sold off the Kinlochewe section of their estates in 1920. In 1945 the property was split up, when a Mrs Greig bought the Beinn Eighe division; it was from her that the Nature Conservancy took over the ground that is now the nature reserve. By the early 1960s, it was reckoned that the deer stalking all round Kinlochewe had been ruined by hikers, climbers and 'bus loads of tourists'.

The Nature Conservancy put a lot of effort into managing the woodlands and the red deer herds, culling about thirty beasts every year. From the visitor's point of view, perhaps the most notable amenity is the Glas Leitire nature trail, which meanders over the hillside near the picnic site at Loch Maree, a little way to the left of the main road junction. Round that way, there are several projects run jointly by the Conservancy, the Commission and private landowners.

In a way, it's a pity that so much of Wester Ross is owned by institutional landlords like the Forestry Commission, the National Trust for Scotland and the Nature Conservancy. Most of the work done by these agencies concerns the wildlife and landscape, and many of their activities are, by definition, concerned with preserving the social status quo. If as much enthusiasm could be generated for the problems of the people of the whole area as for the mountains, eagles and deer, it would be more reassuring. What Wester Ross needs is not so much a Nature as a People Conservancy.

CHAPTER 12

ALLIGIN AND DIABAIG

THE ROAD ALONG THE NORTH SIDE of Loch Torridon begins at the junction near the foot of the glen. Beside a stand of old pine trees, the National Trust for Scotland have set up a small information centre, which is worth a visit by motorists and walkers alike, since their property extends most of the way towards Diabaig. Details are given of the animal and plant life, and of the best ways through the mountains. One of the NTS booklets includes some advice to motorists that should be heeded throughout the whole of Wester Ross: 'The courteous driver on a single track road will remember that passing places are designed to enable other cars to pass or overtake. Car registration numbers including the letters ST or JS probably represent a vehicle belonging to a member of the local population who has his job to do and may be in a hurry. Please use the nearest passing place and give way to him to ensure that he is not delayed.' To this could be added a warning that drivers should keep to the passing places on their own side of the road. It is not polite, just dangerous, to pull into a right-hand passing place to let an oncoming car go by, because it will be heading for the same place; the drill, if there is no passing place on the nearside of the road, is to stop alongside the one on the right, and let the oncoming driver make the little detour. The roads of Wester Ross are plastered with tyre marks deposited hurriedly when visitors from the south forget this simple rule.

The Alligin and Diabaig road curls along under the dominating bulk of Liathach, with Torridon Mains, now the home of a Trust warden, across the arable land at the foot of the glen. Soon it comes into Torridon village, sometimes known as Fasag, a settlement of pleasant houses and bright gardens that seems in great danger of being engulfed by rocks and debris that have come down the great scree runs of Mullach an Rathain. There's

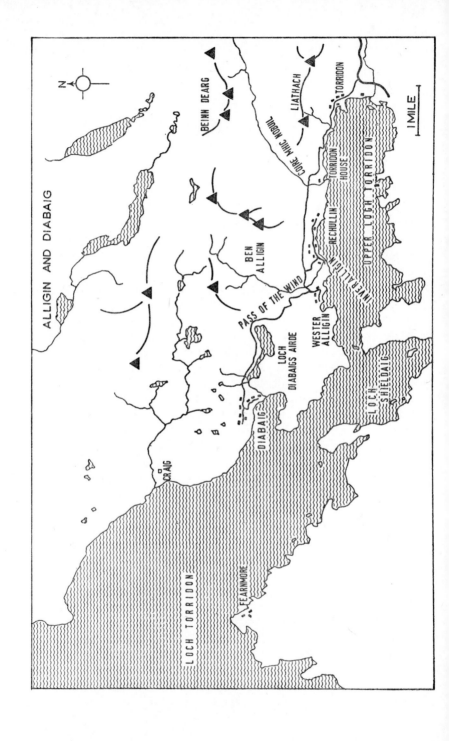

ALLIGIN AND DIABAIG

N

BEINN DEARG

LIATHACH

COIRE MHIC NOBUIL

TORRIDON

BEN ALLIGIN

TORRIDON HOUSE

RECHULLIN

PASS OF THE WIND

INVERALLIGIN

WESTER ALLIGIN

UPPER LOCH TORRIDON

LOCH DIABAIGS AIRDE

DIABAIG

LOCH SHIELDAIG

CRAIG

LOCH TORRIDON

FEARNMORE

1 MILE

a little peninsula known as the Plock, sticking out towards the low water mark; it was used in the past for open-air church services, and for a kind of local assembly where the men would meet to mull over the affairs of the day.

Naturally, this district north of the loch had a long spell under Mackenzie control, and the Mackenzies of Torridon ruled the place from the middle of the seventeenth century until the middle of the nineteenth. Although they were much fewer in number than many of the other Mackenzie families, in Gairloch, Applecross and Kintail, they kept on the right side of their more powerful relatives by a series of judiciously arranged marriages. Most famous of them was John Mackenzie, the third laird, who was a kind of pin-up for Jacobite ladies during the stirring days of the Forty-five. At the retreat from Culloden he and his men fought under Macdonald of Keppoch; when their chief was killed, the outnumbered Keppoch men were about to flee before the Redcoat advance, but young Torridon is said to have rallied them with words that are always quoted in any book about him: 'Keep together, men. If we stand shoulder to shoulder, these men will be far more frightened at us than we can be of them. But remember, if you scatter, they have four legs to each of your two, and you will stand singly but small chance against them.'

Mackenzie of Torridon survived the rebellion, but had a price put on his head after it. Later, this was removed when that same Macdonald of Sleat who died in the barracks at Glenelg and was either a traitor or a loyalist, according to your view of Scottish history, pointed out: 'Young Torridon is so popular with the ladies that if you hang him, half of them will hang themselves.'

It was another John, the sixth laird, who had to sell off the lands of Torridon. After passing through different hands, in 1838 they were bought for £12,150 by a Colonel McBarnet, who had made his fortune as a plantation owner in the West Indies. From the very start, McBarnet's ownership was a disaster for the Torridon people.

He gave some help to the tenants who emigrated during the potato famine of the 1840s, and was said to have bothered himself little about payment of the crofters' rents, but that was about the full extent of his interest in the people. He spent nothing at all on any improvements for his smaller tenants, took away their best land and formed a single large sheep farm which he then rented out to an incomer from the south; these incoming sheep farmers were mostly, like himself, unwilling to spend much of their time in the north-west, and rarely visited their farms. It was only as he grew older that McBarnet came to live for longer spells at his Highland estate, but his treatment of the crofters never mellowed.

In 1859 he turned most of the crofters out of the original village of Fasag and pulled down their houses; the ones who were left had little more than garden ground on which to plant potatoes. The local people were not allowed to keep sheep, which was the privilege of the single farmer to whom all the grazing had been rented out, and the only cow in the district was at the inn. Nine years later, after McBarnet's death, a new factor called Adam Currer appeared on the scene. Despite being warned off by the trustees for McBarnet's sons, he cleared away the remaining crofters on the Fasag side of the loch, and settled them on land at Annat taken away from the already miserable holdings of the people there. The land at Annat was almost exhausted, and always liable to flooding from the storm tides; so the condition of the people grew even worse. What saved them, as it did many of the west coast people, was the herring fishing; but they were still able to do little more than keep themselve alive.

Fortunately, the McBarnet trustees soon sold the property off, and the new owner turned out to be perhaps the best landlord Wester Ross has ever seen. Duncan Darroch took over the estate in 1873, paying £63,000 for Torridon and Ben Damh, an indication of how land prices had soared during the past thirty-five years. Unusually for a Lowlander who bought over a Highland estate, Duncan Darroch seemed to have a historical connexion with the place. Away back in the sixteenth century, when the Macdonells of Glengarry were in control of Torridon, one of them was a well-known cattle thief called MacGille Riabhaich. A great fighter too, he was at the Battle of Flodden in 1513 when James IV's army was smashed by the English. On one of his cattle raids to the Western Isles, this Macdonell had run out of food when he suddenly stumbled on a camp of local men who were settling down to a hearty meal from a great pot of stew suspended over a fire. Macdonell, armed only with the branch of an oak tree, but almost maddened with hunger, hurled himself at them, flailing blows from his hefty cudgel, and chased all the local men away. Hooking the pot over the end of his stick, he trotted off happily to his own camp and handed the food out round his men. Because of this exploit, he came to be given the name of Darach or Darroch, the Gaelic for oak, and the family is said to have started from him.

Later, there was a Duncan Darroch who made himself a fortune as a merchant in Jamaica. In 1784 he came back to Scotland and bought himself the estate and barony of Gourock in Renfrewshire, for which he paid £15,000. Fifteen years later he applied to the Lord Lyon King of Arms for recognition as chief of the Darroch family, a branch of the Macdonells who had previously moved from Torridon to the island of Jura. It is said that the Lord Lyon remembered the old story about the oak branch, and decided that it should be included in the new coat of arms. The Darroch arms, in fact, are a fine mixture of West Indian and West Highland symbols, including a three-masted ship under full sail between three oak trees, a negro with a dagger, and a pair of alligators as supporters.

Confusingly enough, all the heads of the Darroch family since then have been called Duncan. The one who bought Torridon was the fourth of the line, thirty-seven years old at the time, a Cambridge man who was a qualified barrister. As soon as he bought Ben Damh and Torridon he turned them into a deer forest; but it was done in an entirely different way from usual. Duncan Darroch had a great umbrage against sheep, which he considered were the quickest way to ruin the grazing on a West Highland estate. The sheep he cleared off Torridon, however, did not belong to the crofters, since the previous owner had forbidden them to keep any of their own, but were the estate flocks which had been taken over by the McBarnets after their sheep-farming tenant went bankrupt. Darroch's view was that turning the place into a deer forest was a much sounder idea, because it left the lower arable ground available to the crofters; and the hill grazings, which the crofters' cattle were able to share with the deer, were greatly improved after the sheep were turned off.

One of the first things he did was to give back the former Fasag crofters the ground below Liathach that had been taken from them when they were evicted to Annat, and the present Torridon village dates from that time. As croft land, he gave them some of the fine alluvial ground near the mouth of the river, and Torridon Mains was run as a very productive home farm. Darroch made sure that the crofters' fields were securely fenced against any raiding deer, which was a great deal more than many Wester Ross landlords were prepared to do. His tenants throughout Torridon were able to cut as much timber as they needed for house repairs; peat and seaweed were available without restriction; he supplied them all with oat seed and potatoes for planting; there was plenty of employment on estate work; and he was always ready to advance money for building boats and buying cattle. The only thing he insisted on was that they shouldn't keep sheep, which interfered with the deer forest grazing; but as they didn't have sheep anyway, that wasn't much of a hardship. On one special occasion, though, he did help some of the crofters to buy sheep, but that's a story for a later part of the chapter. The tenants couldn't complain about not getting their fair share of the limited amount of arable ground that Torridonian geology had made available; when the Royal Commission met at Shieldaig, the only complaint was that they would be better off with some more hill grazing. George Mackenzie of Fasag voiced the general opinion when he told the commissioners: 'For my part I think our proprietor is the best in the whole north.' Even with these unequalled conditions, there wasn't enough of a living to be made at crofting and loch fishing to stop many of the young men from taking jobs in the east coast fishing fleet.

This happy state of affairs continued until Darroch's death in 1910. As a stone put up by his widow at the roadside beyond the village announces, his Torridon tenants gave their laird, who by then spent almost all his time among them, a tribute that only the old clan chiefs could previously command. He died at Torridon House, the mansion he had built to the west of the village, but his body was to be laid to rest at Gourock, many miles away in the Lowlands. The inscription reads: 'This stone was erected in 1912 by Ann, widow of Duncan Darroch, of Gourock and Torridon, in memory of the devotion and affection shown by one hundred men on the estate of Torridon, who, at their own request, carried his body from the house here on its way to internment in the family burial place at Gourock.'

Gourock had benefited too from Duncan Darroch's liberality. Towards the end of his life, when he stayed most of the time in

Torridon, he would make a yearly visit south to his other estate, and the councillors of Gourock rarely laid some philanthropic scheme before him in vain. His successor gave parkland to the town, and then the mansion house and its grounds were sold to the council for a very reasonable sum; after the second world war the house was demolished, but the grounds are now a public park. The present head of the family is the seventh Duncan Darroch, and still lord of the barony of Gourock; but the family's connexions with Wester Ross and Clydeside are mostly gone, and he lives in Surrey.

Not long after buying the estate, Duncan Darroch had sold off the Ben Damh section to the Earl of Lovelace; so when Torridon was bought after his death by Lord Woolavington, it was only the north side of the loch that was involved. That south of England title disguised the person of James Buchanan, whose fortune had been made in the Black and White whisky firm. He didn't come to Torridon very often, and sold it in 1925 to Sir Charles Blair Gordon of Montreal. Sir Charles was a director of many Canadian companies with interests in insurance, mining, banking, textiles and railways; he was a member of the executive committee of the Canadian Pacific Railway. During the first world war he was vice-chairman of the Imperial Munitions Board in Ottawa, and a principal negotiator for British war supplies from the United States. His knighthood came in 1918. Latterly, the Gordons spent a fair part of the year at Torridon. Sir Charles died in 1939 and eight years later the estate was sold to Richard Gunter from Aldwark in Yorkshire, but a small western part of the property was held back.

Richard Gunter more or less made his home at Torridon, his spell of ownership being the first since Duncan Darroch's time when the estate had a resident proprietor for most of the year. He died in 1960, and is buried in the modern part of the old graveyard over at Annat. The Earl of Lovelace then bought over Torridon to add to the Ben Damh property that one of his predecessors had acquired when Duncan Darroch separated it from the northern part of the estate. After Ben Damh House was converted into a hotel, the Lovelaces came to live at Torridon House; when the fourth Earl died in 1964, Torridon was accepted by the Inland Revenue in part payment of death duty, and was transferred three years later to the National Trust for Scotland.

The present Earl, who succeeded to the title when only thirteen, retains the mansion house and the fine policy woods round about.

Passing the Darroch stone, the Diabaig road winds along the water's edge, with a hillside above it covered in rock, heather and bracken. It's a very pleasant stretch of road, and Queen Victoria seemed to enjoy herself thoroughly when she picnicked here on 15 September 1877. This was during the holiday she spent at Loch Maree Hotel, over the mountains at Talladale on the Kinlochewe–Gairloch road; one result of the holiday is a beauty spot near Talladale that ever since has borne the name of Victoria Falls.

Accompanied by Princess Beatrice, attended by the Duchess of Roxburghe, and escorted by General Ponsonby and the inevitable John Brown, the Queen drove in a carriage round by Kinlochewe and Glen Torridon, noting the day's activities in her diary: 'We came to the Upper Loch Torridon, which is almost landlocked and very pretty. In the distance the hills of Skye were seen. Village there is really none, and the inn is merely a small, one-storied, "harled" house, with small windows. We drove beyond the habitations to a turn where we could not be overlooked, and scrambled up a bank, where we seated ourselves, and at twenty minutes to three took our luncheon with good appetite. The air off the mountains and the sea was delicious, and not muggy. We two remained sketching, for the view was beautiful. To the right were the hills of Skye, rising above the lower purple ones which closed in the loch. . . . We were nearly an hour sitting there, and we got down unwillingly, as it was so fine and such a wild uncivilized spot, like the end of the world. There was a school, standing detached by itself, which had been lately built. The property here belongs to a Mr Darroch, whose two little boys rode past us twice with a groom. An old man, very tottery, passed where I was sketching, and I asked the Duchess of Roxburghe to speak to him; he seemed strange, said he had come from America, and was going to England, and thought Torridon very ugly!

'We walked along, the people came out to see us, and we went into a little merchant's shop, where we all bought trifles . . . the poor man was so nervous he threw almost everything down. I got some very good comforters, two little woven woollen shawls, and a very nice cloak. We had spoken to a woman before, but she could not understand us, only knowing Gaelic, and had to ask another younger woman to help.

'A little farther off the road, and more on the slope of the hill, was a row of five or six wretched hovels, before which stood barelegged and very ill-clad children, and poor women literally squatting on the ground. The people cheered us and seemed very much pleased. Hardly anyone ever comes here.'

At the entrance to Torridon House, which is out of sight in a wooded valley, the private driveway keeps straight along the lochside, while the public road bears to the right uphill. Soon there's a double hairpin bend, and then the road winds up and down through the top of the pinewood that protects the mansion house nearer the shore. A suitable place to stop and have a look around is beside a stone bridge over the magnificent ravine formed by the river that comes down the Coire Mhic Nobuil, the steep valley separating Ben Alligin from Liathach. The effect is completely hidden from a passing car. The river has cut an enormous trough in the rock above the bridge, filled by a splendid waterfall at the northern end. Just before the bridge is the start of a footpath, signposted by the NTS, up the valley to pass between Beinn Dearg and Liathach, then between Liathach and Beinn Eighe, to come down into Glen Torridon by the Great Black Corrie and rejoin the public road at the Lochan an Iasgaich bridge. Using this path and a stalkers' track at the western side of Beinn Eighe, it is not too strenuous to reach the remote and spectacular Coire Mhic Fhearchair.

Beyond the Coire Mhic Nobuil bridge, the public road climbs up into barer country beyond the limits of the Torridon House woodlands, along the lower slopes of Ben Alligin. There is deer fencing here, a good reminder that although the Trust properties are no longer strictly speaking deer forests, there are still plenty of these fine animals about. During the world wars the Torridon forest was a prohibited zone that couldn't be entered without a special pass; but poachers got in both then and in the after-war years, and Richard Gunter was concerned during his ownership of the estate to build up the deer stocks again.

As the road climbs above the loch, there are splendid views in every direction, with Ben Alligin, Beinn Dearg and Liathach behind, and the peaks of the Coulin and Ben Damh deer forests across the water; Ben Shieldaig and the North Applecross hills are out towards the open sea, and on a clear day there's always the chance of a glimpse of the mountains of Skye.

Not many literary types have come this way and left their impressions of this superb sea loch. One who did was Swinburne, who travelled down Glen Torridon and spent a night beside the loch; if his poem *Loch Torridon* is less well known than some of his more claustrophobic works, the imagery is not unfamiliar:

. . . And the dawn leapt in at my casement: and there, as I rose, at my feet
No waves of landlocked waters, no lake submissive and sweet,
Soft slave of the lordly seasons, whose breath may loose it or freeze;
But to left and right and ahead was the ripple whose pulse is the sea's.
From the gorge we had travelled by starlight the sunrise, winged and aflame,
Shone large on the live wide wavelets that shuddered with joy as it came;
As it came and caressed and possessed them, till panting and laughing with light
From mountain to mountain the water was kindled and stung to delight.
And the grey gaunt heights that embraced and constrained and compelled it were glad,
And the rampart of rock, stark naked, that thwarted and barred it, was clad
With a stern grey splendour of sunrise: and scarce had I sprung to the sea
When the dawn and the water were wedded, the hills and the sky set free.

From this part of the high road, which was built as a rough track in Duncan Darroch's time, there's a sudden revelation of the most beautiful setting of the scattered little village of Alligin, its houses dotted here and there on the hillside down near the sea. Out towards the open water is the narrowing of the upper loch with the outer reaches, apparently blocked from here by the peninsula that runs north from Shieldaig; but the channel is just a little way out of view to the right.

The high road dips down for a while and comes to a junction

where the left turn leads downhill again into the village. Over to the right of this village road the Alligin Burn falls down a deep-cut gully that's almost hidden by a casual spread of birches. Round a bend, and the view is out over the loch to the great depression of Loch Damh and the peaks around and behind it; from Ben Damh, its long ridge seen more grandly end-on from this viewpoint, the mountains range away eastwards to the summits on the edge of the Coulin deer forest.

The road to Alligin dates only from twenty years ago, and it was about then that the Torridon–Diabaig road was first given a tarred surface. Before then, the Alligin people who had cars were forced to leave them on the high road and walk down one or other of the steep paths that ran to the water's edge.

Beyond a rock cutting, the road comes down to a junction at the start of the village. In fact, the settlement is much more spread out than a first-time visitor might imagine. The part hereabouts, being at the foot of the Alligin Burn, is known by the rather attractive name of Inveralligin; some way to the east, reached by a coast road that heads back towards, but not as far as Torridon House, is the collection of houses known as Rechullin, the Hillside of the Holly; farther west, but reachable by car only after a return to the high road, is Wester Alligin.

At Inveralligin there is a triangle of common grazing ground between the burn and the main part of the village over to the left. The shoreline is stony, with a great selection of sandstone pebbles, worn down from the rock that was created 750,000,000 years ago. There are several old cottages on the hillside reaching up to the high road, but also a number of superbly situated bungalows looking out over the lochside from elevated positions, built just before the National Trust for Scotland put rather a damper on modern design.

The lane that leads to the right at the first junction, round the edge of the sheep grazing ground and beside the Alligin Burn, leads to a parking place beside a wooden bridge over the rocky mouth of the burn, beyond which are a few houses and the local post office and shop. A little way round the lochside from these splendidly situated houses is the old schoolhouse, long since abandoned, now that all the primary school children go to Torridon village. It is now used as a field centre by children from Rutherglen Academy, a school just outside Glasgow. It's a sad statistic that seventy years ago there were as many people living at the post office corner as spend the whole year nowadays in the entire settlement of Inveralligin and Rechullin.

Back at the little bridge, there's a most peculiar jumble of great natural sandstone blocks, with an old church building perched almost out of sight on the top. Going back round the central area of grazing ground, the road continues beyond the foot of the hill down from the high road, past a varied selection of cottages and larger houses as it meanders back towards the head of the loch. There was a youth hostel here for a while, but it has now moved to Glen Torridon. Many of the houses are up the hillside, often on the sites of older croft cottages; there are also vague remains of long since abandoned crofts all along the hill. The apparently haphazard numbering of some of the houses refers to the positions of the original crofts. Until the middle of the 1960s the coast road stopped dead at the edge of Inveralligin, and anybody wanting to get as far as Rechullin had to tramp along a narrow pathway or slither down from the high road; now a reasonable tarred road has been blasted out of the lochside cliffs, and heads above the rocky shore to the very last house in the village. Beyond Rechullin is a poorly kept path to the parish church, which lies in a most awkward position near the water's edge between Rechullin and Torridon House. In Lord Woolav-ington's time the estate came to an arrangement with the local people that created a right of way along the mansion house driveway from the entrance nearer Torridon village.

The whole settlement here has a most attractive situation, with some of the finest views from any village in the north-west. It takes only the most casual glance, however, to realise that the history of Alligin is not much different from that of most of the other West Highland townships which had to survive the hard days of the nineteenth century, when the crofters and fishermen whose families had lived there for generations were the least important concern of the landlords who took over from the old clan chiefs.

Inveralligin and Rechullin fared much better under McBarnet than Fasag and Wester Alligin, because there were no real clearances here, although the people still suffered from the with-drawal of their hill grazings when most of the estate was rented out to a single sheep farmer. Even so, conditions were pretty miserable. The Rev. George Macleod, a Free Church minister, told the Royal Commission of 1883: 'When I went to Alligin, as missionary and teacher in 1870, the condition of the people was most deplorable, the children were almost naked, and many of the aged people very ill off for want of clothing. I have known families who for days, perhaps for weeks, had no other food than shell-fish.' The Alligin crofters managed to survive until Duncan Darroch came, after which the situation eased considerably. Before the first world war there were twenty-two crofts at Inveralligin and Rechullin, and the fishing was good enough to allow a fish-curer to keep in a fair way of business. The place was as near self-sufficient as possible, although there wasn't much of a margin for any bad times.

It was the Great War that ruined Alligin as a place in which it was possible to make a reasonable living. There were, to begin with, perhaps as many men of the Torridon estate killed in action as live in Alligin today. When the survivors came back, times were hard for fishermen. The price of boats and gear went up substantially after the war, although the fish prices remained much the same; in the 1920s there were still some locally owned fishing boats available, but not enough men to form crews. The fishing petered out until today there isn't a boat going out from the main part of the village, and only one from Wester Alligin. The community became more remote with the stopping after the first world war of the MacBraynes' service, which provided a boat once a fortnight, when the dinghies would row out from Torridon, Alligin and Diabaig to gather supplies.

Times became very hard between the wars, and most of the people had no choice but to leave and find work elsewhere. Recently, the old familiar degeneration of the community has taken place. Although there are plenty of good houses at Inveralligin, many of them are occupied only during the holiday season, and most of the others belong to retired people; no more than thirty people live here all the year. On this part of the coast, most of the people are in their sixties, seventies or eighties; there is practically no work to keep the younger families in this beautiful district. There's a chance of looking after sheep, or working at the Loch Torridon Hotel, or taking a job with the county roads department, but almost nothing else. One family who came from the south a few years ago started a business in hand-made toys, but that's no more than the exception that proves the rule.

Even cattle are a rarity at Alligin now; most of the milk comes all the way from Dingwall, away on the other side of the county, and as an example of the crippling transport charges that make the cost of living in these west coast districts of Scotland higher than anywhere else on the mainland of Britain, the price is nearly half as much again as in the Lowlands. Altering this difficult way of life is not part of the remit of the National Trust, which seems to be more concerned with attracting visitors and preserving the picturesque, and there seems little hope that anything will ever be done to improve it. What makes the situation here all the more maddening is that, despite talk of Plockton or Lochcarron or Applecross, Alligin is the most perfectly situated village in Wester Ross, a delight to the eye but an almost impossible place in which to make a living; and there seems to be no doubt that authority prefers it that way.

Continuing along the high road, it isn't far to the top of the next hill, where another tarmac road goes down to the left towards the lochside through the partly derelict crofting township of Wester Alligin. The Ordnance Survey and Bartholomew's both mark this place as Alligin Shuas, but nobody in Torridon, even among the Gaelic speakers, can understand where they got that name from. In its day, and that means right up to the first world war, Wester Alligin was a fair sized community divided into twenty different crofts, much the same number as Inveralligin. Today the rough grassy hillside that slopes to the sea is littered with the ruins of cottages and crofting land that has gone rank and sour.

The Wester Alligin people were badly treated once McBarnet bought over the estate in 1838. At that time each of the crofters had fifteen sheep and half a dozen cows; with a share of the loch fishing this was an adequate living, even if not far removed from the general peasant level. A few years later the trustees of McBarnet's estate proposed to the Wester Alligin tenants that if they would give up their sheep, the estate would pay them £50 every year to rent the grazing ground from them, so that it could be included in the single large sheep farm which took up most of the Torridon property by then. The tenants discussed the scheme and finally agreed; but the £50 was paid to them for only one year, after which they had neither sheep nor land nor rent.

Duncan Beaton, a crofter/fisherman from Wester Alligin—there's still a family of that name there today—told the Royal Commission of 1883 how McBarnet's agents acted after that: 'Matters then went from bad to worse. One hardship was endured by us after another. No sooner did we lose our stock of sheep than we were deprived of grazing for our cattle . . . now we were not allowed to keep any save one cow, the calf of which we were forced to sell or kill before it was six months old. It is only fair to add that our rental was reduced from £5 to £3, but notwithstanding this reduction we were in poorer circumstances than when we possessed the grazing. Our grievances were further increased by the fact that we were at the same time deprived of about one-fourth part of the arable land for the benefit of the proprietor's shepherds. In consequence of all this we gradually fell into arrears as we possessed nothing that we could sell save one calf.'

Duncan Beaton was giving his evidence at a time when Darroch was the landlord, and he said that things had got very much better under the new owner. The old hill grazings above Wester Alligin that had once been at the crofters' disposal, but had been swindled away from them by McBarnet's agents, were given back to be used by the cattle from the whole of Alligin. At Wester Alligin too, under some pressure from the crofters, Darroch broke his normal rule and allowed them to bring in sheep again. Since they hadn't been allowed to graze sheep under the McBarnet regime, the tenants had to build up new flocks. Darroch advanced them money for this, and sent his farm manager with one of them to the market at Muir of Ord, where the nucleus of the new flocks was bought and paid for. In the whole of the Torridon estate, only the Wester Alligin tenants had asked to be allowed to graze sheep once again; the others were perhaps more realistic. Although Darroch put no obstacles in their way, the Wester Alligin men made a very poor show at re-establishing themselves as small sheep farmers. A few years later, having made nothing of it, they decided to sell their flocks before their condition deteriorated even more, and paid off the outstanding loan from the proceeds. Even at that time crofting at Wester Alligin contained some of the seeds of its own destruction: in 1883 one of the

holdings was in forty-three separate patches, no one of them
touching any of the others.

Between the wars, Wester Alligin went the same way as the
rest of the village. It suffered too from the removal of the steamer
service; once it had been possible to sail from Wester Alligin to
Diabaig for sixpence, and Kyle of Lochalsh was within easy reach.
While many of the houses at Inveralligin became holiday homes,
at Wester Alligin most of the ones abandoned by the families that
had lived in them for generations simply fell to pieces. Now
there are only half a dozen occupied. The croft land on the slopes
between the high road and the loch, never very good because of
the thin covering of soil, has mostly reverted to a wilderness;
but there are still Wester Alligin sheep grazing higher up on the
slopes of Ben Alligin. The only boat that goes fishing out of
Alligin is owned by a family here; but the fading away of the
local fishing boats doesn't mean that the fishing itself has deteriorated: in the winter of 1969/70 there were many of the inshore
east coast boats operating in the loch, sometimes as many as thirty
of them at one time. They took something like three thousand
crans of herring, and practically cleared the loch. Loch Torridon
is not short of fish: just of people.

Until the middle of the 1960s the tarmac stretch down from
the high road didn't extend beyond the first house in Wester
Alligin. One of the local residents fought a long battle with the
county council, pointing out that Wester Alligin was about the
only place in the district where there were a fair number of
children, and what were the chances of them staying there after
leaving school if they were so neglected by the authorities that
they didn't even have a road? The campaign worked, and the
road was extended almost to the lochside. There are not, of
course, all that many youngsters in the place, but the total
population is so small that they make a significant alteration in
any average-age calculations, even allowing that the oldest person
in Wester Alligin is over a hundred years old.

When Sir Charles Gordon's family sold off the Torridon estate
to Richard Gunter, it was the Wester Alligin part that they
retained for themselves. It may have been for sentiment, or they
may have meant to build a house on it; but Sir Charles's sons
were all in Canada, and after the National Trust for Scotland took
over the rest of the Torridon property, they handed over the

extra two thousand acres of Wester Alligin to be reunited with the rest.

Beyond the Wester Alligin road-end, the high road to Diabaig forces its way through rough bouldery country over the Bealach na Gaoithe, the Pass of the Wind. From time to time there are great slabs of exposed rock by the roadside. Although the road across the pass has been very much improved over the last few years, it still follows very largely the difficult hairpinned line of the older road; the original track to Diabaig can be seen taking a more direct line over the hills. There are one or two places where the road widens dramatically, but, as at Ardaneaskan, it soon narrows down again. Drivers will find it impossible to see over the bonnets of their cars at one or two of the crests.

At a newly built parking place to the left of the road, there's a sudden view over Loch Diabaigs Airde, away down in a depression below the road, which has to snake right and left around the eastern end. There are dampish remains of old crofting ground near the loch, and a stiff hillside on the southern edge. This is the end of the National Trust for Scotland property: going west, the country is part of the extensive Gairloch estate, one of the few places in Wester Ross still owned by the Mackenzies.

Loch Diabaigs Airde means Upper Diabaig Loch, but the little settlement of that name, beside the narrows on the north shore, has more or less faded into oblivion. Towards the west end of the loch, there comes into view the tremendous ravine down which it drains into Loch Diabaig, which is just an inlet of outer Loch Torridon. Around here, and higher up on the Pass of the Wind, the road is often blocked for short spells in winter, when snow builds up in great drifts over the exposed countryside.

Beyond the west end of Loch Diabaigs Airde there's a gate and a parking place, and then a sudden view into the unexpected and magnificent amphitheatre in which the little village of Diabaig is situated: three-quarters of a circle of steeply sloping ground that sweeps almost without interruption down to the rocky bay. There are cottages at the roadside, and more down by the water's edge, with steep patches of crofting land at an unlikely angle in between.

The road down to Diabaig has one of the steepest gradients in Scotland; almost out of the question on a hard winter's day, it is also stiff enough for a contractor's lorry that's based in the place to be kept away up at the top of the hill. About halfway down the sharp cornered road there's a turning off to the right, which takes a narrow, winding and unpredictable course high above the north side of the bay, past more croft cottages to finish at the local post office house. There are, of course, many ruined cottages and places where the once arable ground has gone back to nature. From the post office, there's an incomparable view of the great curving hillside that sweeps down to the loch, under a ringed rocky ridge. There are patches of grass among the crofts on the hill, but also many places where the rank growth of bracken has spread. Here and there, outcrops and buttresses of bare rock take over.

Grazing at Diabaig there are more goats to be seen than any-thing else. They are kept for their milk, and can find enough to eat as well as keeping their feet on the steeply sloping hillside. There used to be goats at Alligin too, although they have long since been given up. As happens almost everywhere that goats are kept, some of them have become half wild and now live on the higher slopes north-westwards round the coast. There is more crofting done at Diabaig than at Alligin, although most of the Diabaig sheep graze in the roadless area beyond the village on the way to the remote youth hostel at Craig, or on the slopes of Beinn Dearg over towards Liathach. A footpath leads from the post office away above the lochside to the hostel at Craig, and farther round the coast to Red Point, at the end of one of the public roads that radiate from Gairloch. Near Red Point there is a salmon netting station that used to be run by the Powrie family who have many fishing interests on this coast; but it seems to have been given up for the last year or two.

In *A Hundred Years in the Highlands*, Osgood Mackenzie recalled a story about one of the Diabaig tenants told by his uncle, who had been the estate factor. Norman Mackenzie, one of the crofters, was discovered distilling some illegal 'mountain dew'. Since he was only distilling it to provide some decent spirits for the guests at his own wedding, being unwilling to offer his friends 'the horrid Parliament whisky', he couldn't understand why the estate should remind him of their normally very strict rule that anybody who was involved in the smuggling trade should be evicted. Eventually, he gave himself up to the county Sheriff at Dingwall, where he spent a day or two in jail awaiting trial, was brought to court and fined £30 with the option of another thirty days inside. The factor, who had sent the Gairloch law agent to Dingwall as well, knew that Norman Mackenzie had some money salted away, and prepared to make him a loan of the £30 to pay the fine. 'But the few days in the far too cosy jail had quite dispelled Norman's sense of degradation, so he declined to pay the fine, and at the end of the month he came home, if a sadder and wiser man, at any rate not a poorer one!'

Back at the start of the post office road, the way to Lower Diabaig lies down the last stretch of hill towards a line of houses near the pier. The shoreline here is rocky and stony, and there are some fishing nets and dinghies lying about. There is still a little loch fishing done from Diabaig, although it has been more or less abandoned at Alligin. There was a busy fish-curing business before the first world war here too, but the inter-war years saw a great decline at Diabaig, as at other places up and down this coast; in this village, as at Alligin, the average age of the people is fairly high. Some of the houses offer accommodation to visitors, but the way of life among the Free Church folk makes it impossible for some of them to take in visitors who want to leave on a Sunday. Because of the scattered Free Church congregations, and the shortage of ministers, it's not unusual to find a church service taking place on a weekday, held by a visiting minister from another parish.

Looking at the place from the pier, the impression is still of a great green amphitheatre with rocky outcrops above; the ravine that plunges down from Loch Diabaigs Airde reaches the sea a little way farther on. It's a steep hillside too on the north side of the bay, below the post office road, with wooded cliffs rising up out of the sea. Suggestions have been made from time to time that the post office road should be extended all the way round the coast past Craig and Red Point to meet up with the network of public roads that radiate from Gairloch. It would be a difficult road to build, and if it ever came about, the reason would have nothing to do with the welfare of the Diabaig people, but would be the result of some decision about what an advantage a continuation of the present road system would be to the tourist traffic.

Diabaig is probably doomed, like many of the other settlements mentioned in this book, to a future as nothing more than a collection of holiday homes for people who leave at the end of the summer and return to the cities; that, and a retirement centre where the pension book is the most significant feature of the local economy. There is no doubt that official thinking regards the north-west Highlands as little more than a recreation area for people from the congested districts of the south. Administrative energies and the activities of the various agencies that have found themselves in the landowning game are directed at showing off the area to summer visitors: a praiseworthy aim, for this magnificent country should be available to everyone; but only if coupled with some kind of help to make year-round living in these beautiful lochside districts possible for younger families. From the administrators' point of view, concentrating on the summer tourist trade is the easiest and cheapest way out.

These doleful thoughts, however, are not likely to affect the first-time visitor who travels over the Pass of the Wind to Diabaig, especially into the golden glow of a summer dusk. Torridon is possibly equalled, but not surpassed, in the majesty of its soaring mountains and sparkling lochsides. It will be an unforgettable experience when you and the sun dip down to Diabaig, towards the glorious light of the western sea.

INDEX OF PLACES